Grassroots Liberals

Royce Koop

Grassroots Liberals
Organizing for Local and National Politics

UBCPress · Vancouver · Toronto

20 19 18 17 16 15 14 13 12 11   5 4 3 2 1

Printed in Canada on FSC-certified ancient-forest-free paper
(100% post-consumer recycled) that is processed chlorine- and acid-free.

Library and Archives Canada Cataloguing in Publication

Koop, Royce,
  Grassroots Liberals : organizing for local and national politics / Royce Koop.

Includes bibliographical references and index.
ISBN 978-0-7748-2097-4 (bound); ISBN 978-0-7748-2098-1 (pbk.)

  1. Liberal Party of Canada. 2. Political participation – Canada. 3. Canada – Politics and government. I. Title.

| JL197.L5K66 2011 | 324.27106 | C2011-900899-8 |

e-book ISBNs: 978-0-7748-2099-8 (PDF); 978-0-7748-2100-1 (epub)

Canadä

UBC Press gratefully acknowledges the financial support for our publishing program of the Government of Canada (through the Canada Book Fund), the Canada Council for the Arts, and the British Columbia Arts Council.

This book has been published with the help of a grant from the Canadian Federation for the Humanities and Social Sciences, through the Aid to Scholarly Publications Program, using funds provided by the Social Sciences and Humanities Research Council of Canada, and with the help of the K.D. Srivastava Fund.

UBC Press
The University of British Columbia
2029 West Mall
Vancouver, BC V6T 1Z2
www.ubcpress.ca

For my parents,
Leroy and Wanda Koop

Contents

Tables and Figures

Acknowledgments

Seventy-six grassroots party activists agreed to be interviewed for this research, and many others spoke informally with me. Many of them bought me coffee, invited me out to gatherings, introduced me to their friends and colleagues, drove me back to wherever I was staying, and gave me tours of their towns and neighbourhoods. One insisted on packing me a lunch at the conclusion of our interview, and another towed my car out of a ditch after I slid off the road and walked to his farm. I am grateful to all of them for their time, insights, and generosity.

Many people commented on and improved this manuscript at various stages of research and writing. They include Gerry Baier, Amanda Bittner, Michelle Garvey, Angela O'Mahony, Hilary Pearse, Susan Scarrow, Allan Tupper, and Graeme Wynn. Special thanks are owed to Chris Kam, Ben Nyblade, and Campbell Sharman. My greatest intellectual debt is to Ken Carty, who was around from the beginning to the end of this project and who spent many hours over the past several years reading and critiquing drafts of this work. The final product is immeasurably better as a result.

I was supported financially while researching and writing this book by a Canada Graduate Scholarship doctoral fellowship from the Social Sciences and Humanities Research Council of Canada and a graduate entrance scholarship from the University of British Columbia. Both institutions have my thanks. I revised the manuscript while a University Postdoctoral Fellow in the Department of Political Science at Memorial University of Newfoundland and am grateful for the financial support as well as the generosity of the members of that department.

Emily Andrew at UBC Press guided this book through the review process, and I appreciate her expertise, patience, and professionalism a great deal. Thanks are also owed to Megan Brand for overseeing the book's production process. I also appreciate the comments and suggestions made by the anonymous reviewers.

This book would not exist were it not for my parents, Leroy and Wanda Koop, who have always been supportive of my education and scholarly work. Mom and Dad are well acquainted with pounding campaign signs into the ground and working in campaign offices. I hope that they will see my admiration for them and people like them in the pages that follow.

My greatest debt is to Denisa Gavan-Koop. Denisa commented on every thought, critiqued every figure, and edited every line, several times. More importantly, she made the journey worthwhile. Thanks, Diggy-D.

Grassroots Liberals

Introduction

The years 2006 to 2009 were not pleasant for the Liberal Party of Canada. After having been in office for thirteen years under the leadership of Jean Chrétien and later Paul Martin, the party was defeated in the 2006 election by the rejuvenated Conservative Party. Martin resigned as leader and was replaced by Stéphane Dion, but the party struggled to renew itself under Dion's leadership and was again defeated in the 2008 election. For a party that won eighteen of the twenty-seven Canadian elections held since the expansion of the franchise in 1918, this experience on the opposition benches was a shock, especially to party activists who had commenced their participation during the solidly Liberal 1990s. Nevertheless, just as it had following previous defeats, the party turned its attention to the task of organizational renewal.

In the past, the processes of renewal were often intimately linked to Canadian federalism and the presence of Liberal parties in the provinces. Out of office, the national party was generally able to fall back on its provincial "cousins," particularly when those cousins themselves were in power, and draw on their strength in the provinces to reconstruct a national organization capable of defeating the Tories (Wearing 1981, 13). But that option was no longer available to the national party leadership in the period following the 2006 defeat. Part of one of the party's former rebuilding efforts around the middle of the twentieth century had been a process of organizational disentanglement from provincial Liberal parties, with which the national party had shared important structural linkages. Fifty years later that process seemed to have fully culminated: provincial Liberal cousins in 2006 were seemingly unsympathetic to the national party (Ontario), suspiciously close to the national Conservatives (British Columbia), or, as in Saskatchewan, dead. The national Liberal Party in 2006 therefore appeared to embark on the process of rebuilding all on its own.

The party focused its rebuilding efforts in this period on the organizations that it maintains in each of the nation's constituencies. Following Dion's departure as leader in 2009, party elites reaffirmed this focus in a report entitled *Every Voter Counts: The 308 Riding Strategy.* "At present," the authors observed, "many of the Party's Electoral District Associations ... are poorly organized, and some are near dormant." The report emphasized "a number of initiatives ... to revive EDAs and rebuild the Party's presence in areas where we are considered weak" (Liberal Party of Canada 2009, 11). Party reformers argued that the Liberal Party as a whole could only be rebuilt on a foundation of strong organizations in the ridings. Michael Ignatieff, the party's next leader, took this advice in the summer of 2010 when he embarked on a cross-Canada barbeque tour, one goal of which was to engage local activists and reinvigorate the party's grassroots organizations.

This discussion illuminates two key aspects of the institutional context within which the Liberal Party organizes for politics in Canada. First, federalism mandates two distinctive levels of electoral competition, and parties can organize themselves to compete at the national and provincial levels in distinctive ways. Some parties adapt through organizations capable of contesting both national and provincial elections, whereas others steadfastly restrict themselves to a single level. Second, the use of geographically defined constituencies to elect members of Parliament means that the parties must maintain local organizations to select and support local candidates if they hope to win overall. Given the diversity of these constituencies, these tasks fall for the most part to grassroots Liberals in the ridings.

On their own, these two topics have received substantial scholarly attention, particularly from analysts of Canadian party politics. Yet they have not, with a few notable exceptions, been studied in an interconnected manner. How are the constituency organizations of Canadian parties linked between the national and provincial levels? What does the organization of these local groups say about the overall integration, or separation, of national and provincial politics in Canada, especially since most Canadians who participate in political parties do so in the ridings? Do Canadians really live in "two political worlds," to use Donald Blake's (1985) phrase? Or do grassroots Liberals and other partisans sometimes construct local political worlds that encompass both national and provincial politics?

Answering these questions requires a re-examination of Canadian parties' organizational adaptation to federalism, with emphasis placed on their organizations in the ridings. *Grassroots Liberals* undertakes such an examination of the Liberal Party in a multi-level context. Rather than investigating formal linkages between national and provincial parties' permanent structures and elite campaign groups, this study turns the spotlight on the activist bases, constituency associations, and campaigns that comprise the parties' local organizations.

This introduction sets the stage for the analysis that follows. First, I account for federalism as an institutional context that shapes the structures of political parties. I then explore the organizational responses of parties, emphasizing how scholars have previously conceptualized and described party organizations at Canada's national and provincial levels. Next I lay out the defining characteristics of the Liberal Party's constituency organizations – particularly their special, autonomous places within the party's wider structures – and raise the broad questions that structure this inquiry. The introduction closes with an outline of the following chapters.

Federalism as an Institutional Context

Political parties organize themselves partially in response to incentives embedded in the institutional environments within which they compete for public office. Much of the academic literature on party organizations situates those parties within a strictly national, unitary context (Deschouwer 2006, 291). Yet federalism constitutes a vastly different institutional environment, so any account of party organizations in such states must take into account the opportunities presented and the challenges posed by multi-level institutions.

In terms of opportunities, federalism adds locations in which political parties can compete for power. This multiplies the sources of office benefits for parties. In addition, federalism provides parties with opportunities to use provincial organizations as building blocks to construct strong national organizations. The result is that national and provincial parties are able to draw on the strengths of one another, particularly while in power at one level but not at the other. And by maintaining linkages with parties in the provinces, national parties are able to maintain organizations that exist close to citizens. In response to these opportunities, parties can compete at both levels of the federal state, and there are numerous organizational forms adapted to do so.

In terms of disadvantages, the prospect of competing for power at both the national level and the provincial level poses the risk of diluting efforts, exhausting party workers, and depleting donors' bank accounts. National and provincial party elites at the two levels might also come into conflict with one another, straining linkages between the two levels. Such strains are particularly dangerous when elites are in government at both levels and have vested interests in asserting themselves against one another. In response to these disadvantages, some political parties disengage from one level of competition entirely, instead focusing on either one level of partisan activity.

Federal structures themselves contain incentives to certain forms of party organization. Three aspects of these structures can be identified. First, the extent to which taxing and spending powers are centralized or decentralized exercises an influence on party organizations. In general, elites organize parties to maximize their own power given the distribution of resources within federations. Centralization of resources within federations creates incentives for the development of aggregated national organizations (see Chhibber and Kollman 2004). In contrast, decentralization of resources enhances the rewards associated with provincial office and therefore creates incentives for the development of strong, autonomous provincial parties. Canada is a decentralized federation, which should encourage the development of autonomous provincial parties (Thorlakson 2009, 164-65).

Second, the method of multi-level power division – how responsibilities are defined between the national and provincial levels – also contains incentives for the development of different types of party organizations. Overlapping policy competencies and shared administrative responsibilities between the national and provincial levels encourage cooperation between governments. This method of power division encourages the maintenance of organizational and elite linkages that facilitate cooperation between the two levels. In contrast, systems of federalism characterized by largely separate spheres of policy competence for national and provincial governments mean that parties at the two levels are free to operate without regard for the other level of the state (see Chandler 1987). Organizational linkages between parties at the two levels are therefore largely unnecessary within this institutional context. Canada's system of "dual federalism" therefore contains incentives for the development of decentralized party organizations (Thorlakson 2009, 165).

Third, characteristics of the multi-level electoral regime have important consequences for the organizations of political parties, particularly their campaign structures (see Deschouwer 2006, 296). Simultaneous national and provincial elections provide incentives for national and provincial parties to develop common campaign structures to contest elections that occur on the same day, whereas different election dates entail national and provincial campaign strategies that reflect the realities of "second-order elections" at the provincial level (Reif and Schmitt 1980).

Of more relevance to this study is the drawing of constituency boundaries at the national and provincial levels. Coterminous boundaries at the two levels mean that national and provincial parties can more easily cooperate in performing their duties both between and during election campaigns, so common constituency organizations are likely to result. But different boundaries complicate linkages between the two levels, so national and provincial parties are forced to maintain separate structures in distinctive geographic spaces (also see Bradbury and Russell 2005, 27-28). National and provincial elections in Canada occur on different days, and constituency boundaries are distinctive in every province except Ontario. These electoral regime characteristics therefore contain incentives for the development of separate, autonomous national and provincial parties.

These three aspects of Canada's multi-level institutions suggest that Canadian parties encounter substantial incentives to foster organizational decentralization or separation between the two levels. But while characteristics of federalism provide incentives to adopt particular forms of organization, party elites might have a fair amount of freedom in choosing how to adapt their parties to these incentives. Although the "ultimate" sources of party adaptation are found outside parties (Katz and Mair 1992, 9), the pre-existing nature of party organizations must also be taken into account, since the extent to which particular multi-level forms can be imposed on parties depends on distributions of intra-party power (see Koelble 1991). Parties characterized by strong hierarchical patterns of power are likely to be characterized by consistent patterns of integration or separation throughout the organization. But more loosely organized parties characterized by devolved locations of power and mutual autonomy – what Eldersveld (1964) refers to as "stratarchical" parties – might be unable to adapt a single organizational response to the opportunities and challenges posed by federalism.

Party Organizations in Multi-Level States
The question, then, is how have Canada's political parties responded to this multi-level institutional context? Smiley and Dyck provide two conceptual approaches to understanding party organization in federations. Both follow Riker's (1964, 129) famous contention that political party organization is the key factor influencing the centralization or decentralization of multi-level systems. However, political parties are

not the primary focus of his analysis, and Riker does not rigorously define centralized and decentralized parties.

Smiley (1987, 103-4) operationalizes Riker's independent variable by distinguishing between integrated and confederal party systems. Integrated systems have crucial organizational and behavioural linkages between parties at the national and provincial levels, whereas the parties of confederal systems are characterized by single-level autonomy. In defining organizational indicators of such systems, Smiley argues that parties in integrated systems have shared nomination and policy formulation processes, common campaign organizations, and common mechanisms for raising and spending money between the two levels. Distinctive processes at the two levels, in contrast, characterize parties in confederal systems. Smiley marshals his framework to explore the nature of the Canadian party system and finds that it is, with some exceptions, strongly confederal in comparison with other multi-level systems (117).

Although Smiley examines the nature of the Canadian party system, he is cautious in applying labels to the parties themselves. In contrast, Dyck (1992, 1996) categorizes Canadian parties on the basis of their linkages between the national and provincial levels. Dyck (1996, 160) distinguishes between three types of parties. *Integrated* parties are those with substantial linkages between the two levels; *confederal* parties are those in which national and provincial branches operate separately from one another; and *truncated* parties exist only at a single level. He conceives of these parties as archetypes, with real-world examples occupying a continuum that ranges between them.

These party types are defined by a series of organizational indicators. Strongly integrated parties are characterized by shared party membership, shared staff, common mechanisms for fundraising and spending money, common campaign organizations, and common leadership selection processes. In contrast, confederal parties issue autonomous national and provincial memberships, have distinctive offices and staff, raise and spend money on their own, and campaign without the assistance of the party at the other level (Dyck 1996, 161). With several caveats, Dyck argues that the New Democratic Party (NDP) can be understood as an integrated party, whereas the Progressive Conservative Party was a confederal party. The Liberal Party occupies a middle ground, sometimes semi-integrated and sometimes semi-confederal (163).

These are the findings that one would expect in a decentralized multi-level state where the method of power division and the electoral regime also favour the development of strong, autonomous provincial parties.

Drawing on Smiley's and Dyck's conceptual approaches, other scholars have come to the conclusion that national and provincial parties in Canada have largely separated their organizations since the 1950s and have, as a result, seen the development of distinctive party systems at the national and provincial levels (see, e.g., Wolinetz 2007, 183). Wolinetz and Carty (2006, 54), for example, commence their contribution to a volume comparing national and subnational party organization and competition in a number of multi-level states by clearly setting out this seemingly unique character of Canadian party politics: "Over time, provincial parties and provincial party systems have become increasingly separate from federal parties and the federal party system ... Most provincial parties are now organizationally distinct and feel no obligation to adhere to a common party line ... The result is a series of federal and provincial party systems that are anything but congruent." It appears, then, that Canadian parties have dealt with the challenges of multi-level institutions by simply opting out – by establishing distinctive organizations and, as a result, party systems at each level with few linkages between them. One of the consequences of this bifurcation has been the weakening and fragmentation of party identifications by Canadians so that by 2000 only about a third of respondents to the national election survey reported identification with the same party at the national and provincial levels (Wolinetz and Carty 2006, 64). In other words, Canadian partisans appear to have come to inhabit two political worlds at the national and provincial levels (Blake 1985).

Before accepting this conclusion, however, we should focus on an aspect of Canadian political parties that has been largely ignored: their organizations in the ridings. In neither Smiley's nor Dyck's accounts are the local organizations of Canada's parties examined as indicators of linkage between the two levels. The implicit line of thought appears to be that local organizations will follow the trends of the wider party: separation of national and provincial parties will necessarily be accompanied by separation on the ground. Indeed, Franks (2007, 26) explicitly makes this argument: "There are ... stark separations at all levels from constituency organization to party headquarters between provincial and national parties bearing the same name."

However, empirical evidence calls into question the view that separation in the upper reaches of the party is matched by separation on the ground. There are several examples. First, in his survey, Carty (1991, 49) found that 64 percent of national constituency associations focus to some extent on both national and provincial politics. In contrast, only 36 percent of the associations surveyed reported an exclusive focus on national politics. Second, in their study of campaign workers in two Ontario constituencies, Jacek et al. (1972, 194) found significant cross-involvement by local activists in national and provincial elections. Third, Smiley (1987, 117) tentatively notes variation within the parties themselves. "Confederalism is most marked at the higher levels of party organization," he notes. In contrast, "in the constituencies the same persons often carry out both federal and provincial party activity." Finally, this speculation is borne out by studies of Canadian party membership: in a 2000 survey, 74 percent of national Liberal party members were also members of provincial Liberal parties (Koop and Sayers 2005, 14).

Although Canada's national and provincial parties have formally separated, many of the constituency organizations of the national parties appear to be making their own way when it comes to establishing linkages between the two levels. These preliminary findings suggest that the loosely structured Liberal Party has been unable to adopt a single response to multi-level institutional incentives from the top to the bottom of its organization. Such intra-party variation indicates that any account of the Liberal Party's multi-level form requires some examination of its organizations in the ridings as well as the broader party organizational forms that are able to encompass these constituency structures.

Constituency Organizations

Scholars have argued for some time that the changing structure of party politics has rendered the local organizations of political parties and the members that staff them redundant or even a nuisance (Katz 1997, 145). Declining membership numbers, weakened linkages between parties and citizens, the professionalization of parties, and a new dependence of parties on the state rather than members for funding all suggest that local organizations are of little continuing use to political parties. However, a more recent Revisionist School has asserted the important roles played by local party organizations in linking state to society (see, e.g., Clark 2004). Local organizations provide activists with opportunities to select the personnel that staff government and shape party policy. Extensive local organization boosts the public legitimacy of political parties. Well-staffed local organizations also provide parties with personnel to staff campaign organizations and can be tapped for fundraising purposes. And the view that national election campaigns are strictly national events has been challenged by recent work demonstrating that local campaigning has important electoral consequences (see, e.g., Denver et al. 2003; Whiteley and Seyd 1994).

Constituency party organizations in Canada consist of three components. The first component is the local activist base, which encompasses local members and sympathizers. Constituency associations, the structures that the parties maintain in each of the ridings, are the second component of these local organizations. Although constituency associations encompass the entire local membership, they are provided with leadership by their local executives – small groups of local elites – and are sometimes attached to local auxiliary units. Executives organize local contests to nominate party candidates, so local members have retained the right to select the personnel that staff public office. The local campaigns, which manifest themselves in the lead-up to elections as nominated candidates construct organizations, are the third component. Campaigns are staffed by members of the candidate's inner circle who perform specialized tasks, secondary workers who are available on a regular basis to help with labour-intensive tasks, and sympathizers who drift in and out of campaigns (Sayers 1999, 68-71). Although campaigns are formally separate from the local association, in practice many of the personnel that staff the association executive participate in campaigns as well.

In a diverse country where national electoral victory is dependent on winning in individual ridings, the major parties have always relied on these local organizations to engage grassroots activists, maintain riding-level structures between election campaigns, and nominate and support candidates. An impressive national campaign is useless if the party cannot win in more ridings than the other parties, and doing so requires both competent candidates and local organizations to support them. Because many constituency contests are competitive and there are no runner-up prizes in these plurality races, riding campaigns can impact national election results by altering only a small percentage of local votes (Carty and Eagles 2005, Chapter 8). Recognizing this, Canadian parties often allocate more money for local than for national election campaigns (see, e.g., Stanbury 1991, 586).

Given the diversity of Canadian society, national parties must find ways of appealing to a wide range of frequently conflicting regional and local interests. The decline of national-provincial organizational linkages means that the national Liberal Party has come to rely on its constituency organizations to adapt the party's national appeals to these distinctive regional and local interests. Furthermore, the lack of any substantial extra-parliamentary organization means that the national party must maintain direct linkages with its riding organizations (Sayers

1999, 4, 216). This relationship between the party in central office and the parties on the ground is enumerated through a franchise bargain that grants leaders the power to formulate policy and constituency organizations the right to select candidates for public office (Carty 2002, 733-34). The key to this arrangement is a great deal of autonomy for both actors within their respective spheres.

Local autonomy is assured under the terms of this arrangement in return for the constituency organizations' disciplined support of the party in public office (Carty and Cross 2006, 97). In return for this support, local Liberals enjoy the autonomy necessary to adapt their organizations and operations to the unique ecological, geographic, and competitive conditions of each constituency. This autonomy also allows grassroots Liberals to construct organizations that best reflect their own unique goals as activists, since officials in the upper reaches of the party have little interest in enforcing constituency organizations' compliance with a particular organizational template and virtually no capacity to do so. The result is that different forms of Liberal constituency organization can be observed as one travels from riding to riding.

The Liberal Party's loose, stratarchical structures hold important consequences for understanding how the party is linked between the national and provincial levels. If the constituency organizations of the Liberal Party are relatively autonomous from the national party leadership and exhibit differing organizational forms in response to local demands and activist wishes, then those local organizations also have the capacity to structure themselves in an integrated manner and operate accordingly, with organizational overlap across the national and provincial levels resulting. In short, it is reasonable to expect that some constituency parties will take advantage of their autonomy to organize themselves in ways that link national to provincial when doing so makes sense within the context of their own local environments.

This understanding of the Liberal Party and its local organizations underlies the three sets of questions that structure this inquiry. First, is the national Liberal Party linked to provincial parties through its organizations in the ridings? If so, to what extent? And what are the local behavioural and structural mechanisms through which those constituency organizations integrate national and provincial politics in the ridings?

Second, do the Liberal Party's constituency-level organizations exhibit diversity in how they are linked between the two levels? Variation in the overall organization of these local parties suggests that they do, and preliminary empirical evidence demonstrates that local constituency associations do differ in their focus on national and provincial politics (Carty 1991, 49). Some local organizations might therefore maintain integrated structures that span national and provincial parties, whereas others confine themselves to the politics of a single level. This then begs the question of what exactly is responsible for the development of integrated local parties in some ridings but not others. Since constituency parties are necessarily adaptive to the conditions of the ridings that they exist within, it is reasonable to expect that the sources of variation can be found mainly in the ridings themselves. As a result, these sources of variation are not easily detectable without close observation in the ridings.

Third, what are the consequences of integrated local organizations for any wider understanding of the Liberal Party and its role in Canadian politics? What lessons do the experiences of the party provide for analyses of political party organizations in other multi-level states, particularly states that employ geographic units of election and representation? Formal processes of national-provincial separation have prompted several scholarly portrayals of the Liberal Party as a single-level organization that disengages entirely from the politics of the provinces, with important consequences for how Canadians identify with and participate in national and provincial politics. But the portrait of the Liberal Party that emerges from this study is significantly more nuanced and demonstrates that the party in fact serves to link national and provincial politics through many of its constituency organizations.

The Liberal Party
This study focuses exclusively on the Liberal Party of Canada and the linkages that it maintains with parties at the provincial level, particularly provincial Liberal parties. Selecting a single national party for analysis was motivated in part by methodological reasons: by doing so, I was able to increase the depth of analysis and construct a richer account of the organization that the Liberal Party has evolved within the context of Canada's multi-level institutions. Many of the findings of this study can be applied to the Conservative Party and particularly the NDP. However, by focusing exclusively on the Liberal Party, this book also makes an important contribution to the limited literature on the Liberal Party of Canada.

Such a contribution is valuable given the electoral success of the Liberal Party and its impact on the development of the country as a whole. Of the forty national elections held since Confederation in 1867, the Liberal Party has won twenty-three (58 percent). This pattern became more pronounced following the expansion of the franchise in 1918: the Liberals won eighteen of the twenty-seven national elections (67 percent) held since 1918. One might think that political scientists would be intent on understanding the type of organization that the Liberal Party has evolved to attain such a record of electoral success. But this has not been the case; the party has generally been the recipient of less academic attention than the NDP and the minor parties that have occasionally appeared at the national and provincial levels.

When the subject of academic attention, the national Liberal Party is often analyzed as merely one aspect of the wider national party system (see, e.g., Carty, Cross, and Young 2000). Thick descriptive accounts of the national Liberal Party have tended to focus on particular regions and provinces (see, e.g., Smith 1981) rather than on the party as a whole. Whitaker's (1977) and Wearing's (1981) rich accounts of the national Liberal Party organization constitute important exceptions. However, recent accounts of the party have been more focused on party leaders and election campaigns than on the party organization (see, e.g., Clarkson 2005). In contrast, this study explicitly examines the Liberal Party organization in a multi-level context.

Outline

Chapter 1 situates this analysis of the Liberal Party of Canada in a historical context and outlines the empirical framework employed in the book's analytical chapters. Traditional accounts of the relationship between federalism and Canadian parties maintain that the Liberal Party was strongly tied to provincial affiliates until roughly the 1950s, when reformers turned their attention to constructing a single-level national party capable of campaigning on the basis of broad, pan-Canadian themes. The result has been distinctive national and provincial Liberal parties with few organizational linkages between them. But this conception is challenged by the realities of organization and party life in the ridings. I close the chapter by presenting a conceptual continuum used to study the party's local organizations and describing the constituencies that I selected as case studies.

Chapters 2, 3, and 4 marshal this conceptual continuum to describe the three aspects of the party's constituency organizations and how they link national to provincial in the ridings. Chapter 2 focuses on local Liberal partisans and the activist bases that they comprise. I pay particular attention to how and why grassroots activists participate in national and provincial politics as well as the consequences of these different forms of participation for the party as a whole. Chapter 3 focuses on constituency associations and how they are linked between the national and provincial levels, if at all. Chapter 4 concludes the descriptive section of the book by exploring several examples of integrated and differentiated local campaign organizations.

Chapters 5 and 6 turn to explaining variations in local party organization across the ridings. Chapter 5 argues that local integration and differentiation can be traced back to characteristics of the ridings within which these organizations exist. Chapter 6 explores how elected members – national members of Parliament (MPs) and provincial members of legislative assemblies (MLAs)[1] – influence the development of local organizations that are most conducive to their own goals.

Chapter 7 concludes the book by drawing the local narratives contained in previous chapters together into a comprehensive account of the Liberal Party in a multi-level context. Traditional accounts maintain that Canada's national and provincial Liberal parties, like voters, exist in two political worlds (Blake 1985). But Chapter 7 discerns between four distinctive types of local political worlds in the ridings. The chapter constructs portraits of each of these local political worlds – the types of party organizations that they encompass and the factors influencing their development – and explores the consequences of this understanding of the Liberal Party for both Canadian politics and the study of political parties in other multi-level states.

---

[1] Members of provincial legislatures in Canada have several titles. I use the term "MLA" to refer to these representatives from all provinces.

1
Multi-Level Politics and the Liberal Party

The focus of this book is on how the Liberal Party of Canada is organized between the national and provincial levels of political competition. Many comparative studies have developed ideal-type categories designed to conceptualize the organizational diversity of multi-level political parties (see, e.g., Deschouwer 2006, 292). But these categories necessarily represent snapshots in time; the structures and power relations of party organizations evolve in response to both internal and external influences. A rich understanding of the relationship between federalism and the organization of the Liberal Party therefore requires an accounting of the historical processes that led to the party's current organizational form.

This chapter accordingly charts the organizational evolution of the Liberal Party from a multi-level perspective. It explores how the party has been linked to provincial affiliates in the past and how these linkages have transformed over time. Most accounts of the national Liberal Party maintain that it was largely integrated with provincial cousins until roughly the 1950s, when internal reformers in the party and party leaders in the provinces began to encourage the development of a single-level, pan-Canadian party. This chapter provides an alternative account of the recent historical development of the party by focusing on its local organizations. I argue that the national Liberal Party is best understood not as a single-level party but as an *unevenly integrated party,* integrated in some aspects of its organization but not others. This historical discussion leads into the empirical framework that is marshalled in subsequent chapters to examine the party's constituency organizations as well as a justification of the cases selected and the methodology employed in this study.

The Liberal Party as a Traditionally Integrated Party

The development of Canadian political parties is typically understood within the context of three (and perhaps four) historical party systems. The major parties were organized and appealed to Canadians in quite different ways in each of these systems (Carty 1992, 583). The first system, which existed from 1867 to 1917, was characterized by organizationally weak cadre parties and strong leaders who relied on patronage to sustain the efforts of partisans. The second party system, from 1921 to 1957, was dominated by Liberal Mackenzie King, who practised a unique form of regional brokerage during his long tenure as prime minister. To support this balancing of regional interests, the Liberal Party developed a ministerialist model of party government – characterized by powerful regional ministers and an enmeshing of party and state – that would sustain King in power until the late 1940s but that ultimately weakened the overall party organization (Whitaker 1977). The third party system, beginning in 1963, was characterized by newer professionalized parties and leaders such as Pierre Trudeau and Brian Mulroney, who made personal, catch-all electoral appeals to Canadians. Carty, Cross, and Young (2000) also argue that Canada entered a fourth party system in the 1993 national election, which saw the Conservatives reduced from 169 to 2 seats in Parliament. This conceptualization of Canadian parties' organizational evolution provides a useful context within which to describe the Liberal Party's development from an integrated party to an unevenly integrated party.

The organization of the Liberal Party in the first and second party systems was weak, so the national party often relied on the organizations of provincial parties for support, particularly during election campaigns. With no meaningful extra-parliamentary structures in place, national party leaders allowed provincial elites to oversee local nominations and provide the machinery necessary for national election campaigns (Wearing 1981, 9-10). National campaigns in this period were therefore agglomerations of provincial organizations. Indeed, national dependence on provincial campaign organizations formed the basis for the Liberal victory in the 1896 national election, and Wilfrid Laurier was sworn in as prime minister for the first time partially as a result of the strength of this federalized arrangement.

This decentralized form of party organization – "the use of the cabinet as the mode of organizing the country" – soon took root (Regenstreif 1963, 216). National ministers under this arrangement were linked to provincial organizations that conducted national election campaigns in their respective provinces. These regional ministers drew on their access to patronage to construct formidable regional and local organizations. As a result, the national and provincial parties maintained linkages with one another, since the national party was largely dependent on provincial organizations to contest election campaigns (Reid 1972, 32). In this period, then, the Liberal Party can be thought of as a *traditionally integrated party* in which there existed organizational ties between the two levels that were crucial to the success of the national party.

Traditionally integrated parties were also characterized by local organizations that the parties relied on to select and support candidates during both national and provincial election campaigns. In traditionally integrated parties, the crucial organizational linkage between the national party and these organizations in the constituencies was routed through intermediary provincial parties. Although differences between national and provincial constituency boundaries mandated formally distinctive national and provincial local organizations, it was usually difficult to distinguish these riding-level organizations from one another (Perlin 1980, 22). These local groups were informally organized, fuelled by patronage, and dominated by groups of local notables who involved themselves in both national and provincial election campaigns. In other words, the personnel of Canada's traditionally integrated Liberal parties coordinated their local structures and resources.

This traditionally integrated party form was well adapted to the incentives offered by federal institutions, where resilient subnational organizations can act as building blocks for a strong national party. Just as patronage fuelled the parties throughout the first party system, so too did it buttress the survival of traditionally integrated party organizations. The crucial "reciprocal benefit" of this arrangement for provincial elites was access to patronage while they were out of power but the national party was in government and vice versa (Smith 1981, 52). Local Liberals could count on largesse from either the national or the provincial government, with the exception of those dark periods when the party sat on the opposition benches at both levels.

Nor was this form of organization embraced by only the Liberal Party; the Conservative Party evolved a similar structure early in the century. Conservative leader Robert Borden, for example, prepared for the 1911 election by reinforcing the national party's ties with provincial affiliates and allies, hoping that premiers and provincial party leaders might strengthen the resolve of their organizations to aid in the national Conservative effort (English 1997, 46-52). As with Laurier in 1896, the effort paid off, and Borden formed a Conservative government following the 1911 election.

Given these advantages, this traditionally integrated organizational arrangement continued into the second party system during Mackenzie King's lengthy period in office and in fact became formalized as regional ministers oversaw the development of resilient sectional organizations rooted in the politics of the provinces (Smiley 1987, 121). Indeed, the dominance of the regional ministers meant that the position of national organizer was effectively abolished in 1940 (Wearing 1981, 21).

There was, however, always a tension intrinsic to traditionally integrated parties. National parties that are reliant on provincial organizations for campaign personnel and resources inevitably find themselves in a position of weakness compared with provincial elites, who necessarily exist closer to the constituency organizations and grassroots activists that are crucial to success in both national and provincial elections. The national party might therefore be at a disadvantage compared with provincial partners. This tension in the party's traditionally integrated arrangements manifested itself in the 1930s and 1940s when Prime Minister King and Premier of Ontario Mitch Hepburn publicly feuded. As Whitaker (1977, 327) observes of this dispute,

> The most immediate weapon which Hepburn could utilize was the control of the provincial leader over the party organization in the province, and the exclusion of the federal party from direct access to the party machinery. Since the Liberal party had never developed separate federal and provincial organizations to any extent, a strong provincial leader could squeeze the federal leaders out of the picture by the simple expedient of dominating the existing party machinery.

When Hepburn ordered his organization to withhold support from national Liberal candidates, activists in the constituencies were placed in a conflicted position, and King was deprived of a large section of the Ontario electoral organization.

The Liberal Party in the second party system was generally understood to be a brokerage party, and the label is sometimes still applied (see, e.g., Merolla, Stephenson, and Zechmeister 2008, 690). Brokerage parties are tasked with standing above the divisions of Canadian society – particularly the sectional divisions nurtured by federal institutional arrangements – and brokering rather than articulating these competing interests so as to avoid exacerbating regional conflicts and thereby threatening the integrity of the state (Carty 2006, 5). But the King-Hepburn conflict illuminates the inherent contradiction between (1) national parties that are charged with brokering provincial interests and (2) the organizational dependence of these national parties on provincial campaign organizations. This was a paradox that would eventually be resolved for the Liberal Party as the 1950s ushered in a new national party system.

As has always been the case with the Liberal Party, organizational deficiencies were ignored until the party suffered at the ballot box. The party's defeat in the 1957 national election spurred an internal re-examination of the traditionally integrated party model and especially of regional ministers' influence over the campaign machinery in the provinces. Electoral disaster in the subsequent 1958 election both marginalized the regional ministers, nine of whom went down to defeat in their own ridings, and lent new urgency to the internal reform program. Party reformers were intent on constructing a pan-Canadian organization that would be capable of contesting national election campaigns without the support of provincial organizations, thus overcoming the paradox of national brokerage parties that are reliant on provincial organizations for their success (Smith 1981, 52).

The key to organizational renewal was to loosen the grip of the old, sectionally oriented regional ministers over the national party organization. Cutting ties with the provincial organizations and constructing an autonomous national campaign organization allowed the national party to run on broad, pan-Canadian themes without fearing Hepburn-style retaliations from provincial allies. Even the quintessential regional minister, Jimmy Gardiner of Saskatchewan, recognized in this period that the party's traditionally integrated structures desperately required reforms, if only because the failing provincial Liberal parties represented poor organizational bases for the national party (Smith 1981, 53).

The influence of these reformers – particularly Keith Davey as national organizer from 1961 to 1966 – meant that the party began the process of extricating itself from dependence on provincial party organizations following the 1958 defeat. What the reformers advocated and what developed was a parallel set of national and provincial Liberal organizations. The reformers, for example, developed new mechanisms for policy formulation at the national level without input from provincial elites. In addition, national campaigns were run by a centralized campaign committee as well as campaign chairpersons in each province, all appointed by the leader. Notes Smiley (1987, 10), "this centralized pattern of control left little decisive influence in federal campaigns for the provincial wings of the party." Indeed, there was little room for the influence of regional ministers and the provincial organizations in a national party that was increasingly embracing modern techniques of organization and campaigning. Although national and provincial party leaders could construct informal alliances prior to election campaigns (Clarkson 2005, 41-42), the deep-seated linkages between the central components of the national and provincial parties were dissolving.

Some provincial elites were caught off guard by the initiative of reformers in the national party. This was especially true for provincial Liberals in Saskatchewan, where the national and provincial organizations had previously been strongly integrated (Smith 1981, 65). But other provincial elites encouraged separation, since formal affiliations between parties at the two levels were increasingly problematic by the 1950s for provincial leaders. This was because the evolution of provincial societies had led to the rise of successful third parties at this level and, consequently, the development of new provincial party systems. Cairns (1977, 715) observes that "parties at different levels of the federal system exist in different socioeconomic environments, respond to different competitive situations, and are products of particular patterns of historical development, and historical accidents." Incongruence between the national and provincial party systems in British Columbia and Quebec, for example, strained traditionally integrated party organizations in those provinces as far back as the 1940s as provincial leaders struggled to respond to distinctive provincial demands while maintaining friendly relations with the national party (Black 1972, 122; Rayside 1978, 508). Provincial party leaders wished for free rein in responding to the distinctive incentives embedded in their respective party systems without having to account for the wishes and actions of the national party. The leader of the provincial party in Alberta, for example, argued for organizational separation so that he would be freed from "the albatross of having to explain every asinine move Ottawa makes" (quoted in Smiley 1987, 111). Provincial elites were increasingly likely by the 1950s to approve of and encourage processes of disentanglement.

Old party hands, confronted with the 1958 election defeat, argued that the best way to regroup was to elect provincial Liberal governments that would in turn act as building blocks on which the national party could be rebuilt – in other words, a return to the traditionally integrated party form (McCall-Newman 1982, 18). This argument did not carry the day, and in fact party reformers ruled out any return to the traditionally integrated organization following the party's return to office after the 1963 election (Smiley 1987, 110). As a result, the third party system beginning in 1963 differed from the two previous systems in that national and provincial party organizations appeared for the first time in Canadian history to be disentangling. A key point not explored in previous accounts of Canada's historical party systems is that the pan-Canadian electoral appeals that characterized this system were made possible by the separation of the national Liberal Party from its previous benefactors in the provinces.

Since Canadian parties are dominated by their leaders, separation was assured once those leaders came to identify their own interests with the disentanglement of national and provincial organizations. Formal separation was therefore reinforced by the increasing importance of intergovernmental negotiations that were a characteristic of the third party system, for national and provincial government leaders were keen to minimize partisan obstacles to effective negotiations at first ministers' conferences (Painter 1991, 284). Cairns (1977, 716) argues that in the third party system "party solidarity across jurisdictions [was] sacrificed for the greater good of intergovernmental agreement." Incongruence between the national party system and those of several of the provinces also reinforces the organizational separation of parties at the two levels, since the differing competitive demands placed on national and provincial Liberal parties means that they might in fact have little in common. Many national Liberal activists in British Columbia, for example, argue that the provincial party in that province has more in common with the national Conservative Party than the national Liberal Party; given such perceptions, a return to any form of traditionally integrated organization is out of the question.

It therefore appears that Canada's national and provincial Liberal parties have evolved from traditionally integrated to single-level parties and that any meaningful organizational linkages between the parties have been severed. Whereas provincial organizations had previously acted as intermediaries between the national party leadership and the organizations in the ridings, Lester Pearson's goal of "a direct link between federal electoral districts ... and the national office of the party" appeared to have been realized (quoted in Smith 1981, 53). This process of organizational separation culminated in the formal separation of the national and provincial Liberal parties in Quebec in 1964, Ontario in 1976, Alberta in 1977, and British Columbia in 1993 (Smiley 1987, 111). Formal separation was largely a symbolic acknowledgment of the practical separation of the national and provincial parties that had already taken place.

The Liberal Party as an Unevenly Integrated Party

What was taking place in the constituencies while these dramatic processes of national-provincial disentanglement were playing out? As it turns out, not a great deal, for the fundamental aspects of constituency organization and campaigning in Canada have never changed significantly. Constituency associations still consist of groups of local elites who come together occasionally to organize picnics and nomination meetings; local candidates still shake hands, drop in to local establishments, give speeches, and encourage supporters to get out to the polls on election day. In other words, there is not much about Canadian party organization "that would surprise constituency politicians of earlier generations" (Carty 1991, 184).

In the same way, many of the ridings' entangled national and provincial organizations did not change significantly throughout the twentieth century. As events swirled around them, the constituency parties tended to retain their old integrated organizations. The result has been that the Liberal Party in many ridings has maintained organizations that span national and provincial politics in terms of both local structures and personnel. These organizations are integrated between the two levels rather than divided between them. The result is that the Liberal Party can be understood as an *unevenly integrated party,* integrated between the national and provincial levels in some aspects of its organization but not others.

There are two interconnected reasons why many national and provincial groups in the ridings have not disentangled their organizations. Local organizations within the overall structure enjoy the necessary autonomy to withstand any attempts by the party in central office to impose particular forms of organization on them. Constituency party activists are typically resistant to reform efforts imposed from the outside, and the freedom of grassroots Liberals to structure their organizations in the ways that they choose to do so are enumerated in the party's franchise bargain. Cut off from the pressures facing the party in Ottawa, the local groups have maintained organizational forms that are best adapted to their own particular needs, and this extends to their organization between the national and provincial levels. Local party activists are generally somewhat conservative in their "fondness ... for existing practices" and in the sense that they tend to stick with what has worked in the past; for many grassroots Liberals, what works are local structures that are integrated between the national and provincial levels (Russell 2005, 214).

Integrated organizations work for many Liberal activists because these organizations have several advantages over local parties that are differentiated between the two levels. This is true with respect to local structures, personnel, resources, and party life. Integrated organizations are better suited to coordinating the efforts of local personnel and directing local activists to service at the level where they are most needed. Integrated constituency parties also make more efficient use of local resources than do differentiated organizations. Rather than marshalling dual sets of resources at the national and provincial levels, integrated organizations meet demands at both levels with the same resources (see Carty 1994, 138; Whitaker 1977, 416). Integrated organizations offer (1) enhanced opportunities for grassroots activists to pursue their own goals at both levels and (2) an expanded party life that encompasses both national and provincial politics in the ridings. So, though party leaders might face incentives to achieve disentanglement, elites in the ridings frequently face incentives to foster integration.

These inherent benefits of local integration, however, are not experienced equally across all constituencies. This is because other factors rooted in the politics of the ridings can themselves render local integration either undesirable or unworkable. Research in the ridings revealed three such factors.

The first factor is the structure of national and provincial party systems, which constitute the key competitive context within which integrated and differentiated organizations develop. There are three aspects of this context that can complicate local integration. First, parties might be present at both the national and provincial levels, but their competitive positions within these systems might be vastly different. In some provinces, the national Liberal Party is a force to be reckoned with, yet provincial Liberals struggle to win votes; the inverse is also true. Second, parties might be truncated: successful at one level but entirely absent from the other (Thorlakson 2009, 161). Such truncation can be a result of electoral decimation at a single level (the Saskatchewan Liberal Party, for example, was historically dominant but is now uncompetitive) or of deliberate design by elites at one level, as was the case with the national Reform Party (Stark 1992, 144). Third, parties might be present at both levels but nevertheless advocate quite different policies (Blake 1982, 710). Given that the competitive demands confronting leaders of national and provincial parties can be distinctive, ideological dissimilarity between the two levels often occurs naturally since Canadian parties do not have common policy formulation processes. Even if such processes existed, party leaders would pick and choose the parties' policies and campaign themes. As will be seen, British Columbia's national and provincial parties are typically viewed as ideologically distinctive.

When the same parties are competitive at both levels, and those parties are ideologically similar, then activists face few party system obstacles to becoming involved at both levels. It is also easier for local organizations to build linkages between the two parties in the ridings. But when there are competitive differences between the two levels, and parties of the same name are ideologically distinctive, then activists confront obstacles to participation at the two levels. Local activists who wish to construct linkages between national and provincial organizations must find new ways of bridging differing competitive situations at the two levels and of reconciling parties that occupy different spaces on the ideological spectrum. These are daunting tasks, and differentiated local parties are more likely to result when the national and provincial systems differ.

The second factor that complicates local integration is found in the ridings themselves. Geographic characteristics of constituencies as well as the manner in which their boundaries are drawn between the national and provincial levels can evoke practical obstacles to the development of integrated local parties.

Coterminous national and provincial constituency boundaries encourage the development of integrated local organization in three ways. First, coterminous boundaries provide a common base of operations for both the national and the provincial organizations, facilitating cooperation between them. In these cases, national and provincial organizations service identical geographic areas and respond to identical local demands at both national and provincial levels. Second, since there is only a single national and a single provincial organization in each riding, any cooperative processes are simplified. National and provincial organizations might come to be seen as partners, pursuing identical goals in different electoral realms – this equality is an extension of the relationships between MPs and MLAs in coterminous ridings, which stand in sharp contrast to such relationships in small provinces such as New Brunswick, where MLAs might be viewed as "poor cousins" to MPs (Franks 2007, 38). Third, activists in coterminous ridings that participate in national events and campaigns are able to do so at the provincial level among the same friends and activists. The result is that common riding boundaries decrease the costs of local cooperation and encourage the development of integrated constituency organizations.

Conversely, distinctive national and provincial riding boundaries are obstacles to local integration. When national and provincial boundaries are distinctive, local parties must organize themselves in different spaces and in response to differing demands (Bradbury and Russell 2005, 27-28). The presence of several provincial organizations within the boundaries of a single national riding means that a range of local actors must be recruited to create integrated organizations – the process of cooperation between the national and provincial levels is therefore complicated. Rather than a federal-provincial partnership, integrated organizations in this context must take on the form of an agglomeration of one national and up to eight provincial organizations all operating in different geographic spaces and facing distinctive local demands. And distinctive boundaries also mitigate against participation at both levels, for activists who participate as a group at the national level can find themselves split up into several provincial ridings and therefore unable to participate as a group during provincial elections. For these reasons, distinctive national and provincial boundaries raise the cost of local integration, and differentiated local organizations can result.

The third factor influencing the development of integrated and differentiated local organizations is the preference of MPs and/or MLAs in the ridings. Once elected, MPs wield a significant degree of influence over local organizations, and the paid staff whom they maintain in the ridings often become involved in constituency associations (Sayers 1999, 62). The result is that incumbents play important, though not decisive, roles in shaping the character of their local organizations. This influence extends to whether the organizations are integrated or differentiated. In some cases, MPs encourage the development of integrated local organizations because it suits their electoral goals to do so. But in other cases, for a variety of reasons, MPs are cool to the idea of local integration and act as obstacles to national-provincial cooperation. In these cases, grassroots activists find it very difficult to construct integrated local organizations in direct opposition to the wishes of the local MP. For this reason, MPs and MLAs can significantly raise the costs of local integration.

However, the extent to which incumbents can influence their organizations is limited by local traditions. In some ridings, a long tradition of local integration makes it difficult for incumbents to craft differentiated local organizations. But the absence of such a tradition means that incumbents have greater influence.

Local electoral strength is also related to the development of integrated and differentiated organizations. Integration requires committed local activists willing to reach out to the association at the other level. As a result, ineffectual "paper" organizations are very unlikely to be integrated. However, though local competitiveness is a prerequisite for integration, it is not a sufficient condition. As we will see, some strong local organizations remain differentiated between the national and provincial levels.

Figure 1.1

A continuum of local party organizations

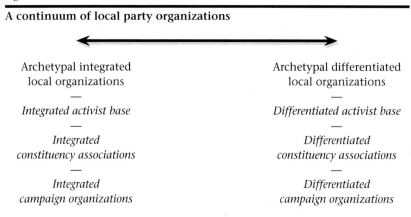

Archetypal integrated local organizations	Archetypal differentiated local organizations
—	—
Integrated activist base	*Differentiated activist base*
—	—
Integrated constituency associations	*Differentiated constituency associations*
—	—
Integrated campaign organizations	*Differentiated campaign organizations*

These factors manifest themselves in varying combinations across the constituencies. Some ridings will be within provinces where the national and provincial party systems are identical; where the policies of parties at the two levels are similar; where national and provincial riding boundaries are congruent; and where the incumbent MP and MLA do their part to encourage cooperation between the two levels. In other cases, there are few similarities between the politics of the national and provincial levels; national ridings are splintered into numerous provincial constituencies; and MPs and MLAs are hostile to one another as well as to organizational cooperation. In the former riding, the costs of integration will be very low. It is therefore possible, even likely, that local activists will pursue organizational integration given its advantages. But the system, regime, and political conditions of the latter riding increase the costs of local integration, perhaps to prohibitive levels. This riding is therefore likely to see the development of differentiated local organizations.

The result is significant diversity in the relative integration and differentiation of local party organizations. Figure 1.1 captures this diversity through an inductively formulated continuum that ranges between two organizational archetypes and lists how three aspects of these local organizations – the activist base, constituency association, and local campaign – manifest themselves in these archetypes.

It is possible to plot constituency parties somewhere on this continuum based on the extent to which their different aspects link national to provincial or differentiate those two levels. Fully integrated constituency organizations exist where all local activists participate in both national and provincial politics, where the constituency associations of the national and provincial parties are fused, and where national and provincial campaign organizations draw on identical personnel and resources. In sharp contrast, fully differentiated constituency organizations are characterized by distinctive activist bases, no linkages whatsoever between the national and provincial constituency associations, and fully separate national and provincial campaigns.

In practice, few local organizations resemble these archetypes; they must therefore be placed on the continuum somewhere between purely integrated and purely differentiated local parties. By investigating the extent to which local organizations are integrated between the national and provincial levels, one can use this continuum to plot local party organizations relative to one another and compare their characteristics across the ridings. The following three chapters explore the three aspects of local organizations summarized in Figure 1.1: Chapter 2 focuses on party activists, Chapter 3 on constituency associations, and Chapter 4 on campaigns. One implication of the academic view that national and provincial parties are separated is that those parties have contributed to the creation of two political worlds for Canadians (Blake 1985). As we will see, integrated and differentiated party organizations engender several different types of political worlds in the ridings.

The Provinces and Ridings
Since this is a study characterized by intensive study of a relatively small number of cases, the selection of ridings in which to explore local party organizations was crucial. Case selection was guided by my initial and ongoing suspicions about which factors influence the development of integrated and differentiated local organizations. Some case ridings were abandoned and others added during the course of the field research as I gained a clearer understanding of the factors involved in developing and maintaining integrated and differentiated organizations. This method of case selection reflects Fenno's (1978, 3) experiences as a participant researcher observing members of Congress in their districts: "I spent a lot of time trying to figure out a priori what types of [constituencies] ... might pose serious tests for, or exceptions to, whatever generalizations seemed to be emerging ... Data collection and data analysis ... proceed simultaneously." Table A.1 in the appendix lists the New Brunswick, Ontario, and BC constituencies studied along with the characteristics that are relevant to this study.

Table 1.1

National and provincial ridings in Ontario, British Columbia, and New Brunswick

Province	National ridings	Provincial ridings	Provincial ridings per national riding
Ontario	106	107	1.0
British Columbia	36	79	2.2
New Brunswick	10	55	5.5

The inclusion of a Maritime province in this study was necessitated by the prevailing academic view that national and provincial parties in those provinces are somewhat more integrated than those in other provinces (see, e.g., Smiley 1987, 117). This is certainly the case in New Brunswick, where the national and provincial Liberal parties continue to share a common party office (also see Whitaker 1977, 389). New Brunswick provides opportunities to explore the Maritime brand of national-provincial party cooperation and to clarify what exactly that cooperation entails.

Ontario ridings were included as case studies because Ontario is the only Canadian province with identical national and provincial constituencies. Table 1.1 contrasts the number of national and provincial ridings in Ontario at the time of this study with those of British Columbia and New Brunswick.

The 1996 Fewer Politicians Act in Ontario linked provincial constituency redistributions to national redistributions (Pond 2005, 171). This means that, with the exception of some northern ridings, national and provincial constituencies in Ontario are identical. National and provincial parties in Ontario therefore organize in identical geographic spaces, organize themselves in response to the same local imperatives, encounter similar obstacles, and compete for support from the same voters. Including Ontario case studies allowed me to explore the impact of co-terminous national and provincial constituency boundaries on local party organizations.

Conversely, including ridings from British Columbia and New Brunswick allowed me to explore the impact of distinctive national and provincial riding boundaries. In contrast to Ontario, British Columbia's national constituencies contained roughly two provincial ridings at the time of analysis; New Brunswick's national constituencies were splintered

Table 1.2

National and provincial election results and effective numbers of elective parties

Province *Most recent election*	Liberal vote	Conservative vote	NDP vote	Effective number of elective parties
Ontario				
National	33.8	39.2	18.2	3.3
Provincial	42.2	31.6	16.8	3.2
Difference	*8.4*	*7.6*	*1.4*	*0.1*
New Brunswick				
National	32.5	39.4	21.9	3.1
Provincial	47.1	47.5	5.1	2.2
Difference	*14.6*	*8.1*	*16.8*	*0.9*
British Columbia				
National	19.3	44.5	26.1	3.8
Provincial	45.8	n/a	41.5	2.6
Difference	*26.5*	*n/a*	*15.4*	*1.2*

into five or six provincial ridings. Whereas identical ridings facilitate processes of local integration, dissimilarity complicates these processes, so local activists in British Columbia and New Brunswick must adapt new strategies to construct integrated local organizations. The selection of ridings from these three provinces allowed me to explore the adaptive behaviours of local activists in three contexts: Ontario, where national and provincial ridings are identical; British Columbia, where national ridings are divided; and New Brunswick, where national ridings are splintered into several provincial constituencies.

Case studies were selected from British Columbia in order to explore the impact of distinctive national and provincial parties and party systems on local organization. To approximate the similarity of the national and provincial party systems in the three provinces studied, Table 1.2 lists the vote shares of the major parties in the 2008 national election; the provincial elections that immediately preceded it; and the effective number of elective parties in each of these elections.[1] These are crude measures of similarity between the two levels, but they do provide an

---

[1] The effective number of parties summarizes the number of parties in a system and weights the count by their relative strength. I summarize the effective number of elective parties (Nv) (Markku and Taagepera 1979).

approximate picture of national-provincial differences in the three provinces studied.

Canadians in Ontario confront very similar choices at the national and provincial levels, and party competition at the two levels in the provinces studied is also comparable. In these provinces, the Liberal and Conservative parties are the major contenders, and the NDP constitutes a third party. This is true at both the national level and the provincial level of electoral competition: the effective numbers of parties at the two levels are nearly identical. The result is that participation at one level in Ontario is easily transferred to the other level, and many Liberals therefore participate in both the national and the provincial parties.

New Brunswick displays similarities between the two levels, but there are also differences. To a large extent, these party system differences between the two levels are due to the differing competitive situations of the national and provincial New Democratic parties in the province: whereas the party is not successful in provincial elections, it collects a respectable number of votes (if not seats) in national elections. This is reflected in the effective number of parties: the national system contains approximately one more party than the provincial system. Although there are differences between patterns of competition at the two levels, the difference for the national and provincial Liberal parties is not extreme.

Ontario and New Brunswick differ sharply from British Columbia, where there are important competitive and ideological differences between party competition at the national and provincial levels. This is particularly true for Liberal partisans. The provincial party system in British Columbia is dominated by two parties, the Liberals and NDP, and the Green Party is somewhat competitive. The situation is starkly different at the national level, where all three major parties are competitors; indeed, British Columbia's leading party at the national level is essentially a fringe party at the provincial level. Of particular note is the different competitive situations of the national and provincial Liberal parties; whereas the provincial party has formed the government in the past three elections, the national party regularly garners fewer votes in the province than the Conservatives and NDP. Given the lack of continuity between the two levels, non-NDP supporters and activists in this context are unable to rely on party labels as heuristics to guide their support for national and provincial parties (Thorlakson 2006, 43).

In addition, the national and provincial Liberal parties in British Columbia are generally perceived to be ideologically distinctive, with the provincial party assuming a right-of-centre position following the collapse of the provincial Social Credit Party in the early 1990s. Cross and Young (2004, 429), for example, note an "affinity" between the provincial Liberal Party and the national Canadian Alliance, a predecessor to the national Conservative Party. Differences between these parties and party systems serve to confuse linkages between the two levels for many activists and voters and are therefore obstacles to the development of integrated local organizations. Including BC ridings as case studies allowed me to explore how activists cope with distinctive national and provincial systems of partisan competition in the process of constructing their own local organizations.

Within each of these provinces, ridings that differ in their geographic, ecological, competitive, and political characteristics were selected. Both urban and rural constituencies were selected in each province. The dilemmas of local party organization differ markedly in these constituencies. So do processes of local integration, for national and provincial parties attempt to engage with one another within either vast, sparsely populated rural ridings or small, diverse urban constituencies. Chapter 5 explores how these riding conditions affect local integration and differentiation.

Ridings were also selected based on the competitive situations of the Liberal Party in each of them. There is significant regional variability in the Liberal Party's competitiveness, with the result that some candidates regularly garner a majority of votes cast while others stand in as "stop-gap candidates" for a party with no real organization or chance of winning (Sayers 1999, 79). A crucial finding of Carty's (1991, 71) study of Canadian constituency associations is that many are in fact "paper associations," groups that exist only on paper so that the parties can make claims of a pan-Canadian presence. Local competitiveness matters for the subject addressed here because national-provincial integration requires some degree of organization in the ridings. Since paper associations struggle to maintain any viable organizational presence, they lack the ability to maintain integrative linkages with organizations at the other level. In most cases, integration requires that local party officials reach out to the party at the other level to construct linkages, and paper associations and other weak local parties lack the personnel to do so. In contrast, more competitive organizations will have sufficient personnel and therefore the capacity to do so. The expectation is therefore that electorally strong parties are more likely to be integrated, whereas weak organizations are more likely to be differentiated.

Tables A.2 and A.3 in the appendix list the most proximate national and provincial election results to the period when I conducted fieldwork.

The national ridings include Liberal strongholds such as York West (in which Judy Sgro won 64.7 percent of the vote in the 2004 national election) and wastelands such as Kootenay-Columbia. Most ridings selected range between these two extremes. There is similar diversity among the provincial constituencies studied, sometimes even within the boundaries of the same national ridings. Within New Brunswick's Acadie-Bathurst, for example, Liberal candidates in the 2003 provincial election won with a clear majority of votes cast in Nepisiguit; narrowly won by less than a single percentage point in the neighbouring riding of Centre-Péninsule; and were decisively defeated in Lameque-Shippagan-Miscou with a margin of 24 percent for the Tory candidate. Including a diversity of competitiveness among the local organizations studied allowed me to explore the effect of electoral strength on local integration and differentiation.

Finally, ridings with and without Liberal MPs and MLAs were selected. The presence of incumbents is naturally related to the competitiveness of local party organizations. However, incumbents play special, privileged roles in shaping the party organizations in their constituencies. Incumbents can be expected to "use the perks of political success to strengthen the organizational resources of [the] local party," with "strong, often highly personal, local organizations" resulting (Carty and Eagles 2005, 37). They result in part from the influence of incumbents on elites in the local party – although these elites cannot always be dictated to – as well as incumbents' willingness to involve their paid constituency staff in the affairs of the party organization (Sayers 1999, 62). The implication of this influence is that, though competitiveness is expected to be related to local integration, incumbents can use their influence over the local party to encourage the development of either integrated or differentiated constituency parties. The questions, then, are why incumbents take these different approaches and how they go about getting their way when it comes to organization in the ridings.

Table A.1 in the appendix lists the partisan affiliations of national and provincial incumbents in each of the ridings studied. In some ridings, such as Ajax-Pickering and Don Valley East, there are Liberal incumbents at both the national level and the provincial level. This raises the question of relations between incumbents at the two levels and their effects on local integration or differentiation. Other ridings have incumbents at one level but not the other (e.g., Richmond Hill and Perth-Wellington). This particular configuration provides opportunities for incumbents at one level to encourage integration by assisting the organization at the other level; however, incumbents might not embrace these opportunities.

Still other ridings have Liberal incumbents at neither level, and the local organizations are accordingly deprived of the perks associated with having an MP or MLA of their own. In New Brunswick and British Columbia, distinctive national and provincial constituency boundaries mean that there will likely be a combination of Liberal and non-Liberal incumbents at the two levels.

Any study that examines a small number of cases inevitably raises questions about why some cases were chosen and others were not. For this study, ridings in British Columbia, Ontario, and New Brunswick were selected for three reasons. First, as described above, they were ideal provinces to explore the factors that appeared to influence the development of integrated and differentiated local organizations.

Second, focusing on a small number of cases allowed me to develop a deeper understanding of how constituency organizations function in each of these provinces. Including more provinces in the analysis would have expanded the width of the analysis but at the cost of depth. And since the question of how the parties organize between the national and provincial levels in the ridings is largely unexplored, it is appropriate to focus on a small number of cases to generate theory about the phenomenon (Small 2009).

Third, qualitative research is costly in terms of time and resources. By limiting the provinces in which I conducted field research, I was able to maximize the number of interviews conducted in each. And by conducting research in only three provinces, I was able to explore several different types of ridings within each. The result is a rich exploration of local party organization in the three selected provinces. The price of this depth is that other provinces with interesting national-provincial party dynamics – particularly Quebec and Saskatchewan – are left out of the analysis. However, the framework of analysis developed in later chapters can and should be applied to party organizations in these provinces. I tentatively explore the implications of this framework for several provinces in the concluding chapter.

The same can be said of the decision to study a single party rather than all three major national parties. The primary drawback of this research design decision is that variability in national-provincial integration among the parties cannot be observed. Since previous studies have demonstrated that such variability does exist, with the NDP more integrated and the Conservatives more decentralized than the Liberal Party (Dyck 1992), this decision prevents this work from exploring the causes of these differences. Furthermore, the effect of different types of party organizations – predominantly cadre for the Liberal and Conservative parties and mass for the NDP – on integration and differentiation cannot be explored. However, the focus on a single party allows for a deeper understanding not only of the Liberal Party but also of the ways that integration takes place in the constituencies. This study draws on observation of a single party to develop inductively an empirical framework that can be applied to other parties, even in other institutional settings outside Canada.

Watching and Talking to Grassroots Liberals

The empirical research for this study consisted mostly of watching local party organizations in action and talking to party activists themselves. The fieldwork for this project took place between January 2006 and June 2007. Participant observation was an important aspect of this field research. I attended association executive meetings, inter-election maintenance events, information meetings, fundraisers, informal functions, and outings of local activists. I also attended nomination contests and worked on a local election campaign.

In addition to this participant observation, I conducted seventy-six semi-structured interviews and engaged in a great deal more informal conversations with local party activists. Most interviewees were members of constituency association executives or had been active in local campaigns. I also interviewed former MPs and MLAs, officials with the national and provincial parties, and a few activists from the national Conservative Party.

The interviews themselves consisted of a combination of scripted and non-scripted questions. The early interviews were largely unstructured as I explored the nature of local party organization. No set interview schedule was ever developed. Instead, prior to each interview, I planned a series of questions and probes specifically for that activist in light of his or her own knowledge and experiences (to the extent that I knew what they were ahead of time). Activists were able to clarify accounts provided in previous interviews and provide fresh perspectives on occurrences within the riding, contributing to the development of several local narratives that make up the case studies contained in the chapters that follow.

Conclusion

Prior to the 1950s, Canada's national and provincial Liberal parties maintained deeply intertwined organizations as the national party relied on its provincial cousins to provide the electoral machinery necessary to win national elections. Following the 1957 and 1958 defeats, the party appears to have moved closer to a single-level archetype as successive party leaders sought to construct a pan-Canadian national party free from the grip of regional ministers and organizations. Yet the party's riding organizations have been free to retain their old integrated forms and in many cases have done so given the inherent advantages of integrated constituency organizations.

One result of many local activists' stubborn attachment to integrated local structures has been the development of an organizational incongruence between the central component of the Liberal Party, which is largely separated from those of the provincial Liberal parties, and the local components in many of the ridings, which are often linked between the two levels. While the Liberal Party in Ottawa has evolved an essentially single-level organization, the Liberal Party in many of the nation's communities has retained organizations rooted simultaneously in both national and provincial politics. This incongruence between the central and local components of the Liberal Party is the defining characteristic of what I refer to as unevenly integrated parties: a type of multi-level party that is integrated between the national and provincial levels in some aspects of its organization but not others.

If Canada's Liberal Party does fit the unevenly integrated party model, then we know a great deal about how the party's central components are separated but little about how its local components remain, to a significant extent, integrated between the national and provincial levels. Accordingly, the chapters that follow analyze the local organizations that the party maintains in the ridings. The next chapter turns to the grassroots activists who staff those local organizations and explores how these activists both identify with and participate in national and provincial politics.

2
Grassroots Party Activists

For as long as he can remember, Tony has been "fighting Tories." A committed Liberal in Saint John, New Brunswick, Tony relishes the opportunity to participate in Liberal election campaigns. He pounds the pavement going door to door handing out pamphlets, calls identified supporters on election day to offer rides to polling stations, and cheers at Liberal headquarters as the results pour in. His love of campaigning also transcends federal boundaries, for Tony can be found putting in time during both national and provincial Liberal campaigns. In this respect, he is not that different from most Liberals in Saint John. Local organizers argue that the vast majority of Liberals in the riding are consistent: they support both the national and the provincial Liberal parties. "You couldn't run an election provincially or federally [in Saint John] without using the same people," argues Carmen, another local activist.

Across the country in British Columbia, Harold is an equally enthusiastic Liberal. He campaigns hard during provincial election campaigns and has worked as a close adviser to his candidate. "To have any impact on the future," he explains, "you had to become involved with the BC Liberals, which I did." But his commitment to Liberal politics does not transcend federalism, for Harold is a long-term national Conservative partisan. His commitment to the provincial Liberal Party is matched, if not exceeded, by the time and effort that he puts into the national Conservative Party in his riding. And just as Tony is representative of Saint John's Liberal activist base, so too is Harold representative of the provincial activist base in his riding, which is a hodge-podge of national Conservatives and Liberals.

Tony and Harold illustrate how being a Liberal in the Canadian federation can mean different things for different activists. For some, it entails a commitment to Liberal politics at the national and provincial levels;

for others, it promptly ends at the division between national and provincial politics. Many scholarly accounts maintain that Canada's national and provincial parties are organizationally distinctive. But spending time among the activists who staff the local organizations of the Liberal Party immediately reveals that many of those activists, like Tony, participate in both national and provincial politics. In so doing, these activists engender a crucial personnel linkage between national and provincial parties, binding them to one another in the ridings. This occurs to the extent that outsiders might find it difficult to distinguish between the national and provincial Liberal parties in many constituencies. This chapter explores party activists, particularly their orientations toward and participation in national and provincial politics.

Studies of political party membership in developed democracies suggest that parties have adapted to new communications technology and the decline of previous social alignments by evolving organizations that are less reliant on party members and activists than were the old mass parties (see, e.g., Katz 1997). Canadian parties do appear to be neglecting the maintenance of their memberships and activist bases, since the rate of party members is dropping and older members are generally not being replaced (Cross and Young 2006, 14-15).

However, the geographic imperatives of Canada's single-member plurality electoral system mean that successful national parties have always relied on activist bases in the constituencies to maintain local party structures and contribute to local election campaigns. Local activists continue to play important roles in the ridings. For example, the personnel of constituency association executives, which oversee the day-to-day operations of constituency parties, are drawn from the local activist bases. Aspiring politicians might clinch the party nomination by appealing to existing activists and party members (Sayers 1999, 76). By supporting nomination candidates and voting in nomination contests, activists reaffirm local associations' right to select party candidates. And activists perform other roles in the local organizations between elections, from turning out at social events to attending regional or national party conventions.

Although the mechanics of national campaigning have modernized, constituency campaigning remains a labour-intensive task. Local activists play important roles during these campaigns, working in close contact with the candidate or as volunteers conducting local canvasses, delivering lawn signs, and getting out the vote on election day, among many other tasks. The presence of a vibrant activist base brings parties significant benefits within the constituencies, particularly as indicators of local party legitimacy (Scarrow 1996, 42-43). Members and activists are therefore a valuable commodity for the parties in the constituencies, and most Canadian campaign officials bemoan a lack of local volunteers (Carty 1991, 167).

Local party activists in federations engage with national and provincial parties in three distinctive ways. First, activists that participate in a party at only the national level or the provincial level are referred to as *single-level activists*. Other activists participate in both national and provincial parties. *Consistent activists* participate in parties that share the same name at both levels. In this study, consistent party activists are generally members of both the national Liberal Party and their provincial Liberal Party. In contrast, *inconsistent activists* participate in different parties at the two levels. These labels are adapted from the academic literature on party identifiers in multi-level states (see, e.g., Jennings and Niemi 1966; also see Jacek et al.'s [1972, 191] classification of local campaign workers, which captures participation across the national and provincial levels as well as intensity).

Inconsistent and especially consistent membership and activist bases can constitute important lines of continuity between national and provincial parties. For example, 72 percent of the members of the national Liberal Party surveyed in 2000 reported holding memberships in the national Liberal Party as well as a provincial Liberal Party (Koop and Sayers 2005, 11). This high percentage of consistent party members is not what one would expect from parties at the national and provincial levels that are formally separated from one another. Despite the formal organizational separation of national and provincial Liberal parties in Canada, many party activists continue to participate in Liberal parties at both levels. Such participation holds important consequences for how the party's local organizations function.

To describe and account for the participation of party activists at the national and provincial levels, this chapter explores activists' perceptions of national and provincial parties, how different motivations to participate lead activists to engage with national and provincial parties, and how activists budget their time within a multi-level context. The chapter closes by exploring the impact of activists' participation at the two levels on the party's constituency organizations. Because this chapter focuses on the behaviours but also the attitudes and perceptions of party activists, wherever possible I have included quotations to allow those activists to speak in their own words.

Thinking about National and Provincial Parties

How do activists conceive of the relationships between Canada's national and provincial Liberal parties? Previous analyses of Canadian parties as multi-level organizations have generally employed batteries of measures meant to assess the extent to which they are linked to one another. Smiley (1987, 103-4), for example, relies on measures of formal organizational linkages between national and provincial parties to distinguish between integrated and confederal party systems. Dyck's (1992) criteria also focus on formal organizational linkages, but Dyck also points to common voters, activists, and members as evidence of integration between parties at the two levels.

This emphasis on objectively assessing the presence or absence of linkages leads Smiley and Dyck to neglect the perceptions of the individual activists and members who participate in national and provincial parties. Even if party constitutions indicate that the national and provincial Liberal parties are separated from one another, it does not necessarily follow that activists will conceive of those parties as distinctive or experience them in a separated manner. To the contrary, activists might conclude from their own experiences in the ridings that national and provincial parties are essentially two sides of the same coin, formal-constitutional separation to the contrary notwithstanding.

Activists derive two conceptions of national and provincial parties from their experiences in the parties. Activists with a *unitary conception* of the national and provincial parties emphasize the commonalities of those parties to the extent that they fail to recognize any separation whatsoever between them. For these activists, national and provincial Liberal parties constitute interconnected branches of a common, expansive Liberal world. In contrast, activists with a *disconnected conception* of national and provincial parties recognize important distinctions between those parties. As a result, they view those parties as fundamentally discrete organizations.

Doug is a party activist from the Ontario riding of Ajax-Pickering. He has a unitary conception of the national and provincial Liberal parties in Ontario: "We're all Liberals and fighting for the same things. It only makes sense that you should be supporting your own party, whether it be federally or provincially. When it comes down to election time, you want to get out there and make sure that the Liberals win at both the federal level as well as at the provincial level." Doug conceives of the Liberal Party in Ontario as a single organization with national and provincial wings. Attached to this conception is the view that the national and provincial parties are "fighting for the same things," which is not always objectively true but which is an important aspect of Doug's unitary conception. And this conception guides his participation: Doug volunteers in both the national and the provincial constituency associations in his riding and participates in both national and provincial campaigns to ensure that "Liberals win at both the federal level as well as at the provincial level."

Carmen, a consistent party activist in Saint John, provides another example of an activist with a unitary conception of the national and provincial Liberal parties in her province. Long prohibited from actively participating in partisan politics by her employment in the civil service, Carmen made up for lost time following her retirement by participating in several municipal, provincial, and national campaigns. Her Liberal family history informs her unitary conception of the national and provincial parties, which in turn shapes her consistent activism.

Carmen betrays her unitary conception of the national and provincial Liberal parties by failing to discern between them in conversation. In describing her local activism in Saint John, she veers back and forth between national and provincial campaigns, rarely bothering to distinguish between campaigns for national Liberal candidates and provincial Liberal candidates. In her unfocused account of her initial involvement in Saint John politics following her retirement, Carmen demonstrates that any distinction between national and provincial (not to mention municipal) has not guided her involvement:

> Okay, the first thing I did: Laura ran for [city] council, so I helped her ... And she almost won. Then we did different things, and then she decided she was going to run for the provincial [Liberal] party. But in the meantime, Paul Zed had run [for the national Liberal Party] in that time ... So when Paul Zed first ran I did the special ballots for that election. Then Laura ran for the provincials here in Saint John, and she spent a whole year working on me: "You'll be my campaign manager." And I wasn't very well that year, so I didn't think that I could do it. But then the election came, and I said, "okay, I'll do it."

The thread of continuity through her involvement is the Liberal Party as a unitary organization, stretching across the national, provincial, and municipal levels.

For some activists, crossover between the national and provincial levels is difficult to justify. But for Carmen, there is no need to discern between or evaluate the policies of the national and provincial Liberal organizations in Saint John because those organizations represent different branches of the same expansive party. Just as Doug's unitary conception informs his participation in both national and provincial parties, so too does Carmen's unitary conception allow her participation in both the national and the provincial Liberal parties with ease.

In contrast to Doug and Carmen, Jordan is an example of an activist who has a disconnected conception of the national and provincial Liberal parties in his home province of British Columbia. A small businessman from Richmond, Jordan commences his discussion of his participation by drawing a sharp distinction between the national and provincial Liberal parties. "I don't consider them [provincial Liberals] to be real Liberals," he explains. "I make no connection between the provincial and the federal parties." Whereas Doug and Carmen speak of a holistic Liberal Party, Jordan and activists like him emphasize the formal-legal separation of the national and provincial parties. His disconnected conception is so strong that he views the provincial Liberal Party as an imposter.

Like Doug and Carmen, Jordan's conception of the national and provincial Liberal parties informs his identification with and participation in the two parties. His strong commitment to the national Liberal Party motivates Jordan to sit on his national association executive and commit a significant amount of time to the local re-election campaigns of his Liberal MP, Raymond Chan. "I worked long and hard on his candidacy for his election," he explains. "That just snow-balled ... Now it's a big part of my life. I do a lot of volunteer work [for the association]." But his disconnected conception of those parties allows Jordan to reject the provincial Liberal Party even as he is very active in the national party. "I haven't done anything at the provincial level," he says.

Peter, a national activist from the Ontario riding of Don Valley East, is another good example of an activist with a disconnected conception. It derives largely from watching and interacting with single-level activists in the province: "There are people who are very discerning and who will be very loyal to the provincial party but object strenuously to the federal party [and vice versa]. So they'll stubbornly stay with the Liberals provincially but not have anything to do with the party at the federal level." What distinguishes Peter from other activists with a disconnected conception is that he views those parties primarily as collections of activists – parties are defined by their personnel rather than by their formal structures. For Peter, the national and provincial parties in Ontario are separated from one another because many activists are not involved at both levels. His interactions with inconsistent and single-level activists have led him to develop a disconnected conception of the national and provincial Liberal parties in Ontario.

This ability to distinguish between formal structures and the participation of individuals allows some activists to develop a more nuanced conception of the relationships between national and provincial parties. Earl, a consistent party activist from New Brunswick, is able to make such a distinction: "There is separation on paper, if you look at the constitution. But when you look at the people that are involved, it's much the same people." For Earl, formal organizational separation holds few consequences for local party life, where local activists link the national and provincial parties to one another through their participation. Like Peter, Earl emphasizes people rather than structures in forming his unitary conception of the national and provincial parties in his province.

Everett, a Liberal activist from New Brunswick, also distinguishes between parties as organizations and as collections of individual activists. He notes that the formal separation of the national and provincial Liberal parties in New Brunswick is mitigated by the joint participation of local activists in Saint John:

> I know that when there's an election, a federal election, every provincial riding worker is asked to contribute a Saturday afternoon or whatever to Paul Zed ... It's a very ... grey line between the two when it comes to working. Obviously, the hard legal aspects of federal and provincial politics, there's a definite line. But when it comes to contributions and "would you help Paul Zed get elected?" the answer is, if you're a Liberal, "yes."

Everett raises an additional point: since the Liberal Party does not offer many opportunities for members to engage with the wider party, activists are most likely to interact with the local organizations. In describing the participation of activists, he makes explicit reference to constituency-level fundraising and campaigning. By distinguishing formal structures from participation, activists like Everett are able to distinguish between the central and local components of the party organization. The central components of national and provincial Liberal parties might be formally separate, Everett tells us, but this does not preclude local participation in the politics of both levels. Formal-legal separation of the national and provincial parties does not necessarily entail separation on the ground, where activists focus their participation.

Activists' conceptions of national and provincial parties are important because those conceptions inform their participation at the national and provincial levels. For the most part, activists with a unitary conception of those parties are consistent activists who both identify with and participate in the national and provincial Liberal parties. Because activists like Carmen see the national and provincial parties as different branches of the same party, it is difficult for them to justify single-level and especially inconsistent forms of activism. Such a unitary conception can therefore be thought of as a filter that rules out inconsistent or single-level activism. In contrast, activists with a disconnected conception of the national and provincial Liberal parties are not necessarily consistent activists. By accepting that national and provincial parties are discrete organizations, these activists open up other possibilities for participation. Some activists, such as Doug, remain consistent partisans despite the formal separation of national and provincial Liberal parties. Others, such as Jordan, become inconsistent or single-level activists.

The Goals and Participation of Local Party Activists
Consistent, inconsistent, and single-level forms of participation are shaped by both the goals that activists bring to their involvement and their constituency environments. This section explores how ideological, solidary (social), and material goals inform activists' identification with and participation in national and provincial parties.

Ideological Goals
Ideological or purposive motivations to engage in activism refer to the policy benefits that activists hope to derive from the election of their favoured party. Ideological activists get involved in parties to make a difference in terms of policy. These goals are important in motivating activists in all Canadian national parties but are generally weaker for activists in the older brokerage parties than for those in the NDP, Bloc Québécois, and the now defunct Canadian Alliance (Young and Cross 2002, 562-63). Nevertheless, the Liberal Party harbours a significant number of ideological "believers," to use the term from Panebianco (1988, 27).

Ideological motivations for some activists encourage consistent identification and participation. This is especially true for activists with a unitary conception of the national and provincial parties. Organizational continuity between these parties in their view links the policy goals of the parties to one another, so ideological motivations reinforce their consistent participation at the national and provincial levels.

In contrast, activists with a disconnected conception of national and provincial parties might rely on ideological evaluations to guide their identification and participation at the two levels. Even activists who recognize a formal organizational distinction between national and provincial parties might be inclined to engage with both parties on the basis of the perceived ideological proximity of those parties to their own beliefs. For consistent activists with ideological goals, the national and provincial parties must therefore be proximate to one another in policy terms.

Louis is a good example of a party activist with a disconnected conception of the national and provincial Liberal parties in New Brunswick, but he relies on ideological assessments of the national and provincial parties to inform his consistent identification and participation. Louis is a long-time party activist in northern New Brunswick who identifies strongly with the Liberal brand and therefore with both the national and provincial parties. His identification with both parties results from his perception that both the national party and the provincial party are distinctly centre-left in their policies and therefore proximate to his own beliefs. "It's basically a question of philosophy," Louis notes. "The Liberals here are a lot more left, centre-left ... The rightful place of the Liberal Party is left of centre. That's their place, as far as I'm concerned. And throughout the years, I think it has proven most of the time to be the case."

Louis recognizes, however, that the ideological proximity of the national and provincial Liberal parties in New Brunswick is not the norm in each province. Instead, provincial Liberal parties can diverge radically from the policy orientation of the national Liberal Party: "As you go west, [the provincial Liberal parties] move more and more to the right. To the point that in BC you have the old Alliance/Reform Party joining with the Liberals and actually forming the government. Which makes it difficult, when the party moves too far to the right, for us easterners and Atlantic people." His separated conception of the national and provincial Liberal parties allows him to distinguish between these parties on an ideological basis. For Louis, the centre-left position of the national and provincial Liberal parties in New Brunswick constitutes an incentive for him to identify with and participate in both parties.

However, Louis also recognizes that the formal organizational division between the national and provincial Liberal parties allows the latter parties to respond to distinctive provincial demands and diverge from the dominant credo of the national party (as he interprets it). As a result, Louis would not be a consistent party activist if he lived in a province where the provincial Liberal Party diverged from his own ideological beliefs. "I know that, if I would be in BC, I would not be a Liberal," Louis explains. "I would probably go for the NDP, which is a lot closer to my philosophy of what the Liberal Party should be to get my vote."

For Carmen, the prospect of supporting a non-Liberal party at either the national or the provincial level is unthinkable. This stance results largely from her unitary conception of the national and provincial Liberal parties in New Brunswick. For Louis, a disconnected conception of national and provincial parties and his strong ideological goals mean that he judges national and provincial parties separately on the basis of their policies, so inconsistent activism is a possibility. His disconnected conception means that he is a consistent activist only as long as the national and provincial Liberal parties in New Brunswick continue to espouse roughly the same policies.

Ascertaining the ideological proximity of national and provincial parties to their own beliefs is particularly useful for activists in provinces such as British Columbia, where the national and provincial party systems differ from one another. Activists in that province are well aware that shared partisan labels do not guarantee ideological similarity between the national and provincial Liberal parties. As a result, ideological activists must rely on their own policy judgments of the national and provincial parties. Consistent activists in these provinces have concluded that the national and provincial Liberal parties are the best locations for them to pursue their ideological and policy-oriented goals.

Natasha provides a good example of such an activist. "I'm very socially liberal and very fiscally conservative," she explains. "So I would say that I'm pretty centre." For Natasha, this centrist ideological position represents the true "Liberal Party philosophy," an ideological placement similar to that noted by Louis: the "rightful place of the Liberal Party." Like Louis, Natasha identifies the true philosophy of the national Liberal Party close to her own beliefs. But she also recognizes that there are ideological differences between the national and provincial Liberal parties in British Columbia. Natasha views parties as collections of individuals who can be organized into factions with differing and sometimes conflicting policy preferences:

> The provincial Liberal Party definitely has factions that are more right leaning. And the federal Liberal Party seems to have factions of people that are more left leaning. The provincial party has those Socred-minded, conservative-minded kind of people. That's the BC Liberals. The federal Liberals have people that are actually more true Liberals, I would say. People that are more true to that Liberal Party philosophy.

As a result, Natasha has ideological disagreements with party members in both the national and the provincial parties. These policy differences, however, take on different forms at the two levels. "Sometimes I get annoyed with people in both parties that are to the right or the left of me," Natasha says. "And usually, in the provincial party, it's people that are to the right of me. In the federal, it's people that are to the left of me."

Despite these differing distributions of ideological diversity in the national and provincial parties, Natasha continues to identify with and participate in both parties. Her consistent activism results from her own evaluations of the ideological positions of the two parties. "Both of them are closest to what I believe in," she explains when asked to justify her consistent activism in British Columbia's national and provincial Liberal parties. By assessing national and provincial parties from an ideological perspective, Natasha is able to cope with distinctive national and provincial party systems in that province.

Natasha demonstrates how national and provincial parties that share a name can nevertheless sometimes appear to activists as ideologically distinctive. Yet consistent activists, particularly those with a unitary conception of the national and provincial Liberal parties, can be quite forgiving and willing to grant the parties some ideological leeway. Such activists recognize that the distinctive worlds of national and provincial politics sometimes place differing demands on the national and provincial Liberal parties but that the parties' responses to these demands invalidate neither their fundamental ideological similarities nor their organizational linkages.

Sadie, a long-term consistent Liberal activist from the Ontario riding of Haldimand-Norfolk, provides an example of just such an activist. Sadie holds a unitary conception of the national and provincial Liberal parties in Ontario that derives from her family history in the party. "It's just my upbringing," she explains. "My family has always been Liberal. We've always been federal Liberals, and we've always been provincial Liberals, and that's just kind of the way it's been. So I've grown up with that." Her long-time unitary conception of the national and provincial Liberal parties in Ontario allows her to justify their apparent ideological divergence:

> I think on a general level they are [ideologically similar]. I think that the way they express those [perspectives] in terms of policies can sometimes be quite different because obviously federal and provincial demands can be quite different at times ... But I think at a general level,

> if you boil it down to its base, it really is the same all around ... I think
> in the end the goals of both the federal and provincial parties are gener-
> ally the same, and I think that's why I support the party overall.

That Sadie refers to the national and provincial Liberal parties in Ontario
as "the party overall" betrays an underlying unitary conception of the
two parties. Working from this perspective, she explains away apparent
ideological divergence between the two parties by taking note of the
different demands that those parties face at the national and provincial
levels.

Natasha and Sadie demonstrate how ideological activists within the
Liberal Party can be quite ineffectual anchors on the catch-all tendencies
of party leaders. "Believers" such as Natasha and Sadie are generally
thought to place limits to toleration on the actions of party leaders, al-
beit in a weakened form for brokerage parties such as the Liberal Party
(Tanguay 1992, 467). However, Natasha and Sadie are willing to tolerate
ideological divergence as long as the parties remain within the bounds
of, to use Natasha's phrase, the "true Liberal Party philosophy." The idea
of a true Liberal Party philosophy calls to mind Christian and Campbell's
(1990) classic argument that national parties in Canada are not necessarily ideological but do embody fairly broad ideological coalitions.
Ideological activists in the Liberal Party seem to perceive the existence
of such a coalition and use it to guide their participation at the national
and provincial levels. But they interpret this coalition in different ways.
One gets the impression that Natasha and Sadie interpret this ideological
coalition as quite broad, whereas Louis has a more narrow, exclusive
conception.

In sharp contrast, ideological motivations and goals for some activists
lead to inconsistent identification and participation. For these activists,
different parties at the national and provincial levels best represent their
own ideological preferences. Guided by their ideological evaluations of
national and provincial parties, such activists participate in an inconsistent manner.

Donald, an activist from the Ontario riding of Don Valley East, is a
good example of an activist whose ideological goals have led him to
inconsistent partisanship and participation. A successful engineer ap-
proaching retirement, he identifies with the national Conservative Party.
However, Donald traces his inconsistent activism to his reaction to the
provincial Conservative government of Mike Harris in the 1990s. "I'm
basically Conservative," he volunteers. "I've pretty much voted Conservative my whole life both federally and provincially ... I voted Liberal

once at the federal level and have regretted it ever since." However, the Harris government's neo-conservative ideology in general and its education policy in particular alienated Donald. "My wife's a high school teacher, and she loves teaching. She took early retirement because she couldn't stand what was going on in the school system. So I thought, 'If it's that screwed up, we'd better get rid of Mike Harris.'" As a result, Donald sought out the provincial Liberal candidate in his riding and signed up to volunteer on the campaign. "Our local Liberal candidate ... was having an open house. So I went down and introduced myself and said 'I'd like to join his campaign.' Mainly to get rid of the [provincial] Conservatives."

However, Donald's policy objections to the provincial Conservative Party and his newfound activism in the provincial Liberal Party did not extend to the national level. As a result, Donald became an inconsistent party activist. "There's a lot of people who look at the ideology of each [national and provincial] organization and work from there," he explains, describing how his separated conception of the national and provincial Liberal parties in Ontario allows him to assess the parties as separate organizations. For Donald, the separation of the two parties allows him to come to different ideological conclusions at the two levels and participate accordingly. "The provincial Liberals, I'm comfortable with their platform and their program and what they're trying to do. Federally, I just don't feel like they have any platform or anything. There's nothing there to support as far as I'm concerned."

In some cases, inconsistency is a response to perceived ideological differences between the Liberal parties at the national and provincial levels. Blake (1982, 691-92), for example, argues that party activists cannot identify with national and provincial parties in a consistent manner when there are significant differences between them. Perceived ideological differences between the national and provincial Liberal parties in British Columbia lead many ideological activists to participate in the national or provincial Liberal Party but in a different party at the other level.

Harold, a retired businessman from Port Moody-Westwood-Port Coquitlam, is a good example of an activist whose ideological goals have led him to become an inconsistent party activist within the context of British Columbia's distinctive national and provincial party systems. Harold is a long-time national Conservative activist who brings strong ideological motivations to this activism. "Free enterprise, low taxes, good government" is how he succinctly summarizes those beliefs. For Harold, party activism is a good way to advance his own ideological beliefs. "I firmly believe in the philosophy of the Conservative Party," he explains. "If I want to see that through, I've got to do something about it. You can't sit on the sidelines and criticize."

Within the context of British Columbia's dissimilar national and provincial party systems, ideological goals have led Harold to participate in the national Conservative Party and the provincial Liberal Party. He relocated to British Columbia from Ontario and, faced with a new provincial party system that did not include a competitive provincial Conservative Party, quickly found that the provincial Liberal Party was the best party in which to advance his ideological goals. Harold accordingly became an inconsistent activist, continuing his long-standing participation in the national Conservative Party but also becoming involved in the provincial Liberal Party. However, his newfound inconsistent activism was cause for alarm among his staunchly Conservative family back in Ontario.

> I went home to see my mom, who still lives in Ontario, and I explained to her that I was now doing some work for the BC Liberals. "Who!?" So I had to explain to her that the BC Liberals were a coalition of Conservatives, Socreds, and whoever else. And she's eighty-six, [and she said], "well, I just hope you know what you're doing."

Harold used ideological perceptions of national and provincial parties to adapt his activism to a new environment, an environment that mystifies his family from Ontario, where the national and provincial party systems are very similar. Since doing so, he has come to play an important role in the national Conservative constituency association and in national campaigns in Port Moody-Westwood-Port Coquitlam as well as in provincial Liberal election campaigns in the riding. Just as her ideological evaluations of the national and provincial parties in British Columbia led Natasha to become a consistent party activist, so too did his ideological evaluations lead Harold to inconsistent activism.

In other cases, ideological goals produce single-level identification and participation. Like inconsistent activists, such activists might be responding to differences between the national and provincial party systems. For single-level activists, however, only one party at one level best conforms to their own beliefs; there exists no equivalent at the other level, and such activists therefore withdraw from that level.

Christopher, an activist from the national riding of Vancouver Quadra, is a good example of a party activist whose ideological goals shaped his identification and participation in a single-level direction. Christopher is a young professional but already has wide-ranging experience as a party activist given that he first became involved in Liberal politics at a young age. He commenced his participation as a consistent Liberal activist and brought strongly ideological motivations to his activism. "I saw myself more as wanting to save the world and all that stuff," he says. In this initial period, Christopher refined his progressive views and gained a reputation within the party organization as a proponent of left-wing causes. "I actually carried this reputation I had in the party as a policy wonk," he reports. "Perhaps some might say naive." Rather than being frustrated by the brokerage tendencies of the national Liberal Party, he valued internal party debates over policy.

Christopher joined the national and provincial Liberal parties just prior to the 1994 provincial party convention when the national and provincial organizations were formally separated from one another. The practical effects of this formal separation for activists like Christopher were negligible in the short term: "I basically joined the parties just as they were splitting, at least on a formal basis," he recalls. "But they were still ... quite similar in terms of who was involved." Like other activists, Christopher draws a distinction between the personnel and structures of parties. As a result, formal separation created no conflict for him, and he remained active in the national and provincial parties as well as in his local constituency associations in Vancouver Quadra.

However, his consistent activism was strained in the following years as Christopher observed that the provincial Liberal Party was increasingly diverging from the centre-left position established by the national party. For him, this divergence resulted primarily from an influx of national Conservative and former Social Credit activists into the provincial party. His observations are consistent with Blake's (1996, 78) analysis of the provincial Liberal Party in this period: "Many of the new members were disaffected Socreds whose addition to the Liberal activist group shifted the Liberal Party's position in the ideological spectrum toward the right ... Newcomers are ideologically distinct from veterans ... Those who joined the party following the 1991 election are significantly more right-wing and populist than those with longer-standing ties to the party."

For national Liberals, the movement of national Conservatives into the provincial Liberal Party was cause for annoyance. But for progressive ideological activists like Christopher, the newfound presence of these right-wing "meat-eaters" within the provincial Liberal ranks was cause for alarm. He perceived a shift to the right by the BC Liberal Party, an ideological shift that increasingly distinguished the provincial Liberal Party from its former counterpart in Ottawa. This shift created conflict for Christopher given the strong ideological goals that drive his participation in Liberal politics.

In addition, the presence of a new right-wing challenger to the BC Liberal Party, the provincial Reform Party, created incentives for the BC Liberals to consolidate their own right-wing support. Christopher naturally disapproved of this strategy: "I had some concerns about the rightward drift [of the provincial party] at the time and particularly the explicit strategy of edging out the Reform Party. I saw the strategic merit behind that particular strategy. But I was still quite blindly idealistic at the time, and I had some concerns." Ultimately, his response to this newfound ideological divergence between the national and provincial Liberal parties was to cease his participation in the provincial Liberal Party and focus his energies on the national party, which he thought had remained closer to his own ideological views. "I let my membership lapse back then," he recalls.

Although Christopher has ceased his involvement in the provincial party, he maintains social ties to activists in the party. These ties, however, are not strong enough to overrule his ideological instincts and persuade him to renew his participation in the provincial party. Instead, Christopher has become a party activist who focuses his participation on a single level. The result is that he has invested significant amounts of time in the national constituency association in Vancouver Quadra, taking on leadership roles in that association and in the party as a whole. Christopher is therefore a good example of an activist whose ideological goals played a role in shaping his single-level activism.

Solidary Goals
Activists can also pursue solidary goals through their participation in political parties. Solidary goals refer to the relationships and recreational opportunities that individuals seek through their partisan involvement. The solidary rewards of partisan participation declined as the social bases of mass parties disintegrated over the course of the twentieth century (Scarrow 2000). However, local party organizations in particular continue to provide solidary rewards to activists. Relationships between local activists are forged and developed during inter-election maintenance events, election campaigns, and the high drama of election nights.

Solidary rewards play an important role in maintaining the participation of party activists (Young and Cross 2002, 567). Many activists become involved in party politics to pursue material or ideological goals. But the continued participation of many of these activists is sustained by the relationships formed during their initial participation in parties and the recreational activities that local party organizations offer. Having joined a group bound together by friendships, solidary activists face new incentives to follow the pack and participate in its activities.

For many solidary activists, connecting with a welcoming local group encourages participation in the same party at both the national level and the provincial level. This occurs when activists join pre-existing groups of consistent activists, whether these are informal circles or organized more systematically within the organization of the local constituency association.

Carmen, an activist in the national constituency of Saint John, provides a good example of a party activist whose consistent activism has been motivated by solidary goals within the local activist base. For Carmen, party life is defined in terms of relationships and human contacts. Her participation in nomination and election campaigns is not an altruistic act, she explains; rather, it is a "two-way street" in which her dedication is rewarded with social contacts and relationships. "I had a great time [working on an election campaign]. I met all kinds of great people ... So it's not a one-way street. Anyone who thinks it's a one-way street is a fool. They won't have any fun with it either. I had a lot of fun with it."

As Carmen became more involved in her constituency party, she developed meaningful social bonds with other local activists. Whereas other activists emphasize loyalty to the candidate or an ideological commitment when accounting for their own partisan activities, Carmen emphasizes social bonds with other activists. *Fun* is therefore a word that appears frequently in her descriptions of her participation in local party events and campaigns, and Carmen is not alone in this respect. Her participation is animated by the relationships that she has developed within the local Liberal activist base, which comes together between and during election campaigns in Saint John:

> We had a great team in that [campaign] office. We had lots of fun. We had all sorts of inside jokes. You know, we're very supportive of one another. I think we were all kind to one another. We looked out for one another, and that's what kept us going ... I just think that that helps.

When you have a group of people that like each other and have a common goal and are going to be supportive of one another.

Members of the pre-existing activist base that Carmen entered are engaged, for the most part, at both the national level and the provincial level. "Far and away the majority of people [in Saint John] are involved in both parties," explains Tony, a local party organizer. As Carmen developed social relationships with other activists, she faced solidary incentives to participate in national and provincial Liberal campaigns. As her friends signed up to work on both national and provincial campaigns, her positive experiences on previous campaigns provided incentives for her to volunteer in other campaigns at both national and provincial levels. "We had fun working together wherever we were," she confirms.

Carmen illustrates the strong influence that social relationships can have on activists' participation in national and provincial parties. But it is important to keep in mind that the local activist base in Saint John acted as an intermediary between her solidary goals and her consistent participation. Carmen originally built a social network within the context of a consistent activist base that was engaged at both the national level and the provincial level. Within such a context, solidary relations pushed her to participate in the national and provincial Liberal parties, lest she feel left out of the group.

But this is not the case in every riding, for many contain pre-existing activist bases of mostly inconsistent partisans. Within such ridings, solidary incentives lead to inconsistent activism. Once activists enter such circles, the social bonds that bind them to other members of the group provide strong incentives to follow the pack and participate as inconsistent party activists.

Helen, from the BC riding of Kootenay-Columbia, is a good example of an activist who is motivated by solidary goals to participate inconsistently. Her activism commenced in the national Reform Party, which reflected her ideological goals, and continued in the national Canadian Alliance and the national Conservative Party when the party transformed in 2000 and 2004. Helen originally developed a strong attachment to the national Reform Party and a hostility to Liberal politics. "We were supporters of [Reform Party leader] Preston Manning and his thinking," she explains. "We felt that we were definitely conservative thinkers, and we liked what we heard." Her activism at the national level was first motivated by ideological goals.

Since Manning eschewed formal linkages between the national Reform Party and any provincial party, Helen, who had never before been involved in politics, commenced her partisan participation as a single-level activist (Stark 1992, 144). Following her initial participation, she developed strong solidary attachments to the group of national Conservative activists in her community. "I think what happened is that I formed friendships with these people," she explains. "Then we started to do other things like have lunch. And then, when an election came up, it was kind of fun because we were going to be working together again." Although Helen was first motivated by ideological concerns, she soon encountered solidary incentives to continue to participate at the national level. These motivations reinforced her single-level activism in the national Reform/Alliance/Conservative parties.

However, Helen became involved in the provincial Liberal Party in the lead-up to the 2001 BC provincial election. She received encouragement to do so by the social network that she had joined through her involvement in the national Conservative Party. As other members of her social network signed up to support the provincial Liberal candidate, Helen felt more and more tempted to join in. "I have to say that I got involved provincially because Jane and Marie were also supporting [the provincial candidate]," she explains, naming two of her national Conservative friends. Solidary goals were therefore influential in convincing Helen to participate in the provincial Liberal campaign despite a partisan and ideological discomfort with the party.

As a result, Helen has evolved from a single-level to an inconsistent activist largely in response to solidary incentives. To engage in single-level activism would mean that she would miss opportunities to participate in the activities of her friends at the national and provincial levels. And to engage in consistent activism would likely confuse or even alienate large segments of that social group. In these ways, solidary goals within the context of Kootenay-Columbia's local activist base provided Helen with powerful incentives to become an inconsistent activist. It is a striking outcome given her former hostility to the Liberal brand in Canada, and it illustrates the influence of solidary incentives for activists like her.

The involvement of both Carmen and Helen in national and provincial parties is related to their solidary connections to activists who participate at both levels. In contrast, solidary activists who join social groups involved at only one level of the state tend to confine their participation to a single level. These activists do not extend their participation to both levels partially because their social networks provide them with no reason to do so.

Jordan, a committed national Liberal activist from British Columbia's Richmond constituency, is a good example of a single-level activist. As we saw, he has a distinctively disconnected conception of the national and provincial Liberal parties in British Columbia, and this conception informs his single-level activism. But Jordan, who values his friendships with local Liberal activists, is a member of a partisan social network that is not connected to the national and provincial Liberal parties. When asked to describe the multi-level activism of the members of his social network, Jordan responds by reaffirming his separated conception of the national and provincial Liberal parties:

> I think most people are like me. I think they're federal Liberals ... They seem to be more in tune with the federal Liberals than with the provincial Liberals ... There's a divide there between the two [parties] for most of them. And this is only my opinion, but that's the way I feel about it, that most of the people are federal Liberals. They're very committed to the federal Liberals, and they differentiate between the two [parties].

The important point here is that this is Jordan's perception of his social network. Jordan thinks that most of his friends are, like him, single-level activists, but he is not completely sure. What he does know is that a sharp line is drawn between the national and provincial Liberal parties within this social group and that he faces no pressure from this group to participate in the activities of the provincial Liberal Party. As a result, Jordan encounters no solidary incentives to cease his single-level activism and begin to participate in provincial politics. His social network can therefore be contrasted with those of Carmen and Helen, who faced significant solidary pressures to participate at both the national level and the provincial level.

Material Goals
Another reason that activists join and participate in local party organizations is to pursue material goals and economic benefits. These rewards have always attracted Canadians to party activism in the ridings. In the first party system from 1867 to 1917, widespread patronage led to an almost complete politicization of the civil service as the parties rewarded supporters with jobs. Turnover in the government saw widespread replacement in the bureaucracy, so activists worked hard for

local candidates in the hopes of gaining employment and government contracts as rewards (Carty 1992, 564). Civil service reform in 1921 led to the development of a more professional and independent bureaucracy and therefore deprived the parties of the ability to stack the civil service with supporters.

Despite this, the potential to secure economic benefits – from party jobs to government patronage – continues to motivate Canadians to become active in political parties. This is especially true for the Liberal Party, for material incentives are more important in spurring participation in the Liberal Party than in the other national parties. This has much to do with the party's historical electoral success and commensurate ability to distribute favours to activists (Young and Cross 2002, 560).

Activists with material goals tend to treat their partisan participation as they would a business: they consciously decide on a plan of action that is meant to produce the biggest payoff in material rewards. Two strategies employed by activists to reap material rewards can be discerned.

First, some activists with material goals diversify their participation in national and provincial parties. These activists participate in these parties with the view that, by maximizing their interactions, they maximize their chances to be rewarded in some way. Diversifying is also a strategy meant to minimize risk; if the activist strikes out with the national party, he or she might still receive some benefit from the provincial party (or vice versa). Activists who pursue a diversifying strategy might involve themselves in the same parties or different parties at the two levels and are therefore always consistent or inconsistent.

Second, some activists with material goals focus their efforts on one level or the other. The logic behind this strategy is that activists, by focusing on a single party, can maximize their chances of receiving material rewards from that party. If an activist hopes to receive a job from an MP, for example, that activist might focus her participation on the national level, expending time and effort on constituency association activities and the re-election campaign in the hope of making an impression on the MP. For these activists, participation in the politics of the other level distracts them from their primary goal and should therefore be avoided. Activists who employ a focused strategy to gain material benefits are necessarily single-level activists.

Material goals with a diversifying strategy might lead to consistent activism at the national and provincial levels. Tom is a good example of a party activist whose material and careerist goals inform his consistent activism. Originally from the Restigouche region of New Brunswick, he became involved in the Liberal Party as a teenager and was captivated by the prospect of a career in politics. After participating in student politics, Tom arrived in Ottawa to finish his postsecondary education but quickly found himself swept up in Liberal politics.

Tom encountered two opportunities in Ottawa that shaped his future participation in the national and provincial Liberal parties. First, the Liberal MP who represented Restigouche offered Tom employment as a staffer. For Tom, employment on Parliament Hill reinvigorated the careerist goals that had originally motivated his party activism. This job also opened doors for Tom within the national Liberal organization. For example, he was elected to the executive of the national Young Liberals of Canada auxiliary and played an important role in that organization. As a result, he was able to familiarize himself with the national Liberal organization and develop personal contacts throughout it.

Tom was presented with his second opportunity when he took a new job from the same MP, this time as a constituency office worker in his home region. Having already made a name for himself in the national organization, he returned to New Brunswick with an opportunity to familiarize himself with the Liberal organization in his home province and build contacts there. As a consistent party activist, Tom worked with both national and provincial Liberals in New Brunswick. However, consistent activism also represented a diversifying strategy: by participating at the national and provincial levels in New Brunswick, Tom hoped to multiply his own opportunities in the province.

His diversifying strategy allowed him to pursue subsequent opportunities at both the national level and the provincial level in New Brunswick. When a provincial redistribution resulted in a vacant constituency in his new city of residence, Tom hastily constructed a local organization to contest the Liberal nomination. Drawing on his experience and profile in the national and provincial parties, Tom won the provincial Liberal nomination contest in his riding but narrowly lost the subsequent race against the Progressive Conservative candidate in the 2006 provincial election. Despite this setback, Tom took an important position with the provincial Liberal Party in Fredericton and continues to play a key role in the party.

From a broad perspective, Tom's diversifying strategy for political activism has been remarkably successful at obtaining careerist rewards. As a consistent activist, Tom was able to pursue opportunities with the national and provincial Liberal parties depending on the circumstances that he found himself in at the time. In Ottawa, he was employed by and advanced in the national party. Back in New Brunswick, he continued to be employed by the national party but also worked in the provincial party organization. As a result, Tom was able to seamlessly switch his focus to the provincial level when an opportunity to pursue elected office arose. When that effort was unsuccessful, he rebounded by returning to a party job, this time with the provincial rather than the national Liberal Party. His experiences therefore illustrate how careerist goals can lead to consistent activism.

In sharp contrast to Tom, activists who pursue material goals with a focused strategy typically become single-level activists. They hope to derive material benefits from one level or the other by focusing specifically on that level. Everett, a professional and partner in a small Saint John firm, is a good example of a single-level activist with material goals. He differs from Tom in that he is uninterested in employment with the national and provincial parties and laughs at the prospect of running for office. However, Everett is very interested in obtaining government contracts for his firm. His party activism has always been motivated by material goals. His original involvement in his local party was spurred by his relentless search for "the big plums":

> We received a fair share of provincial government work ... Generally, they farm it out in an equitable manner. Except for the big plums, like a big hospital or something like that. So, during my liaison with the local Liberal people, I was asking, "how does one position oneself to get more work, to get the big plums?" That sort of thing. The short answer was, "if you want to hit a home run, you've got to step up to the plate. Why don't you come to a meeting?"

As a result, Everett attended the annual general meeting of his local provincial constituency association and, despite this being his first involvement with the party, was elected to the local executive. "When they see a professional walk in to a riding meeting," he explains, "they immediately assume you're going to be on the board of directors, and they vote you in. That's what happened." Convinced that local involvement was the best route to securing government contracts, Everett allowed himself to be nominated to sit on the executive, and since that initial involvement he has sat on the provincial executive in his riding for over ten years.

Everett is a good example of a party activist with material goals because he consciously shapes his participation at the national and provincial levels to maximize his chances of meeting those goals. This is apparent even in the organization of his small firm. When Everett took on a partner in his firm, he paid special attention to the partisanship of his new partner:

> My friend, who is now my business partner, was thinking of coming to New Brunswick. He grew up here ... I said, "if you're going to come back, one of us should be a Liberal, and one of us should be a Tory." And I said, "unless you are deeply rooted in the Liberal Party of Canada or the Liberal Party of Ontario" – because that's where he was at the time – "I am currently going down this [Liberal] road, and you should look at the Tory side." And he said, "fine, I have no problem with that."

By convincing his partner to commit to the provincial Conservative Party, Everett hoped to make his firm competitive for government contracts even when the Conservatives were in power. And this strategy proved to be successful: on arriving in Saint John, Everett's new partner, a former Liberal, commenced a long period of activism in his local Conservative organization. The partner played a major role in the re-election campaigns of a Conservative MLA and cabinet minister. The motives behind this participation, according to Everett, were clear: "That's what I did for you, so, if there's a chance for you to butter my bread, I expect you to do it." And, Everett happily reported, this activism had finally culminated in the firm receiving "a major plum" from the then Conservative provincial government.

From the commencement of his activism, Everett has focused almost entirely on the provincial Liberal Party. This commitment to the provincial level derives from his assessment of the level of government from which his firm is most likely to receive contracts. For Everett, activism at the national level is a waste of time because it is unlikely to result in material benefits, at least in the form that he prefers. Instead, Everett has adopted a focused strategy that allows him to concentrate on the provincial level instead of committing time and effort to both the national party and the provincial party.

The Local Organizational Context

Ideological, solidary, and material incentives combine in certain ways with activists' local environments to produce consistent, inconsistent, and single-level participation in Canadian political parties. However, the party organizations themselves – national, provincial, and local –

provide incentives for activists to engage with national and provincial parties in certain ways. Characteristics of the activist base as a whole, constituency associations, and local campaigns come together to shape activists' involvement at the national and provincial levels.

Either the local organization or the wider party organization can provide activists with strong incentives to identify with and participate in the same parties at the national and provincial levels. This is especially true when the local constituency association structures are integrated. Harry, a young professional from the Ontario riding of Richmond Hill, is an example of a party activist whose identification with national and provincial parties was shaped by the integrated form of the local party organization. Harry commenced his partisan involvement by joining the national Liberal Party. However, his disconnected conception of the national and provincial Liberal parties in Ontario allowed him to reject the provincial party. "It's funny because, when I joined [the national Liberal Party], I wasn't that much against the provincial Conservatives, and I think I even said that I'd join [exclusively] for the federal Liberals," he explains. Harry was sympathetic to the provincial Progressive Conservative Party and its leader, Mike Harris. Accordingly, he was initially an inconsistent party identifier.

This inconsistency in party identification, however, was immediately strained by the relatively integrated constituency association structures in Harry's Ontario riding. "The first meeting [I attended] was a provincial-federal meeting," Harry explains. "I said, 'well, I'll get involved since it's a better way to get to know people.' It wasn't really because I considered myself a provincial Liberal." His initial involvement in the provincial Liberal Party therefore resulted from his desire to conform to the expectations of local party officials and the organization that they comprised.

Over time, however, as Harry participated in national/provincial meetings and party activities, his sympathy for the provincial Conservatives waned, and he instead developed an identification with the provincial Liberal Party. "I guess the more you get involved in politics, the more you realize how much you don't know," he admits. "And I started to understand what was wrong with the provincial Conservatives, and that's what made me a provincial Liberal." Harry's identification with the national and provincial Liberal parties had shifted from an inconsistent to a consistent form largely as a result of the integrated nature of the local organization.

Constituency association executives in strongly integrated ridings have a tendency to reject inconsistent party activists. This tendency also reinforces the consistent identification and participation of activists such as Harry. For him, involvement in either of the two parties necessitates consistent identification:

> I find that in Ontario, to be a provincial Conservative and a federal Liberal makes you a lot of enemies. Anyone who would be in those circumstances generally will pick one or the other, either they'll say "I'm a federal Liberal" or "I'm a provincial Conservative." Very few will try to do both at the same time. I think, realistically, if you do try to do that, you're going to have nobody trusting you on either side.

Listening to his pointed critiques of the national and provincial Conservative parties, I was amazed that Harry had in fact commenced his partisanship as an inconsistent activist who was sympathetic to the provincial Conservatives. His strong, consistent partisanship illustrates the potential impact of local structures on the identification and participation of activists in the national and provincial parties.

In other cases, aspects of the local party organization discourage consistent partisanship and encourage inconsistent or single-level forms of partisanship. Christopher encountered such organizational disincentives to engage in consistent activism within the BC Liberal Party. Recall that he ceased his involvement in the party as a result of his perception that the party had become too ideologically conservative. His ideological objections to the provincial Liberal Party saw him evolve from a consistent Liberal activist to a single-level activist at the national level. However, Christopher also faced organizational incentives to cease his activism in the provincial Liberal Party. He thought that being a consistent Liberal was increasingly frowned on in the provincial Liberal Party following the election of Gordon Campbell as leader:

> There has been active encouragement from the leadership of the BC Liberal Party to not have people in important positions take any role in the federal political process because of the coalition nature of the BC Liberal Party. If you work in a minister's office or you are an MLA, you're strongly discouraged if not directed to not participate at all in federal politics because they're concerned with that causing rifts in the BC Liberal Party.

One way that officials in the provincial Liberal Party attempt to maintain their coalition between national Liberals and Conservatives is to avoid the perception that the party is too closely aligned with either of those two national parties – this is the "coalition nature" of the party to which Christopher refers. Within such an organizational context, activists who are actively involved in national politics might find it difficult to advance in the BC Liberal Party. Christopher encountered these organizational pressures within the provincial party. However, he also thought that that pressure was applied more to national Liberals than to national Conservatives:

> Federal Liberals felt that that [rule] was perhaps more enforced when it came to the federal Liberal Party than it was when it came to the federal Reform, Alliance, or Conservative parties ... There was certainly a perception that the leadership was more tolerant of activity amongst BC Liberals in the Alliance or the Conservative Party than they were of activity in the federal Liberal Party.

Christopher abandoned the provincial Liberal Party to become a single-level activist largely because he disapproved of the newfound ideological conservatism of the provincial party. However, his identity as an ideological progressive is intertwined with his identity as a national Liberal. His increasing ideological discomfort with the provincial Liberal Party therefore coincided with his perception that national Liberal activists like him were increasingly unwelcome in the party: "The meat-eaters, as they're called in the BC Liberal Party, were gaining ascendancy and were allowed to do so by the party leadership while [national Liberals] ... were perhaps being edged out a little bit."

Christopher's single-level activism is a product of both ideological and organizational incentives. The provincial Liberal Party had diverged too far to the ideological right for Christopher. However, wrapped up in this ideological movement was a newfound rejection within the party of national Liberal activists. Finding the provincial Liberal Party inhospitable to both ideological progressives and national Liberal partisans, Christopher accordingly left the party to become a single-level activist.

Harry entered the national Liberal Party in Ontario as an inconsistent activist but quickly encountered organizational pressures to consistent activism at the two levels. In contrast, Christopher entered the national and provincial Liberal parties in British Columbia as a consistent activist, but he encountered organizational pressures that discouraged this form of activism and instead led to single-level participation. Both Harry and Christopher succumbed to these organizational pressures. The presence of consistent, inconsistent, and single-level activists shapes local party organizations, but the experiences of Harry and Christopher illustrate that pre-existing party organizations also shape the perceptions and participation of individual activists.

Activism and Time in a Multi-Level Context

Most activists who commit time to political parties in the constituencies do so as volunteers. Local participation can therefore be a high-cost activity and might consume significant amounts of time (Whiteley, Seyd, and Richardson 1994, 110). Some activists are willing to spend a great deal of time on party business, but most face time constraints and therefore must budget the time that they commit. Federalism complicates that process by adding another layer of political competition in which activists can become involved.

But federalism also presents time-strapped activists with a number of ways to budget the time that they commit to politics in the constituencies. Activists generally adopt one of four strategies. First, activists focus their participation on the administrative tasks of the local constituency associations. Second, they focus their energies on local campaigns rather than on constituency associations. Third, they prioritize their participation with either the national party or a provincial party. And fourth, they disengage themselves entirely from activism at one level of the state and become single-level activists.

The first strategy that activists employ to conserve time in a multi-level setting is to focus on certain aspects of party activity with both national and provincial parties. By limiting their participation, activists develop specializations within the structures of the local party and limit the time expended on party business while still participating at both national and provincial levels. Although participation in national and provincial politics can sometimes be overwhelming, these activists respond to the challenge by limiting their involvement.

Some activists enjoy the ongoing organizational challenges posed by involvement in the national and provincial constituency associations. These activists can be referred to as *local administrators*. They typically run for election to the constituency association executive at the national and provincial levels and involve themselves in the day-to-day organization of the local party. Local administrators engage in activities meant to preserve the integrity of the local party organization. They elect leaders; hold meetings; maintain local party records of members, volunteers, and donors; and organize outreach events in the riding, among other activities (Beck 1974, 1231). Participation in the constituency association consumes a steady amount of time, though local administrators generally commit more time in the lead-up to nomination contests and during election campaigns.

Peter plays important roles in both national and provincial constituency association executives in the Ontario riding of Don Valley East and is therefore a good example of a local administrator. He sits on several committees for both associations and actively participates in organizing inter-election events in the riding. Furthermore, Peter regularly attends regional party meetings and represents Don Valley East at these meetings. His administrative tasks at the local level consume a steady amount of time over a long period. "Many of my colleagues don't ... get so involved," he explains. "But because I'm retired, I guess I have the time. So I sit through a lot of meetings." Peter, like other local administrators, finds that participation on the local executive is an attractive form of activism in the local party. He is therefore willing to commit time on an ongoing basis, and work in local constituency associations can entail a significant amount of effort.

Focusing on administrative tasks in the national and provincial constituency associations allows local administrators to develop specialized skills in the ridings. Some executive members, for example, enjoy the challenges of working with membership lists and keeping in touch with long-time members. These local administrators assume the role of membership secretary for both the national association and the provincial association, and they work in this capacity to maintain contacts with local party members and activists. Others are skilled organizers who contribute to the planning of both national and provincial inter-election maintenance events. Still others view themselves as bagmen and seek donations for the national and provincial associations. In Fundy Royal, an executive member used his skills as a desktop publisher to create newsletters for the national and provincial associations to send out to members.

Working in both the national and the provincial associations allows these local administrators to fine-tune their specialized skills. Since these skills are of value, many local administrators believe that they are making a significant difference by lending their talents to both the national and the provincial parties, and other executive members are generally quick to confirm this. By working in similar capacities in the national and provincial associations, these local administrators constitute a thread of continuity between the two associations.

For other activists, however, working in such an administrative capacity is mundane. "There's guys like me who don't get involved on the executives," says Tony, an enthusiastic campaign worker from Saint John. "I was president of a riding for a year, and I don't want to do it again." Instead, activists such as Tony are drawn to the periodic exhilaration of election campaigns. These local activists can be thought of as campaigners or sporadic interventionists, terms that capture both the substantive and the temporal aspects of their participation (Dowse and Hughes 1977; Verba and Nie 1972, 118-19). In this study, activists who budget their time between the national and provincial levels by focusing on national and provincial election campaigns are referred to as *local campaigners*.

Tony is a good example of a local campaigner. "I'm more of a campaign guy. I do it to fight those battles," he says. "I really like campaigning. I fell in love ... when I first got involved. I rolled my sleeves up ... Nothing could make me happier than to go door to door [during a campaign]." For Tony, the ongoing administrative tasks associated with the local constituency associations hold little appeal compared with the drama of local election "battles."

The same is true for James, a party activist from York West, who expresses satisfaction that local administrators such as his friend Jason are in the riding to perform tasks that he does not want to undertake. "I don't like to get involved in all this nitty-gritty stuff," he explains, referring to the administrative work of the constituency association. "That's not my forte. Leave it to guys like Jason. They know all the rules and regulations. I'm not that kind of person." James values local administrators such as Jason because they allow local campaigners to focus on the aspects of local party politics that most interest them.

Since they are consistent or inconsistent activists, local campaigners participate in both national and provincial election campaigns. In this capacity, activists are presented with opportunities to develop their own specializations, such as working with campaign signs and phone lists. By focusing exclusively on campaigns rather than constituency association business at the national and provincial levels, activists can reconcile their consistent participation with restraints on their time and develop a specialization in some aspect of local campaigning. Local campaigners' willingness to perform the same tasks in both national and provincial campaigns means that they constitute a link between those campaigns. Indeed, candidates and their campaign managers often seek reputable local campaigners from the other level to carry out specialized tasks in their own campaigns.

Successful constituency campaigns require an appropriate mix of inner-circle members, secondary workers, and casual workers (Sayers 1999,

68). In the same way, successful local parties always contain a combination of local administrators and local campaigners. The literature provides a relatively good picture of the ratio of local administrators to local campaigners in the ridings: cadre-style constituency associations are generally characterized by a small oligarchy of committed local administrators, whereas campaigns generally draw on the efforts of a larger number of local campaigners. Cross and Young (2004, 440) report that 86 percent of Liberal Party members have volunteered with local campaigns, compared with 59 percent who have served on their local riding association. Working as a local campaigner is clearly a more widespread form of budgeting time between the national and provincial levels.

The third way that activists budget time between the national and provincial levels is to prioritize their activities at one level. These activists can be referred to as *local prioritizers*. Consistent or inconsistent prioritizers cope with time constraints by focusing the majority of their time at one level or the other. A common form of prioritization is for activists to maintain a long-term commitment to the constituency association executive at one level while participating on only election campaigns at the other level, for example by hosting a lawn sign in their front yards and attending party rallies. In this way, such activists prioritize their activism at one level while maintaining their commitment to both national and provincial parties.

James, a consistent Liberal activist from the riding of York West, is a good example of a prioritizer who concentrates his activism at the national level. He serves a variety of roles in the national party, from leadership roles in the constituency association executive to labour-intensive roles on the re-election campaigns of the national incumbent member, Judy Sgro. Although he identifies strongly with both the national and the provincial Liberal parties, constraints on his time force James to concentrate his activism at the national level and neglect the provincial level. "I don't really get involved in the provincial level," he explains. "You've got to remember, I still run a business. So I don't have that much time to spend."

Yet, despite his time constraints, identification with the provincial party means that James is occasionally tempted into participation in provincial activities, especially election campaigns. One gets the impression that provincial Liberals know that he enjoys being involved, so they tempt him into participation against his better judgment to exploit his finely tuned specializations, for he is a walking encyclopedia of local campaign strategy. "I'm involved with the others [at the provincial level]," he admits. "Take the nomination campaign that's going on now.

I'll obviously help them. I was out yesterday knocking on doors. I'll try to give it my all because I'm not working full time." However, the temptation to participate at the provincial level creates difficulties for James given his time constraints: "But like I say, I'm very busy with federal politics. I don't have that much time to spend." In James can be perceived an enthusiastic local campaigner who recognizes the need to prioritize his partisan activities but who has difficulty doing so.

Activists are sometimes unable to identify why they prioritize their activism at one level or the other. "I just fell into it that way years ago," says James, unable to account for his prioritization of national over provincial politics. But concentrating effort on one party might reflect an underlying preference for one party over the other. Activists might feel closer to a solidary grouping found at one level or the other, or they might feel ideologically closer to one party over the other. These underlying preferences help to explain why local prioritizers privilege national over provincial activism or vice versa.

Helen is a good example of a local activist who is motivated by these sorts of underlying preferences to focus on one level over the other. She is an inconsistent activist who participates in the national Conservative and provincial Liberal parties. Her inconsistent activism can be traced back to the ideological and solidary goals that she pursues through participation: her ideological beliefs attach her to the national Conservative Party, but her friends have convinced Helen to join them in working for the provincial Liberal Party. However, her primary loyalties clearly lie with the national Conservative Party. This is revealed through the intensity of her participation on national and provincial election campaigns. Helen campaigns strenuously for the national Conservative Party by working in the local campaign office until late at night, but she expends significantly less effort on provincial election campaigns. Although she brings the enthusiasm of a true ideological believer to national Conservative campaigns, Helen is drawn to provincial Liberal campaign events primarily by the opportunity to meet up and interact with friends.

Finally, activists can deal with the time constraints presented by partisan participation by engaging with only one party at either the national or the provincial level, by becoming single-level activists. Such activism itself can be interpreted as a means of budgeting time expended on party activism. Without the need to distribute their time between two parties at the national and provincial levels, such activists focus all their available energy on a single level.

Local Activist Bases in a Multi-Level Context

The previous sections addressed the perceptions and experiences of party activists as individuals. This section turns to the local activist bases comprised by these individual activists and their experiences at the national and provincial levels. To what extent can we distinguish between activist bases linked to both the national and the provincial parties and activist bases linked to only a single party?

Distinguishing between local activist bases by exploring the extent to which activists engage with national and provincial parties allows for the construction of a continuum that ranges between archetypal integrated and differentiated types. Archetypal integrated activist bases exist where the national and provincial parties share a common activist base. In contrast, archetypal differentiated activist bases exist where every activist participates in either the national or the provincial constituency association but not both.

In practice, local activist bases range between these two archetypes. Activist bases composed largely of activists who participate at both the national and the provincial levels tend toward the integrated archetype. Integrated activist bases are intertwined with the national and provincial parties, and their development as groups, complete with informal customs and internal dynamics, reflects this. In ridings such as Ontario's Ajax-Pickering or New Brunswick's Saint John, for example, local activists with roles in constituency associations and campaigns tend to identify themselves as consistent Liberals at the national and provincial levels. Furthermore, it is difficult for activists to identify single-level activists who are active in the riding. In contrast, activist bases comprised largely of single-level activists tend toward the differentiated archetype. In these cases, national and provincial groups of activists evolve separately from one another, developing their own traditions and internal dynamics.

Similar national and provincial party systems facilitate participation at both the national and provincial levels and, as a result, the development of integrated activist bases. In ridings such as Ajax-Pickering and Saint John, these activists tend to be consistent. However, in provinces such as British Columbia, where the national and provincial party systems are dissimilar, integrated activist bases at the two levels can include consistent and inconsistent activists. In Kootenay-Columbia, for example, it is the national Conservative Party and the provincial Liberal Party that share a largely common activist base. Right-wing activists in British Columbia tend to participate in the national Conservative Party. At the provincial level, however, their ideological aversion to the provincial

NDP provides an incentive for these activists to participate in the provincial Liberal Party. The integrated national-provincial activist base in Kootenay-Columbia differs in important qualitative ways from those in ridings such as Ajax-Pickering and Saint John, but it is nevertheless an integrated activist base consisting of activists who participate at both the national and the provincial levels and who have evolved mixed traditions and customs as a group. Indeed, those customs and the internal dynamics of this Conservative-Liberal integrated activist base in Kootenay-Columbia are strikingly similar to those of the Liberal-Liberal integrated activist bases in ridings like Ajax-Pickering and Saint John.

These findings are important because the presence of integrated and differentiated activist bases has consequences for the organization of constituency associations and local campaigns. Constituency association executives in ridings with integrated activist bases tend to be staffed by consistent activists drawn from the local activist base. These executive members are much more likely than single-level activists to construct linkages between the national and provincial constituency associations. In contrast, where differentiated activist bases exist, the association executive is likely to be staffed by single-level activists. Such activists are less receptive to cooperation between the two levels and are therefore more likely to conduct the business of the association in ways that differentiate it from its counterpart at the other level. In these ways, the nature of the activist base has an impact on the organization of local constituency associations.

In the same way, local campaigns in ridings with integrated activist bases are likely to draw on consistent or inconsistent activists to staff the candidate's inner circle and particularly the armies of secondary workers that perform labour-intensive tasks during the campaign. This means that, in both national and provincial campaigns, the same group of activists can be found licking envelopes, knocking on doors, and pounding in signs along the highway. The specializations that activists develop are put to use in both national and provincial campaigns. In contrast, distinctive activist bases mean that national and provincial campaigns draw on very different groups of activists to work during campaigns. Where there are distinctive activist bases, national and provincial campaigns will therefore be quite different from one another. Because local campaigns draw on local activist bases to a certain extent, the presence of integrated or distinctive activist bases necessarily shapes the character of local campaigns.

The academic literature on federalism and Canadian political parties suggests that national and provincial parties in Canada are largely separated from one another. Yet many activists do not conceive of those parties in this manner. Furthermore, those who accept formal separation nevertheless continue to participate in both national and provincial constituency associations and campaigns, with important consequences for the conduct of politics in the ridings. Although separation of national and provincial parties might be evident from readings of those parties' constitutions, the distinction between national and provincial dissolves in many constituencies where local activists fail to distinguish between parties at the two levels in both their perceptions and their behaviours. In these ways, local activist bases bind national and provincial parties to one another in the ridings.

3

Constituency Associations: Organization and Party Life in the Ridings

In most months, Liberal activists from throughout the large rural riding of Acadie-Bathurst drive to the city of Bathurst to attend the national constituency association executive meeting. For some of these local administrators, the drive entails a five-minute ride; however, for activists from the towns of Tracadie-Sheila, Shippagan, and Caraquet on the Acadian Peninsula, the drive can last for over an hour. The commitment of these far-flung activists to the Liberal Party might seem remarkable, but it is also a by-product of the multi-level organization of the national constituency association in Acadie-Bathurst. There is a long-standing local tradition that presidents of provincial associations contained in the national constituency attend monthly meetings and play a role in the administrative activities of the national association as ex officio members. This lends the national executive a federal nature since a significant contingent of national executive members in Acadie-Bathurst are in fact provincial presidents. The presence of these provincial presidents at national meetings provides a glimpse into the strong integration that characterizes most aspects of the national and provincial Liberal parties in the riding.

This account can be contrasted with that of the national and provincial constituency associations in New Brunswick Southwest. In this riding, the national association could scarcely be more different from the provincial association in Grand Bay-Westfield. The two executives are composed entirely of different groups of Liberals. The two executives also have different focuses: the national association struggles to maintain an active profile in a very Tory riding, whereas the provincial association has successfully expanded its membership and public profile through a series of community-based events. However, these maintenance events are planned and carried out exclusively by the provincial association –

there is no cooperation between the executives and no support offered between the two levels. In sharp contrast to their counterparts in Acadie-Bathurst, local elites in New Brunswick Southwest construct two political worlds at the national and provincial levels.

This discussion illuminates two local solutions to the challenges posed by multi-level institutions: integrated constituency association structures in Acadie-Bathurst and differentiated constituency associations in New Brunswick Southwest. Understanding differences in the national-provincial organization of these associations is crucial to understanding the Liberal Party's overall integration between the two levels, since constituency associations represent the continuous organizational presence of the Liberal Party in the ridings and are therefore the fundamental building blocks of the party as a whole. This chapter explores a range of integrated, mixed, and differentiated constituency associations.

Constituency associations carry out a range of local functions between elections, including maintaining the organization, recruiting members and candidates, communicating with party members, organizing (and occasionally manipulating) local nomination races, and preparing for upcoming campaigns (Carty 1991, 60). Although formally similar and tasked with comparable if not identical responsibilities, constituency associations vary widely in their organization and operation across the ridings (Sayers 1999, 6). How constituency associations are structured reflects the imperatives of their ecological and organizational environments. From an ecological perspective, constituency associations grapple with carrying out their functions within individual ridings that vary widely in geography and socio-economic composition (Carty and Eagles 2005, 6). From an organizational perspective, constituency associations are tasked with maintaining the brand of the party as a whole while nevertheless adapting themselves to the local riding context.

The formal separation of Canada's national and provincial Liberal parties suggests that those parties' constituency associations operate at a strict distance from one another. However, parties characterized by decentralized locations of power and mutual autonomy within their organizations necessarily grant autonomy to their different components, and constituency associations enjoy significant autonomy to structure themselves and operate in response to distinctive local demands. This organizational licence means that local activists are free to organize their constituency associations between the national and provincial levels in a variety of ways. Some respond to the unique constellations of incentives contained in the communities that make up their ridings by constructing organizations that span the national and provincial levels.

Figure 3.1

A continuum of constituency organizations

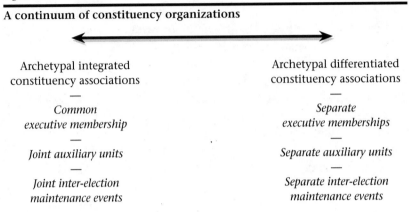

Archetypal integrated
constituency associations

Archetypal differentiated
constituency associations

—

—

Common
executive membership

Separate
executive memberships

—

—

Joint auxiliary units

Separate auxiliary units

—

—

Joint inter-election
maintenance events

Separate inter-election
maintenance events

Others replicate the formal separation of national and provincial parties in their own organizations – these constituency associations have little or no contact with the association at the other level.

Distinguishing between constituency associations on the basis of the number and nature of ties between the national and provincial levels allows for the construction of a continuum that ranges between archetypal integrated and differentiated constituency organizations. Figure 3.1 illustrates this continuum.

Archetypal integrated constituency organizations exist where national and provincial associations are closely linked. Research conducted in the ridings identified three indicators of these integrated constituency organizations. First, constituency association executives, the small groups that provide leadership for the association, are staffed by party activists who participate at both the national and the provincial levels. They can be consistent or inconsistent activists, for both types strengthen linkages between national and provincial associations. Second, any auxiliary units in the constituency such as women or youth clubs are linked in some way to both the national and the provincial constituency associations. Third, inter-election maintenance activities conducted by archetypal integrated associations are coordinated and executed jointly by the national and provincial constituency associations. The result of these linkages is that integrated constituency organizations are effectively (though not formally) unitary across the national and provincial levels; these constituency organizations transcend the division between national and provincial in the ridings and therefore constitute a single organizational world for local party activists.

In contrast, archetypal differentiated constituency organizations exist where there is no contact whatsoever between the national and provincial associations. These organizations differ from integrated constituency organizations on each of the three indicators observed during field research. First, executives in archetypal differentiated constituency organizations are staffed by single-level activists who are active at either the national or the provincial level but not at both. Second, any auxiliary units present are affiliated with either the national or the provincial constituency association. Auxiliary units therefore do not constitute a linkage between the national and provincial associations. Third, national and provincial constituency organizations plan separate inter-election events and do not involve the association from the other level in the planning of these events. These differentiated constituency organizations are effectively and formally separated from one another at the national and provincial levels. As a result, differentiated constituency organizations replicate the formal separation of national and provincial parties, and local activists confront segmented organizational worlds in the ridings.

Conceiving of constituency associations on the basis of their linkages between the national and provincial levels allows for different associations to be plotted somewhere between these two archetypes. Empirical evidence suggests that there is significant diversity in the national-provincial organization of constituency associations: in a 1991 survey, 64 percent of national Liberal constituency associations reported some focus on provincial politics (Carty 1991, 49). Although some national associations confine themselves to carrying out their functions exclusively at the national level, others involve themselves in some capacity in provincial politics. A survey of provincial constituency associations would undoubtedly uncover a similar diversity of involvement at the national level.

The Members of Constituency Association Executives

Executives are the small groups of activists who provide local leadership for constituency associations. Executive members are selected by association members and subsequently elect their own officers, including a president, vice-president, treasurer, and secretary. As members of the local executive, these local administrators maintain the finances and membership lists of the constituency association, plan fundraisers and party activities, organize nomination contests in the riding, and provide support to candidates and incumbent MPs and MLAs (Koop 2010, 897).

Constituency association executives are small and often close-knit groups. These local administrators represent the nucleus of long-term party activists in the community as well as the core of the local organization (Carty 1991, 52; Thorburn 1961, 85). Although the membership of the Liberal Party's cadre-style constituency associations tends to ebb and flow with the electoral cycle, members of the association executive lend stability to the association through their long-term involvement. Executive presidents tend to serve in that capacity for relatively short periods of time, reflecting not intense competition for the position but the propensity of members of sociable executives to pass the position around as an honorific (Carty 1991, 52). Executive members in Grand Bay-Westfield, for example, rotate the position among themselves; however, their responsibilities as executive members do not change as a result. Given the freedom afforded to constituency associations by the wider party organization and the acquiescence of local party memberships, executives play a decisive role in shaping the structure and operation of constituency associations (Sayers 1999, 37).

The presence of consistent and inconsistent executive members is an important indicator of integrated constituency associations for two reasons. First, these executive members bring a mixed national-provincial partisanship as well as experience in both national and provincial politics to their roles. Such executive members tend to extend that perspective and experience to the association as a whole – when opportunities for cooperation between the national and provincial constituency associations arise, for example, these members are likely to embrace them given their attachments to the party at the other level.

Second, consistent and inconsistent executive members can be important means of communication between national and provincial constituency associations. These executive members are in a good position to keep the national and provincial associations informed of one another's activities. Where formal cooperation between the national and provincial associations takes place, these executive members act as go-betweens. Consistent and inconsistent executive members therefore constitute a crucial personnel linkage that facilitates both joint endeavours and coordination of activities and resources between the national and provincial levels.

Don Valley East and Ajax-Pickering are urban constituencies in the Greater Toronto Area (GTA). The national and provincial constituency association executives in these ridings provide good examples of integrated executives. Most executive members are consistent activists who identify with both the national and the provincial Liberal parties. Peter, an executive member in Don Valley East, estimates that a third of the provincial executive also sit on the national executive: "We're atypical in that we have so many executive members on both [the national and provincial executives]. I'd say we're weighted towards being involved at both levels."

In addition, an ex officio rule in Ajax-Pickering and Don Valley East allows for the national constituency association president to sit on the provincial executive and vice versa. Ex officio members are invited to participate in executive meetings and discuss the activities of the executive at the other level but are not permitted to vote with the executive as a whole. Some local activists view the ex officio position as an honorific extended from one constituency association to another, whereas others view the position as a throwback to the period when the national and provincial Liberal organizations were formally intertwined. Still others view the rule as an acknowledgment of the informal national-provincial cooperation that can take place at the riding level despite formal separation of the two parties. "It is symbolic of the relationship between the federal and provincial parties," argues Rod, a member of both executives in Don Valley East.

In any case, ex officio members play a practical role in sustaining lines of communication between the national and provincial association executives. As a result, ex officio members open up opportunities for communication and cooperation between the national and provincial constituency associations. Executive presidents in Don Valley East and Ajax-Pickering maintain communications between the national and provincial executives by attending as many executive meetings at the other level as possible. At these meetings, the provincial president reports on the activities of his association to the national association. Attendance at national meetings also allows the provincial ex officio to keep up to date on the activities of the national association.

A spirit of national-provincial camaraderie pervades executive meetings in Ajax-Pickering and Don Valley East. During the lunches and informal discussions over coffee that inevitably conclude both national and provincial executive meetings, national and provincial Conservative leaders are subjected to equal scorn. Conversation revolves around whatever issues are topical, whether national or provincial. This coffee talk is also related to the electoral cycle: during national election campaigns, meetings of the provincial executive inevitably lose focus and turn to the national campaign at hand. The same occurs at national executive meetings during provincial elections. Indeed, provincial executive meetings might be cancelled during national election campaigns, and vice versa, so that activists can focus their efforts on the ongoing campaign. This national-provincial spirit of camaraderie on the association executives in Ajax-Pickering and Don Valley East reinforces the consistent partisanship of executive members and cements their participation in both the national party and the provincial party.

One consequence of this national-provincial camaraderie is that inconsistent party activists are generally excluded from the group. Such activists typically discover that their inconsistency is incompatible with the integrated association executives in these constituencies. Consistent members of integrated executives are outwardly tolerant of inconsistent members: "You can't hold that against someone," Peter explains. "If they sign up for a membership with us and attend our meetings and help with activities, then we accept them." But distrust generally underlies that tolerance since executive members in Ajax-Pickering and Don Valley East suspect that partisan consistency is related to partisan loyalty. Inconsistency is therefore cause for suspicion, which is perhaps not unreasonable given that inconsistent partisanship is related to unstable voting patterns (Clarke et al. 1980, 107). "We accept [inconsistent members]," admits Rod, "but we don't put them in positions where they'll carry secrets." "If they sit on the riding association, I would think that it [inconsistent activism] [is] a conflict of interest," argues Claudette. For these consistent activists, the relationship between consistency and loyalty is strong enough that inconsistent executive members are considered untrustworthy. "To me, that's like having a spy in your midst," says Claudette. "That's shocking!"

As a result, inconsistent executive members in Ajax-Pickering and Don Valley East find themselves distinctly out of step with the integrated nature of the executives. For these activists, divergence from the local norm necessitates that their inconsistent partisanship be kept hidden. Donald, for example, is a member of the provincial Liberal association executive in Don Valley East. However, he is strongly critical of the national Liberal Party and instead identifies with the national Conservative Party. His inconsistent activism continuously informs his participation in the provincial Liberal executive in Don Valley East:

> I sometimes feel a little bit uncomfortable with it [cooperation between the national and provincial associations] because I don't agree with the

federal Liberals' policies, but, you know, I don't rant and rave or anything like that ... I would doubt that most people know that I don't support the federal Liberal Party ... I would say we [inconsistent members] maintain a low profile ... If they were talking about federal issues, I would just sit back and let them discuss them.

The experiences of inconsistent party activists in Don Valley East and Ajax-Pickering emphasize the strength of the linkages between the national and provincial associations in these ridings. To the extent that inconsistent members are perceived as capable of undermining those connections by ranting or raving about cooperation between the two associations, the wider executive either expects them to conform to the consistent expectations of the group or rejects them. By doing so, integrated association executives remove a potential obstacle to open cooperation and coordination between the two levels.

This strong orientation toward consistent partisanship on the association executives in Don Valley East and Ajax-Pickering has consequences for the constituency association as a whole because executive members dictate the activities and organization of the constituency association. These consistent executive members extend their conception of partisanship to the constituency association by building and maintaining linkages between the national and provincial associations. This tendency is encouraged by the relative passivity of the local membership base and the presence of ex officio presidents from the other association. The result is an acceptance of both formal and informal forms of coordination and cooperation between the national and provincial associations.

In sharp contrast, the presence of single-level activists on association executives indicates that constituency associations are differentiated between the national and provincial levels. Single-level activists lack a mixed national-provincial perspective of partisan politics and, as a result, bring a focused perspective to their participation at either the national or the provincial level. Where a significant number of single-level activists staff the constituency association executive, this perspective extends to the nature of the association as a whole. Single-level activists on association executives therefore do not construct substantive linkages between the national and provincial associations.

The provincial constituency association executive in the Ontario riding of Perth-Wellington provides a good example of an executive that is largely differentiated from the national constituency association. Single-level activists on the executive play a role in differentiating the two associations. Although a few consistent activists sit on the provincial executive, they are outnumbered and do not encourage cooperation between the national and provincial constituency associations. As a result, single-level activists are successful in focusing the activities of the constituency association exclusively on the provincial level.

The factors that shape the single-level activism of executive members in Perth-Wellington are distinctively local. Perth-Wellington is unusual in that it is a rural constituency in southwest Ontario with a Liberal rather than Conservative MLA. The provincial constituency association in Perth-Wellington is a professional organization closely linked to its MLA, John Wilkinson. Prior to his first election victory in 2003, the constituency association was weak and disorganized. Wilkinson sought to construct a strong local party organization that would aid in his future re-election campaigns. To do so, he assigned his former campaign manager and constituency assistant, Adrian, to begin the process of constructing a permanent local organization from the ground up.

Adrian went about recruiting executive members whom he thought could be trusted. The emphasis, as in other rural ridings, was on recruiting executive members from the major population centres of the constituency, providing a ready-made campaign organization with the ability to reach into the disparate corners of the constituency once an election was called. In addition, Adrian himself took on a leadership role on the association executive, providing a crucial linkage between Wilkinson and the constituency association. The result was a competitive and professional cadre-style local organization.

Prior to this activity at the provincial level, the national Liberal Party in Perth-Wellington experienced significant internal difficulties that held consequences for how Wilkinson and Adrian would construct their own local organization. Prior to a 2003 by-election in the riding, the national Liberal association nominated Rick Horst in a competitive and contentious nomination race. The unsuccessful candidate, Brian Innes, appealed this outcome, and the party overturned the result. Innes was successful in the second nomination race, but the local activist base was subsequently polarized between those who had supported Horst and those who had supported Innes. Partially as a result of this local intraparty strife, Innes was unexpectedly defeated in the by-election by the Progressive Conservative candidate, Gary Schellenberger. Although the Liberals had held the riding since the 1993 national election, a divided local activist base and association had contributed to a surprising defeat for the national party.

This loss at the polls intensified conflict between the two segments of the national party's local activist base. Worse still for the local party, elections at the constituency association's annual general meeting resulted in an executive that contained members loyal to both Innes and Horst. As a result, the conflict that characterized the association as a whole was imported onto the association executive. Needless to say, the executive was not very effective in carrying out its responsibilities under these circumstances.

In constructing their own provincial organization, Wilkinson and Adrian hoped to avoid the "poisonous atmosphere" of the national constituency association in Perth-Wellington. Given that the national and provincial constituency associations in the riding had traditionally been integrated, the potential existed for the conflict of the national party to be transmitted to the provincial party. Provincial officials in Perth-Wellington hoped to avoid the conflict of the national association by constructing a differentiated organization at the provincial level, and single-level activists took on a new importance in the provincial executive as a result.

The presence of a significant number of single-level activists on the provincial association executive in Perth-Wellington has resulted in a lack of communication and coordination between the national and provincial executives. The two executives do not cooperate in holding inter-election events or support each other's activities. Given the lack of communication between them, they might not even be aware of these activities. The vastly different competitive situations of these associations – provincial success and national failure – have been sustained in each provincial and national election since the 2003 debacle. The two constituency associations in Perth-Wellington exist in the same geographic space, but their mutual autonomy and distinctive experiences mean that they organize in two political worlds.

The Roles of Local Auxiliary Units

The organization of local auxiliary units is the second indicator of integrated and differentiated constituency associations. Auxiliary units help to maintain the local party organization and provide personnel for campaign teams. Women's auxiliaries in particular have traditionally carried out these roles by mobilizing women into the local organization, even if these units simultaneously functioned to prevent women from advancing within the party bureaucracy as a whole (Whitaker 1977, 195-96). Auxiliary units also allow local organizations to access formerly inaccessible local groups; for example, ethnic and cultural auxiliary units play this role in diverse urban constituencies (Carty and Eagles 2005, 21). Since auxiliary units are organized around a shared identity or set of beliefs, they are excellent locations for activists to pursue solidary or ideological rewards.

Party auxiliaries can constitute formal sections of parties or separate parallel institutions (Lawson 1990, 115). But this is a difficult distinction to make at the local level of the Liberal Party. Although auxiliary units are mandated by the national constitution, they are also largely autonomous from the party. This autonomy lends them the ability to engage with either the national or the provincial constituency association or both in a variety of ways. In practice, linkages between auxiliaries and constituency associations can be confused since there are few clear lines of authority between them. Instead, these linkages are generally sustained by informal relationships.

Although auxiliary units can play an important role at the local level, they are not present in every riding. Sixty-one percent of Liberal constituency associations surveyed in 1991 reported at least one separate branch unit (Carty 1991, 53). The presence of auxiliary units in individual constituencies is dependent on local activists willing to take the initiative to form and maintain such groups. As a result, auxiliary units are more likely to exist in constituencies where there is a large and dedicated activist base.

Auxiliary units are important indicators of integrated constituency associations. In the face of formal separation between national and provincial constituency associations, auxiliary units can provide structural linkages between them and facilitate joint party life in the constituencies. This occurs in two ways. First, auxiliary units can constitute informal intermediaries between national and provincial constituency associations. Second, such units play an integrative role when they accommodate both national and provincial party activists. In so doing, these units provide a context for national and provincial activists to develop solidary and ideological bonds that facilitate cooperation between the two constituency associations.

Local chapters of the national Liberal Women's Commission are sometimes organized in just such an integrated manner. The commission is a loosely organized group of constituency-level women's auxiliaries. These local groups are largely non-institutionalized units and are organized in a loose, informal manner – they exist only where a sufficient number of local administrators are present to sustain such an organization.

This lack of institutionalization is one factor that has led to the creation of several regional women's auxiliaries. The national commission requires at least ten women to found a local club, and these clubs must maintain an ongoing membership of at least twenty-five women (National Women's Liberal Commission 2005, 8). These requirements might seem modest, but ridings often lack local administrators willing to take on the long-term volunteer tasks of constructing local auxiliaries and maintaining their memberships. As a result, local activists sometimes take the initiative to build regional clubs that include several ridings when there are insufficient numbers of activists in every constituency to sustain individual units. By organizing themselves in such a manner, regional women's auxiliaries expand both their memberships and their influence over the national and provincial constituency associations in these ridings.

Members of executives sometimes initiate the creation of a local women's auxiliary, binding the organization to the local constituency association from the outset. In other cases, activists apart from the local executive initiate the creation of auxiliaries as an alternative form of local partisan involvement. In these cases, the auxiliary might maintain a formal distance from the local association executive. The lack of routinization that characterizes these auxiliary units means that, though some clubs identify explicitly as national or provincial Liberal auxiliaries, many are ambiguous in this respect and are open to participation from both national and provincial Liberal members.

This informal organization is apparent in the local women's auxiliary in the Ontario riding of Richmond Hill. When women from neighbouring constituencies contemplated creating their own auxiliaries, the decision was instead taken to transform the Richmond Hill auxiliary into a regional group rather than see the creation of several small auxiliaries. Membership in the auxiliary is therefore not restricted to residents of the riding of Richmond Hill; neither is membership restricted to members of either the national or the provincial party. Despite its roots as a national auxiliary group, the Richmond Hill club declines to affiliate itself formally with either the national or the provincial party and is therefore open to participation from both national and provincial party members.

Some members of the national executive in Richmond Hill view the local women's auxiliary as an exclusively national organization. "Bryon [Wilfert, the incumbent MP], I can tell you, believes that it is essentially his women's club," reports Jenn, an auxiliary member. But these claims are not reflected in the organization of the auxiliary. Instead, its status as a national or provincial organization is unclear, even to its own members. "I can't give you a definitive answer because I'm still trying to figure it out," Jenn responds after a long pause when asked whether the auxiliary is primarily a national, provincial, or unitary organization.

This lack of clarity over formal structure obscures the important informal linkages between the auxiliary and both the national and the provincial Liberal associations in Richmond Hill. This is certainly the case with both the national and the provincial executives. Several members of both executives are also active on the women's auxiliary, and a representative of the auxiliary typically attends both national and provincial executive meetings and presents a report on the club's activities. The auxiliary also advertises and participates in the events held by both the national and the provincial constituency associations.

The Richmond Hill women's auxiliary also mobilizes women as campaign volunteers during nomination races and local campaigns. Members of the auxiliary are especially keen to support the nomination campaigns of other women to increase the number of women elected to public office. The local auxiliary plays this role at both national and provincial levels, encouraging its members to attend nomination contests to support women candidates. The support of the women's auxiliary also provides proof of candidates' progressive credentials, so both national and provincial candidates are eager to gain this support. But more importantly, auxiliary support provides a valuable source of secondary workers for both national and provincial campaigns. By gaining the approval of the women's auxiliary, candidates can expect to receive assistance from members of the auxiliary as well as other women in the riding. By encouraging its members to participate in both national and provincial politics, the women's auxiliary in Richmond Hill constitutes an important personnel linkage between the national and provincial Liberal organizations.

Constituency association executives, particularly those characterized by close relationships, are sometimes cliquish and impermeable. In these cases, auxiliary units can present alternative opportunities for activists to pursue both solidary and ideological goals. This is true for the Richmond Hill women's auxiliary: its members value internal relationships as well as the work that the auxiliary performs on behalf of women. In Richmond Hill, then, these goals are best pursued by auxiliary members through participation in both national and provincial politics. Leaders of the auxiliary encourage members to work for women candidates at both national and provincial levels. Once several members of the auxiliary have committed to doing so, other members face social pressure to follow along, for no one wants to be left out of the activities of the group. As a result, the auxiliary can typically be counted on to deliver secondary workers to both national and provincial campaigns in Richmond Hill.

Despite its confused organization, linkages between the women's auxiliary and the national and provincial association executives in Richmond Hill result in the auxiliary taking on an integrated (and integrative) role. Membership in the auxiliary is open to members of both the national and the provincial Liberal parties. Accordingly, single-level activists are free to join the auxiliary and participate in its activities. In practice, however, the auxiliary provides ideological and solidary incentives for its members to participate in the activities of both the national and the provincial Liberal parties in the riding.

The Young Liberals auxiliary unit in Don Valley East plays a similar role. Although the auxiliary is formally affiliated with the national Liberal Party, it is also informally linked to both the national and the provincial association executives in the riding. The president of the auxiliary sits on both national and provincial executives as an ex officio member. During executive meetings, he or she provides a report on the activities of the auxiliary and advertises youth functions and fundraisers. In turn, both associations encourage and support the activities of the youth auxiliary. The president of the provincial executive, for example, attends the auxiliary's dinners to communicate with youth members and "show the flag and support them."

One result of these shared linkages is that members of the youth auxiliary participate in inter-election maintenance events held by both the national and the provincial associations, since the auxiliary provides incentives to participate at both levels. As is the case with the women's auxiliary in Richmond Hill, the ideological and solidary rewards of participation in the youth auxiliary derive from participation in both the national and the provincial associations. As a result, the same youth members typically turn out to both national and provincial party events in Don Valley East. In this way, the organization's federal-provincial linkages shape how youth members conceive of partisanship. Roger, a youth activist, shrugs when asked to explain why the youth auxiliary is affiliated with both the national and the provincial constituency associations in Don Valley East. "We're all Liberals," he replies. "Why wouldn't we help each other?"

Not all local auxiliaries, however, are linked to the national and provincial constituency associations in their ridings. In other cases, auxiliary units are affiliated with either the national or the provincial constituency association. These auxiliary organizations provide activists with incentives to focus their attention and energy on either the national or the provincial level but not both.

The BC Liberal Women's Commission (BCLWC) is an example of an auxiliary that functions to differentiate the national and provincial Liberal parties. The BCLWC is an auxiliary unit of the provincial Liberal Party and shares no formal linkages to the national party. Unlike the women's auxiliary in Richmond Hill, the BCLWC is largely focused on a single level. As a result, the commission does not work actively to support women who contest nominations at both national and provincial levels. Instead, the commission confines itself to working at the provincial level and does not involve itself in national politics. In sharp contrast to the Richmond Hill auxiliary, social and ideological rewards in the BCLWC result from participation at solely the provincial level.

Despite its single-level organization, the BCLWC is widely perceived as a bastion of national Liberals where national Conservatives are rare. This is perhaps natural given that the national Liberal Party has a similar Women's Commission, whereas the national Conservative Party rejects any such organization for identified groups within the party. The extent to which the BCLWC can play an integrative role between the national and provincial parties in the riding, however, is truncated by the relative weakness of the organization. The BCLWC is largely an elite organization that struggles to attract participation from local activists. In part, this results from the perception that the auxiliary is reserved exclusively for national Liberals; national Conservatives are generally uninterested in participating. Together with its formal separation from any national party, the weakness of the organization causes it to focus on the provincial level rather than on both the national and the provincial levels.

Local Party Life: Inter-Election Maintenance Events

Although their size and vibrancy can vary with the electoral cycle, constituency associations continue to exist and organize between elections. One important role of constituency associations is engaging in inter-election maintenance activities, which can be separated into four categories (Carty 1991, 60). First, organizational maintenance takes place through fundraising and social events as well as membership drives. Second, policy study and development comprise an exclusive activity, carried out by studious local activists who believe that they can make a difference by crafting resolutions for debate at party conventions. Third, communications consist of public meetings and advertising. And fourth, electoral maintenance includes campaign planning and MP/candidate support.

Organizational outreach and communication activities have several benefits for constituency associations and for the party as a whole. These activities present the image of an active party organization at the local level, bolstering the party's legitimacy in the eyes of the public (Scarrow 1996, 42). At open events, citizens are afforded the opportunity to meet and interact with elected officials. Most importantly, these functions help to preserve contact between the party and the activist/volunteer base that local parties attempt to mobilize prior to and during election campaigns.

This role of preserving contact is especially valuable to the Liberal Party for two reasons. First, the cadre nature of the party ensures that the local party's membership rolls and activist base will swell in anticipation of a leadership race, nomination contest, or election and decline shortly thereafter (Sayers 1999, 7). Re-engaging a nascent activist base is therefore a challenge for the Liberal Party, and inter-election events provide opportunities for the association to engage with lapsed members and activists between election campaigns. Second, relatively high turnover rates in Canadian national elections provide an incentive for incumbent members to maintain connections to pre-existing campaign groups in the constituency (Matland and Studlar 2004, 93). Although open contests for Liberal Party nominations attract throngs of new members, incumbent MPs are likely to turn to the same local campaigners whom they have worked successfully with in the past. Inter-election maintenance events give incumbent MPs opportunities to tend to their relationships with these local campaigners, and incumbents' presence at party meetings increases the likelihood that local partisans will attend. For these reasons, inter-election maintenance can be of special significance to local parties with cadre-like characteristics such as those of the Liberal Party.

Inter-election maintenance events are also rewarding for local activists, especially those seeking social or material benefits in exchange for their partisan efforts (Clark 2004, 39). These events offer activists opportunities to interact with friends in the riding or with politicians from whom they hope to derive material rewards. They also provide partisan proselytizers with forums in which to involve their friends. By engaging activists in social gatherings, constituency associations increase the likelihood that activists will participate in future election campaign efforts.

The extent to which inter-election events are coordinated between the national and provincial levels is an important indicator of the integration of national and provincial constituency associations. This integration occurs in three ways. First, national and provincial constituency associations can cooperate with one another to hold inter-election events such as fundraisers or social gatherings. Such coordination can be explicit and open and produce joint national-provincial events. In other cases, cooperation between the two associations is informal and conducted in private, the results of which are exclusively national or provincial events with involvement or support from the other level.

Second, inter-election activities also indicate local integration when they are organized in a manner that allows one association to reach out to the association at the other level. In these outreach events, the organizing association uses informal linkages and relationships to encourage attendance and participation from the other association. Organizers for a provincial fundraiser in Don Valley East, for example, encouraged members of the national association executive to attend by offering tickets at a discounted price.

Third, one constituency association might make a concerted effort to support the association at the other level if the latter is holding an inter-election event. The president of the national association, for example, might announce provincial events at national executive meetings and encourage everyone present to attend. Indeed, integrated associations come to expect such support from the other level, and encouragement from the president is hardly required to get executive members out to such events.

The national and provincial constituency associations in Don Valley East provide examples of associations that cooperate and coordinate with one another in the organization and execution of inter-election maintenance events such as the annual Liberal picnic, a major event for Liberal activists, members, and sympathizers throughout the GTA. Held in a public park, the picnic draws roughly 1,000 Liberals and non-Liberals alike as well as politicians from the national, provincial, and municipal levels.

The Don Valley East picnic is coordinated and hosted jointly by the national and provincial association executives. The planning committee for the event is composed of representatives from both executives, which also provide funding for the event. The picnic is planned as a community outreach event rather than a fundraiser, for organizers hope to attract low-income residents from local immigrant communities to the event. A nominal price is therefore charged for hot dogs and soft drinks, in contrast to a summer barbeque in the neighbouring riding of Don Valley West, where hamburgers and steaks are sold for higher prices to raise funds for the local party. Organizers in Don Valley East reach out to local low-income communities through the picnic, and it is difficult to imagine a better example of a local party organization acting as a partisan ambassador to the community (Scarrow 1996, 137).

Activists from both the national and the provincial associations are called on to serve hot dogs, set up sound equipment, and provide security for the event. Members of the local youth auxiliary are drawn to the event by the opportunity to meet politicians, reconnect with friends from the Toronto area, and eat cheap food. The picnic is in fact a major event for the auxiliary unit, and the auxiliary president helps in its overall planning. Youth members also typically staff the event.

The Don Valley East picnic is an important example of organizational integration at the grassroots level. The event is also significant for the Liberal activist and membership base in the constituency. Such joint events encourage activists and members to develop or maintain a unitary conception of the national and provincial parties in the riding. Formal cooperation between the associations reinforces the perception that "a Liberal is a Liberal is a Liberal" in Don Valley East – indeed, events such as the Don Valley East picnic make it difficult for activists to distinguish between the national and provincial organizations in the riding. The picnic provides consistent activists with opportunities to reinforce their solidary bonds and single-level activists with opportunities to develop such bonds with Liberals from the other level.

This blended perception of national-provincial cooperation at the picnic is further reinforced by the attendance of elected officials from the national and provincial levels in addition to the local MP and MLA, both of whom are Liberals. The picnic provides citizens with an opportunity to interact with both national and provincial Liberal politicians. The impressions derived from these interactions do much to reinforce a unitary conception of the national and provincial Liberal parties in Ontario, formal separation of the two parties to the contrary notwithstanding. So, though joint events such as the Don Valley East picnic reflect the consistent identity of executive members and the local activist base, they also reinforce that consistent identity.

In addition to their annual picnic, the national and provincial constituency associations in Don Valley East actively support separate events held by the other association. When the national association organized a fundraiser dinner, for example, it offered a discount on tickets to members of the provincial association executive. And when the provincial association held a community outreach event at which citizens could trade their old Christmas lights for energy-efficient bulbs, the event was advertised at a national executive meeting, and the national president encouraged those present to attend to support the provincial association. This also occurs when the provincial association hosts open dialogue outreach events at local libraries to boost the profile of the association in the community. In these cases, local integration is strengthened through mutual support between the national and provincial associations.

Unlike the national and provincial executives in Don Valley East, the two executives in the Ontario constituency of Oxford do not plan and coordinate joint maintenance events. But the constituency association executives do work together to maximize the effectiveness of one another's inter-election functions. David, the provincial association president, takes advantage of his position as an ex officio member of the national executive to strengthen the communicative bond that previously existed between the two associations but has since atrophied. "I made a very direct effort to bridge between the federal and provincial riding associations so that there was greater involvement between the two and across the two," he explains. "I made a major effort to try and get the two more receptive to each other and working together a little bit more." For David, his position as ex officio is crucial to maintaining communications between the two executives. "I'm on the [national] executive ... as president of the provincial association," he explains. "I think this is positive in the sense that for things that we're going to be doing that may complement or compete with each other, we can at least get a feel for what's going on."

Communication between the national and provincial associations in Oxford is critical in the planning of inter-election maintenance events, since open lines of communication allow the national and provincial associations to cooperate and support the inter-election events of one another. The annual golf tournament held as a fundraiser in the riding provides a good example of this national-provincial cooperation. Working on the assumption that the relatively small number of Liberal activists and members in the predominantly Tory riding cannot be expected to contribute too often, the national and provincial Liberal associations take turns hosting the annual fundraiser:

> The local golf tournament was one example this past year where we alternate; one does it one year, and the other does it the next. Because of the federal Liberal leadership race, the federal Liberal association

asked if they could run it in 2006 and try to get some of the leadership candidates to come out and attend. And actually they were pretty successful, and they did get some out ... So we made it a big deal, and it was a big splash.

David and the provincial association executive were willing to relinquish the event for a summer to benefit the national association. The presence of leadership candidates was a significant draw for activists and members within the riding, and the national association was best placed to draw these high-profile figures to the riding. David's participation on the national and provincial executives was the key to cooperation on the event. "Because I was on both boards," he explains, "I was able to convey back to the provincial board what was going on and convey back to the feds that we were up to speed on what was happening." Although the national and provincial executives in Oxford do not jointly plan inter-election events, they do cooperate to maximize the effectiveness of local Liberal functions.

In contrast to these examples, inter-election events can also indicate differentiation of national and provincial constituency associations. This occurs when constituency associations conduct their own inter-election activities without reference to the association at the other level. In these cases, constituency associations do not jointly plan inter-election events, do not reach out to the other association with their own events, and do not support the other association. In these ridings, inter-election events provide a context within which a single-level activist base is formed and reinforced through social interactions and contact at either the national or the provincial level.

The provincial constituency of Grand Bay-Westfield, New Brunswick, neighbours the city of Saint John. Although a large rural constituency, it is dominated by the town of Grand Bay-Westfield, which, given its proximity to Saint John, has increasingly become an upscale bedroom community to the larger city. Despite the important linkages between Grand Bay-Westfield and Saint John, the provincial constituency falls not in the national constituency of Saint John but in New Brunswick Southwest; Grand Bay-Westfield occupies a small corner of the sprawling rural national riding. The problem for local activists is that the Liberal organization in New Brunswick Southwest is almost completely inaccessible since it is centred in Saint Stephen, which, as provincial activists emphasize, is a long and sometimes treacherous drive from Grand Bay-Westfield. In this case, the boundaries of the national and provincial constituencies entail formidable geographic obstacles to the integration of the national association executive centred in Saint Stephen and the provincial executive in Grand Bay-Westfield.

Distance between the provincial constituency association in Grand Bay-Westfield and the core of the national constituency association in Saint Stephen limits any possible relationship between the two associations. The face-to-face contact between national and provincial executive members that is crucial to cooperation in Don Valley East and Oxford is ruled out in Grand Bay-Westfield as a result of geographic divisions. "The president [of the national constituency association] is in Saint Stephen in one end of the riding, and we're in this end of the riding. Geographically, we don't see each other much," explains Don, a member of the Grand Bay-Westfield executive. His unitary conception of the national and provincial Liberal parties means that he should be a consistent party activist, but geography intervenes to limit his participation at the national level in New Brunswick Southwest.

However, this separation of the provincial from the national association does not rule out a vibrant party life in Grand Bay-Westfield. The core of provincial party activists who inhabit the association executive in Grand Bay-Westfield in fact bring a strong commitment to public service to their partisan participation. For members of the executive, reaching out to the community through local events and building the local activity base through outreach events is the key to a successful organization. Glenda, a provincial executive member, explains the rationale behind this involvement:

> In our riding, it's been a strong Conservative riding over a number of years ... Our initial goal was to raise party awareness and party involvement. But the question arose: how are we going to do this? So to do that, we decided to raise our community effort ... By doing that, we are raising awareness about the party and building up the party ... We're trying to make people in the community aware that these are Liberal people, and these are Liberal values, and these are the sorts of things that Liberals do.

In this way, members of the association executive attempted to enhance the legitimacy of the Liberal brand in Grand Bay-Westfield by acting as partisan ambassadors to the community. Accordingly, the constituency association in Grand Bay-Westfield is very active, and party life in the riding is vibrant. The constituency association executive hosts numerous functions, all connected to local community groups in Grand Bay-Westfield such as the local food bank. "The first year we had one function, the next year we had three functions. This year we had six functions," recalls Don. "Basically, every other month we have a major function, all community-based functions." By reaching out to the community, the provincial association has successfully recruited several members to the executive. In addition, these community efforts offer significant solidary rewards to local party activists.

But these inter-election maintenance events are entirely single level. Unlike the events held by other associations, the national Liberal constituency association in New Brunswick Southwest does not cooperate with the provincial association in organizing events and does not support the provincial association's events. In part, this results from the lack of communication between the national and provincial association executives. Activists from Grand Bay-Westfield convey a sense of isolation in their description of their community; they occupy one of several geographic pockets within the large rural riding of New Brunswick Southwest. That sense of isolation extends to the local group of Liberal activists on the provincial executive. Without a wider national party community to participate in, the Grand Bay-Westfield activist base has turned inward and focused its inter-election events on building an autonomous differentiated organization through the development and nurturing of linkages to the immediate local community.

Integrated Constituency Associations in British Columbia
The previous three sections explored constituency associations within a context of similar national and provincial party systems. Dissimilar party systems do entail obstacles to local integration, but it is still possible for integrated constituency associations to develop when the national and provincial systems differ from one another, as in British Columbia. Such integrated constituency associations differ from Ontario and New Brunswick associations in both their structures and their functions. These differences, however, do not negate the important linkages that constituency associations can construct between the national and provincial levels in BC ridings.

National and provincial party systems structure the interactions of national and provincial association executives in the ridings. Executive members in Ontario's and New Brunswick's integrated constituency associations tend to be consistent activists and therefore participate in the national and provincial Liberal parties. Executive members also perpetuate this norm within their executives by frowning on inconsistent participation. But in systems where significant differences exist between the two levels, executive members can be inconsistent activists, participating in different parties at the two levels. Both national Liberal and national Conservative partisans staff most BC Liberal constituency association executives. A member of the provincial BC Liberal association executive in Port Moody-Westwood, for example, reports an even split between national Liberals and Conservatives on his executive. This is in sharp contrast to integrated association executives in ridings such as Don Valley East, where executive members have difficulty identifying any inconsistent executive members.

Common executive members can still engender important linkages between the national and provincial constituency associations in British Columbia. The same organizational linkages that characterize integrated constituency associations in Ontario and New Brunswick can exist in British Columbia, but the nature of these linkages differs in two important ways. First, executive members participate in parties at both the national and the provincial levels, and the experiences from both levels inform their roles as executive members. But many of these executive members might participate in different parties at the two levels; their inconsistent experiences therefore contrast with those of consistent executive members from Ontario and New Brunswick. Second, the linkages that inconsistent executive members build between the national and provincial associations will necessarily be informal. Although national and provincial associations in Ontario and New Brunswick might have formally structured relationships, associations in British Columbia are linked informally via social relationships between members.

The provincial constituency association in the BC riding of Delta North is a good example of an integrated constituency association executive that has adapted to this party system context. Like executive members in Ajax-Pickering and Don Valley East, provincial executive members in Delta North tend to participate in both national and provincial politics. But in sharp contrast to those Ontario executives, the provincial executive in Delta North is staffed by a combination of consistent national Liberal and inconsistent national Conservative activists. The configuration of British Columbia's national and provincial party systems dictates that the provincial Liberal Party assume the form of a coalition of national Liberals and Conservatives. The constituency association executive in Delta North, with its mixture of national Liberals and Conservatives, might therefore be thought of as a microcosm of the provincial Liberal Party as a whole.

The provincial executive in Delta North is also similar to those in Ajax-Pickering and Don Valley East in that a significant number of members also sit on an association executive at the other level. One activist estimated that half of the association executive in Delta North also sat on the national Liberal executive and that a smaller proportion sat on the national Conservative executive. Although the largely integrated constituency association executives in Ajax-Pickering and Don Valley East are unreceptive to the participation of inconsistent party activists, the provincial executive in Delta North accommodates these activists. Indeed, its success as a constituency association rests on the executive's ability to maintain the participation of both consistent national Liberals and inconsistent national Conservatives.

An atmosphere of national-provincial camaraderie pervades association executive meetings in ridings with integrated constituency associations such as Ajax-Pickering and Don Valley East. This camaraderie derives largely from their consistent participation and shared experiences in national and provincial politics. Given that activists on the provincial executive in Delta North are active in different parties at the national level, consistent participation cannot similarly bind executive members to one another. Instead, these members have quite different experiences at the national level, experiences that usually include campaigning against one another. The challenge for members of provincial executives is to find ways to accommodate members of the national Liberal and Conservative parties.

Activists from Ontario and New Brunswick sometimes expressed wonder when I described these local party dynamics in British Columbia. "I can't understand Conservatives and Liberals on the same executive. That blows me away!" exclaimed James, a consistent activist from the Ontario riding of York West. "That's like doing business and having the competition sitting in on my meetings." But there are two informal rules that have developed in Delta North and other BC ridings to reconcile the participation of national opponents on the provincial executive.

First, executive members in Delta North are careful to avoid discussions of national politics for fear of fomenting conflict between the national Conservatives and Liberals on the executive. One provincial constituency association president described this as one of her most important roles as president. She succinctly expresses this provincial rule governing provincial executive meetings: "You leave your federal politics at the door."

Natasha, an executive member from the constituency of Port Moody-Westwood-Port Coquitlam, also describes this approach:

[National politics] is just not talked about. A lot of time with the BC Liberals, that's the case. And that's why it's sometimes very easy for federal Liberals and Conservatives to get involved. It's kind of a general rule that provincially we're all friends. We don't talk about our federal affiliations. We talk about federal politics, but we're not going to bring in that divide, and at meetings we're not going to get into those nit-picky debates.

When discussions of national politics do intrude into provincial associa-tion business, other executive members move to enforce group norms and prevent potential conflicts. "Within my riding, it's a very cordial relationship," notes one provincial executive member. "The one time a woman brought it up, federal politics. She was not welcome back after that." In this way, the executive worked to exclude a potentially disrupt-ive influence on cooperation in the constituency association. When national issues divide national Liberals and Conservatives, provincial executive members are expected to "put that [national] partisanship aside and focus on the matter at hand, which is the provincial riding association."

Second, good relations between national Liberals and Conservatives are maintained through close social bonds between the small group of core activists that sit on the association executive. Social relationships are sometimes very important in maintaining participation on constitu-ency association executives. The key requirement for provincial Liberal executives in British Columbia is that activists are able to develop rela-tionships with other executive members without reference to national partisanship. "It's not like it [federal politics] is a taboo subject," Stefan explains. "Everyone jokes about it. Everyone teases each other about it. But it's friendly." When national debates over same-sex marriage pitted national Liberals and Conservatives against one another, the social re-lationships between consistent and inconsistent executive members in Delta North helped to overcome potential conflict between national Liberals and Conservatives. William recalls how this occurred during the lunches that came after executive meetings: "When we'd go out to lunch and we weren't discussing party business, everyone would be teasing everyone about it [same-sex marriage]. We would say 'you're a bigot' and 'you're destroying families.' But it's all in good humour, because it's never going to appear in the minutes of the BC Liberal Party." Social bonds on the executive in Delta North allow consistent and inconsistent executive members to overcome potential conflicts that derive from national pol-itics. Through the adoption of these informal codes of conduct and social bonds, national Liberals and national Conservatives can coexist and contribute to the ongoing success of provincial associations.

Auxiliary units are also important indicators of integrated and differentiated constituency associations in British Columbia. The provincial Liberal Party, for example, supports a vibrant youth auxiliary. With respect to organization, the BC Young Liberals auxiliary (BCYL) is a hierarchical organization. The provincial executive provides leadership for the auxiliary as a whole: its responsibilities include communicating with members, maintaining the organization's membership, and facilitating the formulation of policy resolutions to present to provincial party conferences. Seven regional councils are made up of representatives from each of the provincial constituencies within the region. These constituency representatives in turn assume leadership roles in their ridings, establishing informal local auxiliaries of youth members and often sitting on local association executives. In addition to proposing policy and providing personnel during election campaigns, the BCYL supports a rich array of inter-election maintenance events for youth members. These barbecues, softball games, golf excursions, and trips to amusement parks provide youth members with opportunities to meet MLAs from the party and to strengthen social bonds.

Following the formal separation of the national and provincial Liberal parties in 1991, the BCYL remained staffed by mostly national Liberals. But over time, young activists from the national Conservative Party migrated to the provincial party's youth wing. Like BC Liberal constituency association executives, the youth organization now harbours national Liberal and Conservative activists as well as single-level activists. As a result, the BCYL leadership maintains strict neutrality over national politics to avoid discouraging involvement from either national Liberals or national Conservatives. This neutrality pervades the leadership of the youth organization. A former president of the BC Young Liberals emphasizes its importance:

> In my role as president of the BC Young Liberals ... I work with a group of people that are from various political parties. Some are [national] Liberals, and some are [national] Conservatives. And as president, I think it's my obligation to not have myself seen by them as a competing person on another stage. That they see me just as working with them provincially.

One result of this policy is that the youth organization appears to have few internal conflicts over national issues.

Where they are active, the local groups of the provincial Liberal youth organization generally contain national Liberal and Conservative activists. But this balance shifts in conjunction with the electoral strength of the national Liberal and Conservative parties; auxiliaries in Vancouver are dominated by national Liberals, whereas auxiliaries in the Fraser Valley and the Interior are staffed predominantly by national Conservatives. The predominance of one group of national partisans shapes how local auxiliaries interact with the national constituency associations present. As a result, local clubs in Vancouver are more strongly linked to the national Liberal Party, whereas those elsewhere in the province are more likely to have ties to the national Conservatives. Nevertheless, the mixture of national partisans in local auxiliaries creates imperatives for formal policies of national neutrality.

Youth auxiliaries in British Columbia can constitute important linkages between provincial Liberal constituency associations and the national associations. In the BC constituency of Port Coquitlam-Burke Mountain, for example, Jeff, the president of the local youth auxiliary, sits on both the provincial Liberal executive and the national Conservative executive. Despite a strong commitment to the provincial Liberal Party and former Premier Gordon Campbell, Jeff's political mentor is in fact the local president of the national Conservative association. Jeff attends executive meetings of both the provincial Liberal Party and the national Conservative Party and happily advertises the events of the BCYL at both. In addition, members of both the national Conservative executive and the provincial Liberal executive support the activities of the local BCYL chapter and provide youth members with opportunities to attend and participate in national party events. The allegiance of Jeff and other youth members ensures that the local manifestation of the BCYL constitutes an intermediary between the provincial Liberal constituency association and the national Conservative association.

Informal linkages between local BCYL clubs and national constituency associations sometimes have the effect of drawing youth members into activism at the national level as well as the provincial level. In Port Coquitlam-Burke Mountain, for example, the activism of several youth members in the national Conservative Party ensures that the activities of the national Conservative association will be advertised at meetings of the youth auxiliary. These national Conservatives in the BCYL encourage other BCYL members to engage with the national party, and activists in the youth auxiliary face significant solidary pressures to "follow the pack" in their activities at the national level. When members of the provincial youth auxiliary plan to attend inter-election maintenance events for the national Conservative association, other members face incentives to accompany their friends.

Like its counterpart in Don Valley East, the local BCYL club in Port Coquitlam-Burke Mountain therefore funnels personnel into the events of both national and provincial constituency associations. These informal dynamics, to be sure, are less powerful than those of local auxiliaries in Ontario and New Brunswick, where there exists no rule of neutrality for participation at the other level of the state. Nevertheless, connections between provincial Liberal youth auxiliaries and the national Liberal or Conservative constituency associations can result in those clubs taking on an integrated form, any formal policy of neutrality to the contrary notwithstanding.

Finally, the nature of inter-election events is influenced by the configuration of the national and provincial party systems in British Columbia. In integrated Ontario and New Brunswick constituency associations, inter-election maintenance events are planned jointly, and associations support events at the other level. It is much more difficult for this sort of cooperation to take place in British Columbia, but national and provincial associations can still support one another informally.

The provincial constituency of Port Moody-Westwood is a suburban riding within the Vancouver Regional District, one of three contained within the national constituency of Port Moody-Coquitlam-Port Coquitlam. Although a Conservative incumbent, MP James Moore, represents the national constituency, the provincial riding is represented by a Liberal MLA. The national and provincial constituency associations in Port Moody-Westwood do not cooperate in holding inter-election maintenance events, and joint events held between the two associations are out of the question. At my suggestion that the national and provincial Liberal constituency associations might jointly host inter-election events such as the Don Valley East picnic, a member of the national association executive was succinct in her response: "I think that would be inappropriate."

Other BC executive members are surprised by the official cooperation between national and provincial associations that occurs in ridings such as Ajax-Pickering and Don Valley East. "I think that would be really challenging to do," laughs Natasha at the suggestion, because formal coordination between the national Liberal association and the provincial Liberal association would alienate the segment of national Conservatives that participate on the provincial executive in Port Moody-Westwood. The balance maintained between national Liberals and Conservatives on BC Liberal executives rules out national-provincial cooperation in the planning and execution of inter-election events.

Nevertheless, the national and provincial constituency associations can generally expect to receive support from the association at the other level. Such support is necessarily delivered in an informal manner and is routed through the different social networks that develop within the context of the national and provincial constituency associations. The provincial constituency association in Port Moody-Westwood, for example, occasionally holds fundraiser dinners featuring special speakers. Contingents of both national Liberal and Conservative activists attend these events to support the provincial Liberal Party. The provincial constituency association counts on the support of both national activist bases at such fundraising events, and provincial executive members therefore advertise the events among their social networks in both national associations.

But even providing support in such an innocuous manner illustrates the divide between the two national factions. Local activists gossip about how national Liberals and Conservatives typically separate into their own social groups and sit at separate tables during provincial Liberal dinner events.

Constituency Associations in a Multi-Level Context

Constituency associations display diversity in how they are organized between the national and provincial levels. Although some exist autonomously at the two levels, others evolve integrated structures and are closely linked to one another. Conceiving of constituency associations as existing on a conceptual continuum that ranges between archetypal differentiated and integrated associations allows this organizational diversity in the ridings to be described. This section briefly explores exemplars of integrated, mixed, and differentiated constituency associations, paying close attention to national-provincial linkages in terms of both local structures and how party life is experienced by activists in the ridings.

Strongly integrated constituency associations comprise both affiliated structures and a common national-provincial party life. The classic example of such associations is found in Don Valley East. The national and provincial association executives in that riding are staffed for the most part by consistent activists. In addition, the two executives share a number of members, including ex officio presidents from each level. These conditions have led to the development of integrated local structures in which communications between the two executives flow freely and, as a result, cooperation and coordination between the two levels is common. These structures in turn impact the nature of party life in the riding as the national and provincial executives coordinate inter-election maintenance events. Local activists attend joint events such as the annual Don Valley East picnic fundraiser and, in this capacity, experience a common local party life between the two levels. When the two executives plan their own events, they can expect to receive open support from the executive at the other level, and the same group of activists can generally be found at most national and provincial Liberal events in the riding. As a result, the constituency associations in Don Valley East are good examples of integrated associations close to the left side of the continuum.

In contrast, distinctive local structures and party life indicate differentiated constituency associations, placed on the right side of the continuum close to the archetype. Differentiated associations at the national and provincial levels neither share joint structures nor engender a common party life between the two levels for local activists. Instead, these associations develop separated, autonomous structures that in turn shape the development of a segmented party life at the two levels.

The provincial constituency association in the New Brunswick riding of Grand Bay-Westfield provides a good example of a differentiated constituency association. In this riding, both the structures of the provincial association and the activities and functions that define local party life exist at only a single level. Members of the association executive tend to be single-level activists; although many individual activists identify with the national Liberal Party, they encounter opportunities to engage only with the provincial party in the remote section of the wider national riding of New Brunswick Southwest. Members of the provincial executive have few meaningful linkages to the national executive, and this has consequences for the nature of local party life. Liberal party life in Grand Bay-Westfield is vibrant, but the events, meetings, and functions that make up this life are organized exclusively by the provincial organization and are not supported by the national executive. Local activists in Grand Bay-Westfield therefore experience local party life as strictly single level.

Don Valley East and Grand Bay-Westfield provide examples of strongly integrated and differentiated constituency associations. But what can be said of constituency associations that fall at some midpoint on the continuum? These associations exhibit some characteristics of both integrated and differentiated organizations. One way to explore these associations is to distinguish between (1) the local structures maintained by the association executive and (2) the party life of local members and activists. Mixed constituency associations have integrated structures but a differentiated form of party life or vice versa.

Consider the national and provincial constituency associations in the Ontario riding of Haldimand-Norfolk, which share some characteristics of strongly integrated associations. Local activists tend, for example, to be consistent in their participation; as in many other Ontario and New Brunswick ridings, there exists in Haldimand-Norfolk a long tradition of consistent activism in the riding. Local activists therefore experience a largely common national-provincial party life as they happily attend events and functions planned by both the national and the provincial associations.

But this integration in local party life is less apparent in the structures of the national and provincial constituency associations. The executives do share some members but do not engage in the open cooperation and coordination that characterizes the associations in Don Valley East. For the most part, the national and provincial executives keep to themselves. So, though party life in Haldimand-Norfolk is largely integrated, the structures present are less so, and, as a result, the associations are closer to the centre of the continuum. The key point is that integration between these types of mixed associations is driven by local party activists rather than by local elites. We are likely to see these mixed associations in ridings with long traditions of consistent partisanship, including most constituencies in Ontario and particularly New Brunswick, but in which, for whatever reason, the structural linkages between the two levels have atrophied.

Conversely, constituency associations can maintain structural linkages between the two levels in ridings where there is no tradition of consistent participation. These associations have relatively integrated local structures, yet party life remains largely separate at the two levels. In these cases, integration is driven by local elites, particularly those on the association executive, rather than by grassroots activists.

These mixed associations are likely to be common in western Canada, where, in contrast to many ridings in Ontario and New Brunswick, there is no deeply engrained tradition of joint participation by local party activists. In Port Moody-Westwood-Port Coquitlam, for example, national Liberals and Conservatives must sometimes be convinced to participate in provincial Liberal events and functions. Despite this lack of a common party life, association executives in the riding play an important role in integrating parties at the two levels. In the riding, this is typically an informal role, and linkages between associations at the national and provincial levels are maintained by executive members with personal relationships. To the extent that these constituency associations are integrated between the national and provincial levels, it is local elites rather than grassroots activists who drive that integration.

Although constituency associations can be placed relative to one another on the continuum illustrated in Figure 3.1, their positions on this continuum are not frozen. The autonomy of these organizations means that local activists can adopt new structures and, as a result, adjust their associations on that continuum. In Perth-Wellington, for example, the traditionally integrated national and provincial constituency associations shifted to a more differentiated form. This shift occurred in response to a period of internal conflict in the national association, the reluctance of the provincial association to become embroiled in the conflict, and the eventual commitment of the local MLA to construct an autonomous provincial organization. As a result, a long tradition of integration in the riding was overturned by an episode of internal warfare and the influence of an incumbent, and the national and provincial constituency associations have responded by adopting largely differentiated structures.

Constituency associations can also shift along the continuum in the opposite direction. For example, a history of differentiation between the national and provincial constituency associations in Grand Bay-Westfield appeared to be shifting when a new president of the national executive committed to reaching out and constructing linkages with all of the provincial associations in the riding, even the one in faraway Grand Bay-Westfield. It was unclear at the time, however, how successful these attempts at improvement would be.

These examples illuminate constituency associations' organizational flexibility in response to both internal and external factors. Given that the wider parties give constituency association executives few guidelines on how to organize themselves and lack the resources to police their associations, the local administrators who staff executives evolve their own organizational traditions and rules of conduct. Some small groups, such as in Don Valley East, rely on formal rules and professional relationships to govern themselves; others, such as the executive in Grand Bay-Westfield, evolve loosely structured organizations that fall back on the informal relationships of executive members as the core organizing principle of the group. Just as association executives can be flooded by supporters of a particular nomination candidate, so too can these small non-routinized groups be exposed to new influences that cause them

Table 3.1

Integrated, activist-driven, elite-driven, and differentiated constituency organizations

Integrated	Mixed	Differentiated
Ajax-Pickering[1]	Haldimand-Norfolk[1]	Perth-Wellington[1]
Don Valley East[1]	Oxford[1]	New Brunswick
Richmond Hill[1]	Saint John[2]	Southwest[2]
York West[1]	Fundy-Royal[2]	Vancouver Quadra[3]
Acadie-Bathurst[2]	Delta-Richmond East[3]	Richmond[3]
	Port Moody-Westwood-	Kootenay-Columbia[3]
	Port Coquitlam[3]	

Notes: 1 = Ontario; 2 = New Brunswick; 3 = British Columbia

to adopt a more integrated or differentiated form. So, though one can place constituency associations on the continuum, they are flexible enough to adapt to new incentives and move along that continuum in response.

Nevertheless, associations are unlikely to change in a short period of time. Given that work on the constituency association executive is unattractive to all but a small group of local activists, these administrators are likely to maintain the structures – whether integrated, differentiated, or mixed – that have traditionally worked for them. Even when incumbents or local elites attempt to reshape constituency associations, they might have to overcome long-standing traditions and obstinate local administrators.

Classifying constituency associations as integrated, mixed, and differentiated allows us to observe their prevalence in Ontario and New Brunswick, where the national and provincial party systems are similar, and British Columbia, where the national and provincial party systems are distinctive. Table 3.1 categorizes the national constituencies studied by the types of associations in each riding.

Ontario and New Brunswick ridings tend to be characterized by integrated and mixed constituency associations. Integrated associations in Ontario ridings are formally and openly linked to one another and enjoy joint party activities. Where the structures of the national and provincial associations have for whatever reason experienced disentanglement, such as in Haldimand-Norfolk, integration continues to be driven by an activist base that is strongly consistent. Party life in these ridings is similar to that in ridings with integrated associations despite the lack of enmeshed local structures. The constituency association in Oxford is an example of an association that might be considered integrated. But the few loose forms of cooperation that do exist between the national and provincial associations in that riding mean that Oxford's association has more in common with those in Haldimand-Norfolk than with those in Ajax-Pickering and Don Valley East. Only in exceptional cases, such as in Perth-Wellington, do Ontario constituency associations evolve differentiated organizations in response to idiosyncratic local factors.

In sharp contrast, constituency associations in British Columbia tend to be either mixed or differentiated. Dissimilar party systems at the national and provincial levels mean that there is no tradition of integration or consistent partisanship in the province's ridings. Lacking a tradition of consistent partisanship necessary to build integrated constituency associations, integration in British Columbia necessarily depends on the intervention of elites sitting on the national and provincial association executives. This is the sort of elite cooperation observed in the ridings of Port Moody-Westwood-Port Coquitlam and Delta-Richmond East. Integration of national and provincial constituency associations in these ridings is conducted informally based on personal relationships between executive members in non-routine ways. Differences in the national and provincial party systems in that province play a role in shaping mixed constituency associations as an alternative to the more strongly and openly integrated constituency associations that characterize Ontario and New Brunswick ridings. Where no elites are present to contribute to such integration, differentiated constituency associations result.

Formal disentanglement of national and provincial parties in Canada suggests that local activists follow suit and similarly construct autonomous, differentiated organizations in the ridings. However, the fundamental organizational components of the national Liberal Party, its constituency associations, are often linked in important and meaningful ways with provincial parties. Indeed, most of the national and provincial constituency associations examined in this study maintain some form of linkage to the party at the other level: in only five national ridings studied were the national and provincial constituency associations not linked in any way. Although there are important qualitative differences in the internal dynamics of constituency associations between British Columbia and Ontario, there is a clear tendency among local activists to construct their organizations in ways that link national to provincial in the ridings.

4
Local Campaigns and Grassroots Armies

Judy Sgro has been the MP for York West since a 1999 by-election, and James has been a member of her "inner circle" in each of her re-election campaigns. Prior to each campaign, James begins the process of contacting local Liberals who could be persuaded to work as volunteers. Local campaigns in Canadian elections require "veritable arm[ies] of volunteers" to be successful, and campaigns always seem to be lacking these valuable volunteers (Carty 1991, 167; Dyck 1993, 243). James tackles the problem by assigning callers to contact volunteers from previous elections as well as sympathizers who hosted lawn signs in previous campaigns. Before this begins, however, a crucial task falls to James himself: he calls his contacts in the provincial York West organization and requests the provincial membership list as well as the list of volunteers from the last provincial campaign. The list is readily provided, and James uses it to construct an army of campaign volunteers that consists of secondary workers drawn from both the national and the provincial membership lists.

But in Perth-Wellington, local Liberal elites prepare for election campaigns in a starkly different manner. The provincial organization in the riding is composed of elites who are strongly oriented toward supporting the incumbent MLA. These local elites have crafted a sleek, professional organization that runs professional re-election campaigns in provincial elections and maintains contact with members between elections. However, these elites have little to do with the national Liberal Party, which does not have an MP and is still licking its wounds following a divisive local nomination contest. Indeed, provincial elites make efforts to avoid contact with the national constituency association, and the MLA approves of this.

Whereas campaign organizations in York West are linked between the national and provincial levels, provincial Liberals in Perth-Wellington construct distinctive campaign organizations at the two levels. These examples illustrate two distinctive responses of local campaigners to the challenge of federalism: integrated campaigns in York West and differentiated campaigns in Perth-Wellington. This chapter explores variations in the national-provincial organization of the Liberal Party's local campaign organizations.

Variations in the organization and operation of local campaigns in Canada reflect variations in the geographic and ecological character of the constituencies (Carty, Eagles, and Sayers 2003). The franchise arrangement that characterizes the Liberal Party's wider organization provides tacit recognition of this local imperative by granting constituency campaigns significant autonomy from the party as a whole and from the national campaign. As a result, constituency campaigns in Canadian elections are largely candidate centred – local candidates enjoy significant freedom to organize their campaigns in ways that most closely adapt to the conditions of their individual ridings.

The structures of local campaigns also derive from the circumstances of the nomination contests that precede them. Sayers (1999, 46-48) argues that three local filters on nominations – the appeal of the nomination, the permeability of the local association, and the nature of the candidate search conducted by the constituency association – shape the type of nomination race that takes place, which in turn produces four distinctive types of candidates. These four types of candidates construct campaign organizations that differ in both the nature of the inner circles that surround the candidates and the personnel and resources mustered (87).

If local campaigns adapt to the geographic, ecological, and political realities of the ridings, how then do they adapt to Canada's multi-level institutions? In what ways are national and provincial campaigns linked, if at all? Previous accounts of the formal disentanglement of Canada's national and provincial parties suggest that constituency campaigns conduct themselves without reference to the other level of the multi-level state. National constituency campaigns from this view organize to contest national elections only and have little or no contact with the local provincial party or the provincial campaigns that form to contest elections in the provinces.

Some local campaigns, encouraged by differing national and provincial constituency boundaries, organize and operate in precisely this manner. But the autonomy that local campaigns enjoy from the wider party

Figure 4.1

A continuum of campaign organizations

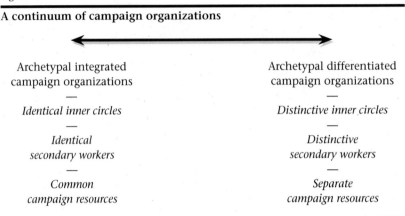

means that campaigns can also be organized in such a way that they are linked to the other level. As is the case with constituency associations, variation exists in the number and nature of these linkages.

Observing the extent to which national and provincial campaigns employ similar or different groups of campaign workers and resources allows for the construction of a continuum that ranges between integrated and differentiated local campaigns. Figure 4.1 illustrates this continuum.

Archetypal integrated campaigns exist where there are significant lines of continuity between the national and provincial levels. Such campaigns have three characteristics. First, national and provincial candidates rely on identical groups of activists to form their inner circles, where these activists advise the candidates and perform specialized tasks during campaigns. As a result, the inner circles of integrated campaigns contain activists with experience in both national and provincial politics. Second, integrated national and provincial campaigns rely on identical groups of volunteers as secondary workers. Third, integrated national and provincial campaigns draw on the same resources at both levels. These resources include office space; computers and computer applications; membership, donor, and sign lists; and the hardware of campaigns such as signs and signposts.

In contrast, archetypal differentiated campaigns exist where there are no bonds between the national and provincial campaigns and are defined by three characteristics. First, the inner circles of national and provincial candidates are altogether distinctive from one another; there are no common inner circle members between differentiated campaigns at the two levels. Second, national and provincial candidates draw on entirely different volunteer bases of secondary workers to staff differentiated campaigns. These groups of workers function as single-level workers, dedicating their time to campaigning at one level but not the other. Third, resources employed during national and provincial campaigns are not shared between the organizations. Differentiated campaigns at the national and provincial levels are therefore largely distinctive with respect to personnel and resources.

As is the case with constituency associations, campaigns generally cannot be classified as wholly integrated or differentiated. Instead, local campaigns typically have characteristics of both. The extent to which such characteristics are present determines the placement of local campaigns on the continuum between integrated and differentiated campaigns. This chapter constructs several case studies of integrated and differentiated campaigns that differ in these three aspects of organization.

The Inner Circle

Candidates' inner circles include campaign managers, official agents, and other activists who perform specialized, complex tasks during the course of the campaign (Sayers 1999, 66-71). Consistent and inconsistent activists in candidates' inner circles are important indicators of integrated local campaigns. This is especially true when both national and provincial candidates trust and invite the same activists into their inner circles. These common inner circle members integrate national and provincial campaigns in two ways. First, inner circle members with experience in campaigns at the other level help to create a perception of unity between national and provincial campaigns when they are visible in their roles at both levels. Second, inner circle members often play important roles as influential figures who help to attract and recruit secondary workers to campaigns. Prominent inner circle members can actively work to recruit volunteers from the party at the other level; indeed, their mere presence in the campaign can encourage volunteers to participate.

Marcelle Mersereau gathered a distinctively integrated inner circle around her during her 2006 campaign in Acadie-Bathurst. Prior to the 2006 election, Mersereau won the nomination to represent the Liberal Party against Yvon Godin, the NDP incumbent MP. Following this victory, she immediately recruited provincial campaign officials into her inner circle to construct an integrated local campaign.

Before describing how Mersereau did so, it is necessary to outline the two immediate challenges facing her following her lopsided nomination race. First, she sought to boost her public profile in the different regions of the riding. Acadie-Bathurst is a sprawling rural riding in northeastern New Brunswick. In addition to the city of Bathurst, the major population centre of the riding, it has two distinctive regions. The Acadian Peninsula in the northeast contains more unilingual French speakers and is generally economically depressed. The Chaleur region in the southwest surrounds Bathurst and is separated from the Acadian Peninsula by language and socio-economic factors as well as by geography. The national riding is divided into seven provincial ridings, four in the Acadian region (Caraquet, Centre-Péninsule, Tracadie-Sheila, and Shippagan) and three in the Chaleur region (Bathurst, Nepisiguit, and Nigadoo-Chaleur).

Given her prior provincial experience, Mersereau was well known in Bathurst and the Chaleur region but was less recognized in the Acadian region. Fritz, a national activist from Bathurst, describes how settling on candidates can be particularly difficult in geographically segmented ridings such as Acadie-Bathurst:

> Candidate selection is probably the worst because you say, "we need to get someone well known." But someone who's well known down in the Acadian Peninsula may not be well known in the Chaleur region and vice versa. We've had candidates, we say, "this person is great," and everyone you talk to in your circle says, "that person's well known." Then you go down to Shippagan, and they say, "we don't know who he is." So that's probably the biggest divider, the popularity of the candidate ... It's hard to find someone whose network extends into the Chaleur region and the Acadian Peninsula.

Mersereau, a well-known public figure from Bathurst, faced a similar problem: she had a public profile in one region but was less recognized in the other. Even where she was recognized in the Acadian region, she lacked deep connections to its communities. Her first challenge was therefore to build up her profile in the Acadian Peninsula, particularly because Godin was popular in the region.

The second challenge for Mersereau was to construct a campaign team from scratch at a late date; indeed, the national campaign was already under way when she was nominated. In addressing this challenge, she accessed the pre-existing provincial campaign groups of secondary workers within the national riding of Acadie-Bathurst by inviting provincial activists into her campaign inner circle. Her 2006 campaign therefore provides a good example of a campaign where inner circle members served to integrate national and provincial campaigns.

The key to accessing these provincial activists was in the national constituency association executive in Acadie-Bathurst. This executive is integrated with the seven provincial association executives contained within the national riding. All seven provincial executive presidents are granted ex officio status on the national executive, and most presidents attend national executive meetings. As a result, these meetings in Acadie-Bathurst are characterized by the presence of a significant contingent of provincial executive presidents, which necessarily means that the focus of these meetings shifts between the national and provincial levels.

The integrated nature of the national and provincial association executives in Acadie-Bathurst extended to Mersereau's 2006 national campaign. The campaign was organized in a federated manner that emphasized the role of provincial association presidents as local campaign coordinators. The first layer of national campaign organizations in Acadie-Bathurst is regional. In the 2006 election, the campaign opened two offices. One coordinated campaign activities in the Acadian Peninsula region, and the other did so for the Chaleur region. The presence of regional offices allowed local organizers to overcome the geographic difficulties posed by a large rural riding. Each regional office comprised desks for each of the provincial ridings in the region. The fundamental organizational components of the national campaign in Acadie-Bathurst were therefore provincial constituencies.

If the national campaign structure in Acadie-Bathurst during the 2006 election was multi-level, then that organization was rooted in the national association executive. During the campaign, the provincial association presidents who sat on the national executive as ex officio members filled the roles of primary campaign coordinators in each of the provincial ridings. Each of these presidents used the desks reserved for them at the campaign's regional offices. These offices allowed the presidents to remain in close contact with one another. The seven presidents were in constant contact with the candidate during the course of the campaign by phone and email. In addition, they met with her as a group once a week during the campaign. In this way, the provincial association presidents entered the candidate's inner circle as representatives of the diverse regions of a large rural constituency.

Drawing on the national constituency association executive and the provincial association presidents who sat on that executive allowed Mersereau partially to solve the two initial problems confronting her campaign. The willingness of the provincial association presidents to enter her inner circle allowed her to construct an experienced core campaign team in the face of severe time constraints. One prominent activist in her campaign team describes the process by which Mersereau drew provincial executive members into her inner circle:

> She made one of the conditions [of her candidacy] that each provincial riding with a sitting member would have their organization work with us. And then the others who didn't have a sitting member provincially, then obviously we had to work with them. And it took about four days – maybe a little more – before all the executives had talked. So at the end of three or four days, we had a commitment from each provincial riding ... that their executive was behind us. So we had seven provincial organizations, and that was how we formed our [campaign] committee.

All of the provincial association presidents had been involved in provincial campaigns in their constituencies. The president from the riding of Nigadoo-Chaleur, for example, had been the "right-hand man" to the provincial campaign manager in that constituency. In that capacity, he had involved himself in most aspects of the campaign and was subsequently able to bring that experience to his role as a member of Mersereau's national inner circle. Pierre, the provincial executive president from Shippagan and the islands, had been an MLA from the constituency and brought a wealth of knowledge about the area and campaigning. In addition, most had been involved in past national campaigns. Mersereau leaned heavily on these presidents for advice during her visits to the Acadian Peninsula.

One way that these members of her inner circle bound the national campaign to the provincial party was by mobilizing secondary workers. The primary role of each provincial association president was to mobilize pre-existing provincial activist bases to participate in the national campaign and to oversee campaign activities within their ridings. Accordingly, these presidents worked to reconstruct the campaign teams that had been in operation during the previous New Brunswick election campaign and drew on their own provincial networks to do so. Provincial membership lists, for example, were used to invite Liberal members to participate in the national campaign.

The national campaign in the provincial constituency of Nigadoo-Chaleur demonstrates the effectiveness of drawing provincial presidents into the national candidate's inner circle. Within Nigadoo-Chaleur, provincial elites had made a concerted effort to recruit executive members from throughout the rural riding. "The riding goes like this: we've got

Beresford, Nigadoo, Petit Rocher, Madran, and Belledune," explains one executive member. "What we did on the executive, we tried to put a director on the executive from each of these localities, which makes it a little stronger." These new executive members were then responsible for recruiting new party members in their own riding. In this way, the strategy of appointing representatives from the riding's communities to the provincial executive has paid off: "By appointing people in that way, we've recruited a lot of [additional] people."

Provincial campaigns in Nigadoo-Chaleur flow from the organization of the executive. In putting together the campaign, the candidate pays attention to spending time in each "pocket" of the constituency. "One of the things we do is, if we get a rally going, we'll have a rally in Beresford. Then the party meeting will be held in Petit Rocher. Then we'll have a fundraiser supper in Pointe-Verte," explains the provincial elite. "We try to give a little bit to each area." The presence of representatives from each of these regions on the provincial executive is essential to such a campaign strategy. "These are close-knit communities. So, if you have a popular person within one community, he's going to attract volunteers ... So this is how we recruit people."

This is a process of campaign organization that is well adapted to rural constituencies. "You have to pick ... movers and shakers from each of the towns," explains one organizer from a rural Ontario riding. "So you have to find that influential person in the town and get them to take you around ... to the coffee shops and the restaurants to try not only to pick up support but also to attract volunteers as well." In Acadie-Bathurst, Mersereau's campaign team accomplished this by tapping into the pre-existing provincial campaign teams in each provincial constituency. By inviting the president of the provincial executive from Nigadoo-Chaleur into her inner circle, Mersereau gained access to this intricate network of local figures and those figures' own networks within the close-knit communities throughout Nigadoo-Chaleur.

The success of provincial association presidents in mobilizing secondary workers was also contingent on the national candidate and the strength of the provincial party in each of the national constituency's provincial ridings. As a former MLA from Bathurst, Mersereau was well known in the Chaleur region. Presidents in the three provincial ridings that comprised that region were largely successful in attracting former provincial campaign workers to participate in the national campaign. But Mersereau was less known in the Acadian Peninsula region. "Provincially, we have a small riding, ... and the people running are all people that we know, that we know very well," explained Louis, from the

Acadian Peninsula region. "As opposed to the federal riding; [the candidate] can be someone from Bathurst that we've never seen in our lives." This was in sharp contrast to the NDP incumbent, Yvon Godin, who was a vocal advocate for seasonal workers in the region. In addition, the provincial Liberal Party is weaker in the Acadian Peninsula than in the Chaleur region.

As a result, provincial association presidents in the Acadian Peninsula region were less successful than their counterparts from the Chaleur region in mobilizing a pre-existing volunteer base for the national campaign. Presidents in the former region nevertheless continued to play an important role as inner circle members within the campaign. When Mersereau travelled to the Acadian Peninsula, for example, the local constituency president would help to organize the events that she attended. "I drove the candidate around when she was in this riding to different places to meet different people, Tim Horton's, and some private homes," notes one president from the region.

The provincial association presidents who staffed Mersereau's inner circle brought a significant amount of previous campaign knowledge to bear on their roles in the campaign. Those experiences were rooted in provincial campaigns in their own constituencies and among their own local networks of provincial activists and workers. These provincial organizations were invaluable to Mersereau given the limited time that she had to construct her organization and the difficulties faced by Liberal candidates in the 2006 campaign. "If we didn't have that organization here in the last election, I don't know who would have run [the campaign]," says one president. "So it's a good thing that that organization is there, because it means that you have something to fall back on." In these ways, the inner circle members bound the national campaign to the seven provincial party organizations in the riding. Most importantly, they functioned to mobilize the pre-existing provincial base of secondary workers in each provincial riding.

Even with this federative campaign organization providing support, however, Mersereau was unable to defeat the NDP incumbent. This was undoubtedly due to the local popularity of the charismatic Godin; he went on to win the riding in the 2008 election as well. But Mersereau also suffered because her organization was constructed only after the campaign had already begun. Falling back on provincial campaign organizations might have provided her with a skeletal campaign structure, but the lack of time undoubtedly prevented provincial association presidents and coordinators from fully mobilizing local activist bases to campaign effectively.

The nature of the national and provincial party systems shapes how common inner circle members integrate national and provincial campaigns. In Ontario and New Brunswick, the same inner circle members tend to appear on Liberal campaigns at the national and provincial levels. But in British Columbia, differing party systems at the two levels can result in inner circle members appearing in different campaigns at the two levels. Provincial Liberal campaigns, for example, are sometimes characterized by the presence of national Liberals and Conservatives in the candidate's inner circle. The number of these inner circle members necessarily varies by campaign. National Liberals dominate some inner circles, whereas national Conservatives predominate in others. In either case, influential inner circle members bind national and provincial campaigns at the two levels to one another.

The provincial Liberal campaign of Iain Black in the riding of Port Moody-Westwood provides a good example of this phenomenon. The riding, located within the national constituency of Port Moody-Westwood-Port Coquitlam within the Greater Vancouver Regional District, is made up of relatively affluent suburbs. Partially as a result, the provincial Liberal Party has been successful in electing members in the riding. The incumbent, Christy Clark, was a high-profile provincial cabinet minister and a former deputy premier who won her final re-election campaign in Port Moody-Westwood with 75 percent of the popular vote.

Clark announced that she would not run for re-election in the lead-up to the 2005 provincial election, sparking a lively nomination contest in the riding. Given the popularity of the BC Liberals in Port Moody-Westwood, potential candidates were attracted to the nomination. The result was a competitive and exciting nomination race between Iain Black, Irene Barr, and Rick Marusik. Black was a low-profile businessman, Marusik was the former mayor of Port Moody, and Barr had stood in the 1996 provincial election as an unsuccessful candidate for the BC Liberal Party in the riding of Port Coquitlam-Burke Mountain. Barr had also been active in the provincial Liberal Women's Commission, serving as its president. Given their previous political experience, Barr and especially Marusik appeared to be higher-quality candidates than Black.

None of the three candidates was well connected to the provincial constituency association. As a result, the embryonic campaign teams for each candidate consisted of family and close friends. The candidates also quickly sought to draft influential figures into their campaign teams. One such influential figure was Harold, a prominent national Conservative in the constituency who sat on the local national Conservative association executive. Barr was the first to attempt to recruit Harold into her campaign team. Unfortunately for her, Harold, despite his view that Barr was hard working and honest, balked at the prospect of her candidacy. Her unsuccessful run for elected office convinced him that she would not be a strong candidate. National Conservatives in the constituency were also dissuaded by her activism on the provincial Women's Commission since it is perceived by many Conservatives as a bastion of national Liberals. Despite the high regard in which he held Barr, Harold ultimately turned down her request for support.

Following this appeal from Barr, Black also attempted to recruit Harold into his campaign. Black did not have a background in politics; nevertheless, his background as a successful businessman impressed Harold. In addition, his politics better conformed to those of the federal Conservative Party than did Barr's perceived views. Whereas Barr's activism on the Liberal Women's Commission was cause for suspicion among local Conservatives, Black was a proponent of the party's fiscally conservative themes. "Iain is a conservative," argues Harold. "He is pro-business, low taxes." Accordingly, Harold was public in his support for Black and took on an important role in his campaign.

Harold quickly developed a close relationship with Black and entered the candidate's inner circle. To Black's opponents, Harold was "one of his main nomination supporters" and subsequently "one of Iain's key guys ... He was very powerful and very effective." When Black subsequently won the competitive nomination race, Harold remained in his inner circle for the duration of the general election campaign. "We're very close," confirms Harold. In this capacity, Harold worked to construct important linkages between Black's provincial Liberal campaign and the national Conservative organization in the riding.

One way that Harold did so was by enlisting national Conservative activists as secondary workers in Black's campaign. His profile in the local community as a national Conservative lent Harold credibility in convincing other Conservatives to sign up to assist Black's provincial campaign. Jeff, a national Conservative from the riding, describes how Harold invited him to join the campaign: "When Iain Black decided to run for the nomination, one of his main nomination supporters was [Harold] ... He said, 'There's this guy named Iain Black running, and he wants to meet you.' And I took an immediate liking to the guy, and we've gotten along really well ever since." Harold's intervention encouraged national Conservatives such as Jeff to participate in Black's campaign; Harold contributed to the construction of a formidable team of secondary workers simply by introducing the provincial candidate to hard-working national Conservative workers.

Harold's efforts illustrate how inner circle members can help to integrate national and provincial campaigns. Harold brought a long history of campaign experience at the national level to Black's provincial campaign. As a member of Black's inner circle, he strengthened the bond between the national Conservative Party and Black's provincial campaign. Most importantly, Harold's presence in Black's inner circle encouraged national Conservatives to take on roles as secondary workers in the campaign.

The example of Port Moody-Westwood also illustrates how inner circle members can play these roles within the context of dissimilar national and provincial party systems. In Acadie-Bathurst, provincial activists in Marcelle Mersereau's inner circle helped to integrate the provincial Liberal Party with the national Liberal campaign. But in Port Moody-Westwood, Harold's presence as a provincial inner circle member strengthened the bonds between the national Conservative Party and the provincial Liberal Party.

This strategy paid off on election day. Port Moody-Westwood was traditionally a strong Liberal riding, but Black was a neophyte candidate running in a riding that had been held by a popular and high-profile incumbent. Constructing a campaign organization that included national Conservatives allowed Black to overcome his weaknesses in the riding, and he easily won the local race in the 2005 provincial election. Having won this initial victory, he went on to be re-elected in 2009.

Acadie-Bathurst and Port Moody-Westwood provide examples of common inner circles in national and provincial campaigns. In other cases, the inner circles of candidates at the national and provincial levels can contain no or very few common members. In these cases, advisers who surround the candidate do not bring experience from the inner circle of the candidate at the other level. Separate inner circles are an important indicator of local campaign differentiation. Whereas common inner circle members represent continuity between national and provincial campaigns, separate inner circles reinforce the autonomy of national and provincial campaigns. In addition, members of separate inner circles do not recruit secondary workers from previous campaigns at the other level. As a result, these inner circle members cause the campaigns that they work on to focus only on a single level.

Most candidates commence their campaigns with an inner circle composed of friends, family, and other close supporters. These supporters do not typically bring important connections to the party at the other level of the multi-level state. Such inner circle members are in a poor position to attract supporters and donors from the other level; they therefore contribute to the development of differentiated local campaigns.

Rob Esselment's 2003 provincial campaign in the Ontario riding of Haldimand-Norfolk provides a good example of a campaign in which single-level activists played an important role in the candidate's inner circle. Esselment's inner circle was largely composed of friends and family who were primarily single-level activists interested in the provincial election campaign. As a result, these activists did not integrate his provincial campaign with the national party by recruiting, for example, members from the national level to work on the campaign. Instead, these inner circle members focused the campaign exclusively on the provincial level.

Over the course of the campaign, however, Esselment's inner circle evolved to include long-term, consistent members of the local Liberal activist base. In part, this reflected the necessity of recruiting campaign volunteers in a riding characterized by a largely consistent activist base. Members of the campaign distinguish between two types of inner circle members: immediate friends and family who were largely concerned with Esselment's provincial campaign, and consistent Liberals who brought experience from national campaigns. "Between family/friends and consistent Liberals, it was half and half," explains Jill, a member of Esselment's inner circle. "We needed some of the consistent Liberals from the area to help us win the nomination, and some of them transferred over to the key campaign group. A few others were family."

Although Esselment's inner circle originally consisted of single-level supporters who were primarily friends and family, reaching out to the local association in Haldimand-Norfolk necessitated the inclusion of consistent Liberals in his core group. "We needed the consistent Liberals because they knew all the other Liberals in the riding," explains Jill. "We weren't intimately familiar with the association or its list of members. We needed long-time federal and provincial Liberals to help us get the endorsements we needed from the main Liberal players in the riding, to help convince existing members to vote for Rob in the nomination, and to help us find new Liberal members to sign up." Although the single-member supporters who originally joined Esselment's inner circle had a differentiating impact on the campaign, this was tempered by the influence of consistent activists who later joined the campaign.

Secondary Campaign Workers

Acquiring an appropriate combination of sympathizers, secondary workers, and inner circle members is crucial to the success of local campaigns (Sayers 1999, 68). Secondary workers and sympathizers who drift in and out of the campaign office present enormous challenges to campaign officials and lend local campaigns their seemingly chaotic character. "There's a lot of people that come and work in campaigns and want to be part of it, and they do their part," explains Jordan, an organizer from the BC riding of Richmond. "Not a lot of effort, but every little bit counts."

Large numbers of secondary workers are particularly important to successful local campaigns. These workers are responsible for carrying out time-consuming and labour-intensive tasks: they pound in campaign signs along the highway, lick envelopes for mail-outs, and walk through entire neighbourhoods during literature drops. A vibrant base of secondary workers lends campaigns an aura of competitiveness that attracts more volunteers (Sayers 1999, 68). As a result, anecdotal accounts emphasize the positive role of a large and motivated group of campaign volunteers (see, e.g., Bell and Bolan 1991).

Yet local campaigns are chronically deficient of these valuable volunteers. Campaigns require on average 150 regular campaign volunteers to be effective, but only 16 percent of campaigns in the 1988 national election reported sufficient numbers of volunteers (Carty 1991, 167). When campaigns lack secondary workers and sympathizers, members of the candidate's inner circle are forced to perform mundane and time-consuming tasks, distracting them from the more specialized tasks that they typically perform during campaigns (Sayers 1999, 69).

Common volunteer bases are an important indicator of integrated national and provincial campaigns since integration is reinforced by the use of common volunteers as secondary workers in local campaigns. National and provincial campaigns in the constituency of Saint John typically share secondary workers, partly because of the largely consistent Liberal activist base in the constituency. As a result, campaign volunteer recruitment in Saint John consists for the most part of mobilizing the same volunteer base during national and provincial campaigns. The volunteer base mustered in Saint John during national campaigns is therefore best summarized as an agglomeration of the seven provincial volunteer bases that are active during provincial election campaigns. "You see the same faces at a lot of these things," explains Tony. "I have a list of Liberal members in Saint John ... When you're working on a federal campaign usually those ... people are all out. When you're working on a provincial campaign, they split up into the different provincial constituencies, the seven constituencies in greater Saint John." The result of this long-standing form of organization is that national and provincial campaigns muster similar sets of activists to staff their campaigns, and campaign managers at both levels have come to depend on many of the same volunteers to carry out the mundane tasks of local campaigns.

For Liberals in Saint John, formal separation of the national and provincial parties is not experienced during the course of their participation in national campaigns. Everett, the president of a provincial association executive, identifies more strongly with the provincial than the national Liberal Party, for the provincial party constitutes a more rewarding incentive structure within which he pursues his purposive goals. Nevertheless, he finds it difficult to distinguish between the national and provincial parties when it comes to campaign work since most local Liberals work on both national and provincial campaigns. As a result, Everett, despite a focused strategy of maximizing material benefits from the provincial Liberal Party, has found himself caught up in national campaign activities given the tendency of local activists to participate in campaigns at both levels.

For many activists in Saint John, participation in both national and provincial campaigns is particularly rewarding. Such participation allows volunteers to perform the same tasks at both levels and therefore develop specializations. For some activists, working in campaign offices is attractive because it allows them to work with friends. In Saint John, a group of women dubbed Pat's Angels – named after the member who acts as the group's de facto leader – have distinguished themselves by working as an informal team on both national and provincial campaigns. The activities of the group are animated by the friendships and solidary relations that exist within the group.

Other volunteers view their contribution as consisting of manual labour, and they therefore enjoy dealing with signs and other labour-intensive tasks. Still other activists value the exhilaration of working on election day and therefore participate in get-out-the-vote activities. By drawing on a similar activist base, national and provincial campaigns in Saint John can tap into the same group of specialists to perform these campaign functions. Both national and provincial candidates in Saint John, for example, typically seek out members of Pat's Angels, reputed to be tough and dedicated local campaigners, as campaign volunteers. In Moncton, an admiring activist describes such a group of "ladies" bound together by solidary relations who work in both national and provincial campaigns:

> There's a lady by the name of Alice. She takes care of Moncton, and she's been an organizer here forever. She came in the mid-70s maybe. And she has her people with her. She has her ladies that make calls [and work as] poll captains and whatnot. She has a list [of volunteers], and every [provincial] election she'll take that list and make it work for the Liberal Party. And when time comes for the federal election, she'll take the same people and contact them and work for the campaign in Moncton. And I'd say that works the same way at the different levels.

In offering their specialized campaign skills to both national and provincial campaigns in Saint John, groups such as Pat's Angels constitute an important linkage between national and provincial campaigns while still pursuing their own goals as partisan volunteers.

Common volunteer bases for national and provincial campaigns in Saint John result partially from the joint national-provincial activist base in the constituency. From the perspective of local activists in Saint John, volunteering as secondary workers in national and provincial campaigns serves to reinforce their dual-level conception of partisanship. National and provincial campaigns, along with meetings of the constituency associations and inter-election maintenance events, punctuate the slow routine of party life in Saint John. By participating in these events, local activists reinforce the social bonds that they have developed at both levels and their partisan commitment to both national and provincial parties. Campaigns, characterized by close teamwork between secondary workers and an air of intense partisanship, are particularly important in reinforcing activists' consistent partisanship. "A Liberal's a Liberal's a Liberal in Saint John," explains Tony. "We'll fight the Tories federally, we'll fight the Tories provincially. We just like fighting Tories."

The volunteer bases of Liberal campaigns at the national and provincial levels in Saint John are relatively similar; the same activists typically sign up as secondary workers in national and provincial campaigns. This consistent participation of local Liberal activists has played a significant part in the recent electoral success of the national Liberal Party in Saint John, formerly an electoral wasteland for the Liberal Party. Candidates now depend on a vibrant community of consistent campaigners to wage ground-level campaigns in the riding. Liberal Paul Zed was successful in the riding in the 2004 and 2006 elections but was defeated in 2008. The

Conservative candidate's margin of victory over Zed in 2008, however, was less than 2 percent, with the result that the local consistent activist base will play important roles in future Liberal campaigns in the riding.

In contrast to Saint John, differences in the national and provincial party systems in British Columbia mean that campaign volunteers can participate in different campaigns at the two levels. Provincial Liberal campaigns, for example, are often staffed by secondary workers who have volunteered for national Conservative candidates. In other ridings, provincial Liberal campaign teams are often staffed by a combination of national Liberals, national Conservatives, and single-level activists. These combinations of volunteers necessarily differ by riding. Anecdotal evidence suggests that the balance between national Liberals and Conservatives on provincial campaign teams reflects the strength of the national party in the area, as is also the case with constituency association executives. The key point is that integration between national and provincial campaign volunteer bases is not ruled out by dissimilarity between the national and provincial party systems.

Wendy McMahon's 2001 provincial Liberal campaign in the riding of Columbia River-Revelstoke provides an example of how national and provincial campaigns can come to depend on similar volunteer bases within a context of different national and provincial party systems. McMahon was a long-time organizer in the provincial party, and her husband, Brian McMahon, had run unsuccessfully for the party in the 1995 election. In contesting the party nomination prior to the 2001 election, McMahon drew on supporters from the provincial organization and from her own network of friends and associates.

McMahon was also able to draw on the national Liberal activist base in the constituency to staff her campaign. She was viewed in the riding as a national Liberal and was a friend of the president of the national Liberal association, who had openly supported her in the provincial nomination contest that preceded the general election campaign. As a result, McMahon was in a good position to recruit national Liberals to work on her campaign, despite uneasiness in some quarters of the national party that the provincial Liberal Party had moved too far to the right in response to the presence of the right-wing provincial Reform Party. McMahon and her inner circle of supporters drew on their contacts and personal relationships in the national party to build a base of secondary workers first for her nomination campaign and then, when she won the party nomination, for her provincial election campaign.

Unfortunately, the national Liberal Party in Kootenay-Columbia was a shallow source of campaign volunteers for McMahon since the national party in the riding is weak. This weakness is reflected in the national party's lack of electoral success in the region; the party has not elected an MP from Kootenay-Columbia or any of its predecessor ridings since 1965.

In sharp contrast, the Conservative Party developed a strong organization in the riding that is centred on the incumbent MP, Jim Abbott. Abbott was elected as a Reform Party candidate in the 1993 national election and was re-elected as an Alliance and finally a Conservative candidate with wide margins of victory in the five elections that followed; for example, he scored 60 percent of the local vote in the 2008 national election. During each re-election campaign, Abbott has relied on a similar group of motivated secondary workers to work at local campaign offices, conduct literature drops, place signs along highways, and organize and attend local events.

The strength of the national Conservative Party in Kootenay-Columbia had important consequences for the organization of McMahon's 2001 provincial campaign. In response to this imbalance of organizational strength between the national Liberal and Conservative parties, members of McMahon's inner circle sought in the lead-up to the 2001 provincial election campaign to supplement her volunteer base with secondary workers from the national Conservative Party. McMahon hoped to draw on the local strength of the national Conservative Party to aid her provincial Liberal campaign.

But doing so was challenging for the campaign given that McMahon was perceived to be a national Liberal; Conservatives in the riding were suspicious of her national partisan sympathies. They were also put off by her perceived support of the national gun registry. Although this was a national rather than a provincial concern, local Conservatives maintain that McMahon could have attracted droves of volunteers in the rural riding had she publicly denounced the registry.

To overcome these obstacles, McMahon's campaign relied on personal contacts to recruit national Conservatives to her campaign. One such contact, Floyd, played an important role in this respect. He was active in the provincial Liberal Party, but he was also well known in the riding as a supporter of Jim Abbott. Like Harold in Port Moody-Westwood, Floyd used his position as an influential figure in the local association of the national Conservative Party to convince wary national activists to work for the provincial candidate. In doing so, Floyd emphasized the organizational separation of the national and provincial Liberal parties to assuage the fears of national Conservatives hostile to the Liberal brand: "I called up the whole Reform [Party] group and just chatted with them ... I went to people that I was familiar with through the Conservatives [and said], 'I'm asking you to join the BC Liberal Party. It has nothing to do with the Liberal Party of Canada.'" His position as an influential figure was important in recruiting national Conservatives for the provincial campaign. For these activists, Floyd's participation signalled that participation in the national Conservative Party and the provincial Liberal Party could be reconciled. This was true even for strongly partisan national Conservatives uncomfortable with the idea of supporting any Liberal party, whether at the national or at the provincial level. Notes Helen, "I've always thought of myself as Conservative. I don't like to refer to myself as a Liberal. I consider myself a Conservative ... I felt that, if there had ever been a provincial Conservative Party, I would have been interested in hearing from them. But we didn't have it." Her strong identification with Conservative politics meant that Floyd's intervention was necessary to convince her to re-evaluate the provincial Liberal Party. "I like Floyd, and I do respect his opinions on things," she explains. "If he supports Jim Abbott, which I did, then I felt that I could trust him in supporting Wendy McMahon. And I would say that Jane [another friend] would probably say the same things that I just said." For the pre-existing group of national Conservative activists in the riding, Floyd's support for McMahon played an important role in spurring their own participation in the provincial campaign.

As a result, national Conservative activists dominated the group of secondary workers who staffed McMahon's provincial Liberal campaign. "I found that the people that were working with me in the office in Jim Abbott's campaign were also the people that were working there for the provincial party," explains Helen. These activists brought a familiarity with local campaigning in Columbia River-Revelstoke. They knew, for example, the best sign locations and the local residents with minivans who could be convinced to drive voters to the polling stations on election day. Local workers who enjoyed transporting signs throughout the constituency with friends during national campaigns, for example, now had the opportunity to do so during provincial campaigns.

In the same way that local volunteers in Saint John play identical roles as secondary workers in national and provincial campaigns, so too did these activists play identical roles in Abbott's national and McMahon's provincial campaigns. In contrast to Saint John, these roles were played out in different parties at the two levels. In this way, McMahon's 2001 provincial campaign demonstrates how secondary workers can bind national and provincial campaigns to one another even within the context of divergent national and provincial party systems. And the participation of inconsistent activists in her campaign contributed to her convincing electoral victory over the NDP incumbent in the 2001 provincial election.

In the same way that common volunteer bases indicate integrated local campaigns, so too do largely distinctive volunteer bases point to differentiated national and provincial campaigns. In these cases, national and provincial campaigns are composed largely of separate volunteer bases. Inner circle members tend to have few connections to the party at the other level and thus cannot recruit campaign workers from that level. Such campaigns therefore muster bases of secondary workers who are largely distinctive from those at the other level. For volunteers in these single-level campaigns, participation reinforces a separated perception of partisanship between the national and provincial levels.

The Liberal campaign of Kwangyul Peck in the riding of Port Moody-Westwood-Port Coquitlam in the 2004 national election provides a good example of a campaign that was staffed largely by single-level volunteers and did not draw on supporters from the other level of the state. In contesting the Liberal nomination against a former mayor from the riding, Peck ran a traditional cadre-style outsider nomination campaign, recruiting large numbers of new members to support his nomination bid. He hoped to win the nomination by recruiting widely from his personal contacts and networks, particularly in the local business and Korean communities. For local activists, Peck was "a very formidable force in the immigrant community, if you can call it that ... He brought in a lot of his Korean students [to the nomination campaign]." Ultimately, his emphasis on recruiting from outside the constituency association proved successful, and he won the local party nomination.

Peck's nomination strategy of recruiting new members to support his nomination bid rather than appealing to the existing membership base in the riding had consequences for his subsequent campaign. Despite his experience as a candidate and his connections to Liberal leader Paul Martin, many local activists in the constituency viewed Peck as an insurgent candidate who had failed to build ties with the local constituency association. Instead of mobilizing the existing Liberal activist base in the constituency, local Liberals thought, Peck had drawn on his personal network of friends and associates to construct a team of instant members. This is a time-honoured tradition in the Liberal Party, but it nevertheless antagonized long-term activists (Docherty 1997, 62). That team subsequently swamped the nomination race. In addition, many local activists were under the impression that Peck's supporters had swamped the association's annual general meeting and elected sympathetic members to the association executive.

Many long-time Liberal activists consequently felt shut out of the process and neglected by Peck's campaign. One national executive member diplomatically explains how the riding association had little contact with Peck's campaign following the nomination contest: "That [the campaign] was mostly Kwangyul Peck and the head office doing a lot of stuff for the riding. But in terms of the riding politics, we take a back seat to let the candidate do what he needs to do." In response, many long-term Liberal activists in the riding committed themselves to "sitting on their hands" during the course of the campaign, making little effort to contribute to Peck's campaign.

Peck, a successful businessman positioned firmly in Liberal leader Paul Martin's centre-right faction of the national Liberal Party, should have been well positioned to appeal to and enlist provincial Liberal activists in the riding in his campaign team as secondary workers. But Peck had criticized former BC premier Gordon Campbell in local newspapers over the provincial government's small business policies, and this episode had not been forgotten by provincial Liberals. Together with a campaign organization designed to rely on Peck's personal contacts rather than existing Liberal partisans, his public criticism of the provincial government served to discourage local provincial Liberals from participating in his campaign. Instead, these potential volunteers sat on their hands throughout the campaign.

Natasha was one such activist. She was distinguished in the riding by her consistent activism. A committed national Liberal who had sat on the national executive, Natasha had also participated in provincial Liberal campaigns and had taken on leadership roles on the provincial Liberal association executive in her riding. As a result, she was an influential figure within the riding among consistent national and provincial Liberals. In this capacity, she might have played an important role for Peck in recruiting provincial Liberals to work as secondary workers in his campaign. Instead, Peck's strategy to win the party nomination and the willingness of his supporters to swamp the national association executive alienated Natasha. "We had a whole big mess here in this riding where a bunch of Korean students took over our riding association in support of one particular candidate," she fumes. "We were mad." As a result, Natasha, far from recruiting provincial Liberals to work as secondary workers in Peck's campaign, was openly hostile to the candidate and his campaign. She is therefore a good example of a long-term provincial Liberal activist who sat out Peck's campaign, contributing to its overall differentiated character.

The single-level nature of Peck's volunteer base indicates that his was a differentiated local campaign. The partisanship of these workers was both temporary and confined to a single campaign at the national level. Whereas Iain Black's local campaign was successful, Peck, facing a relatively popular Conservative incumbent without the support of the local activist and membership bases of his own party, subsequently lost the 2006 general election.

Traditional accounts of Peck would describe him as an insurgent candidate who won the nomination by recruiting instant members and who subsequently built his campaign organization from these outsiders. However, the account presented here situates Peck within a multi-level context as a candidate who constructed not only an outsider campaign organization but also a national campaign organization that was largely differentiated from any party or organization at the provincial level. Within a riding where informal cooperation between national and provincial campaigns occurs regularly, Peck's national campaign appears to have suffered from its differentiation from the provincial Liberal Party.

Campaign Resources

Local campaigns differ in the resources that they marshal during elections. For Sayers (1999, 79), campaign resources generally refer to money, the availability of which differs by type of campaign. Funds are used to purchase advertising in local media outlets and campaign materials. But campaigns also deploy resources to assist with labour-intensive tasks. They include lists of party members, former donors, and previous hosts of lawn signs; equipment for phone banks and public meetings; the wooden or steel stakes used to hold up party lawn signs or their larger counterparts erected alongside busy thoroughfares or highways; computer and communication equipment such as fax machines; the collapsible stalls that campaign workers set up at trade fairs or other public events; and even campaign Winnebagos. Such resources constitute the currency of local campaign strategists – adequate funds allow campaigns to acquire resources, whereas a lack of funds forces campaigns to grapple with their absence.

Campaign resources are generally available to be shared between national and provincial campaigns. Shared resources are an underestimated indicator of integrated campaigns at the national and provincial levels. By drawing on similar membership lists to staff campaigns or similar hardware at the two levels, national and provincial campaigns bind themselves to one another.

But how resources are shared between national and provincial campaigns differs between ridings. In some cases, sharing resources is a natural by-product of close cooperation between national and provincial campaigns. In these cases, resource sharing is conducted in an official and open manner. Such campaigns can come to expect resources from the other level and encounter significant difficulties if they are not forthcoming. In other cases, sharing resources is conducted in an informal manner on the basis of personal relationships between campaign volunteers at the national and provincial levels. This type of sharing can even take place where the national and provincial parties present are separate or where the national and provincial incumbents are hostile to one another. In these cases, informal personal relationships between campaign workers at the national and provincial levels are key to sharing campaign resources.

National and provincial Liberal campaigns in the Ontario riding of York West tend to share secondary workers. The friendly relationship between the national incumbent, Judy Sgro, and the provincial incumbent, Mario Sergio, encourages campaign volunteers to participate in both national and provincial election campaigns. As a result, these campaigns in York West muster similar sets of secondary workers.

Another way that cooperation between the national and provincial parties in York West manifests itself during campaigns is in sharing resources. Of the resources shared, local organizers place particular emphasis on lists of residents who have previously agreed to host lawn signs. Canadian election campaigns typically see great numbers of lawn signs appear throughout the neighbourhoods of the country, yet this phenomenon is "little-remarked" by observers of these campaigns (Sayers 2007, 7).

In preparing to distribute lawn signs throughout the constituency for the 2006 national election, national campaign workers in York West generated a list of local residences that had hosted Judy Sgro signs. Preparing such a list is standard practice. But in addition, the national organizers asked for and received a similar list from the local MLA, Mario Sergio. "In the last election, we had [2,000] or 3,000 names for signs," explains James, a member of Sgro's inner circle. "Mario gave us a list for their 600. So, as soon as they dropped the writ, boom! In forty-eight hours, we had out about 1,500 signs." By obtaining Sergio's list of sign locations, the national campaign was able to expand significantly the number of locations for lawn signs.

Local campaigners are keen to hand out as many lawn signs as possible. Observes Sayers (2007, 8), "campaign teams measure their success by how many signs they erect compared with their opponents, how much of the riding they cover, and who has secured the most favourable sites." A significant number of lawn signs create an aura of support and momentum for the candidate. But a key concern of local organizers is the distribution of lawn signs throughout the riding. For James, lawn signs are ineffective if they are concentrated in a single neighbourhood; instead, they should be placed strategically to cover as much of the riding as possible to maximize their exposure. With the list of provincial sign locations, the number of potential locations for national lawn signs was inflated. The list therefore provided James with significant freedom to plan out effectively the distribution of signs. "We put them out strategically," he explains, relaying his grassroots campaign wisdom. "We spread them out. A hundred here, a hundred there, just to get the whole area covered. Then we fill in the blanks." By expanding the potential number of sign locations through the provincial list, he was in a better position to distribute lawn signs in a manner in which they would be most effective as a campaign tool.

For James, list sharing between the national and provincial campaigns in York West is not a product of informal relationships between national and provincial campaign volunteers; instead, it is a natural manifestation of the close relationship between the national and provincial Liberal organizations in York West. For James, the close cooperation manifested in list sharing is facilitated by congruent boundaries at the national and provincial levels and common bases of secondary workers: "We share lists. We've got that kind of relationship. Why shouldn't you share? You've got to be stupid not to share ... That's the way it should be. If you've got an area with the same boundaries, why shouldn't we work together? We're all Liberals." Sharing sign lists is indicative of the general and natural cooperation that characterizes national and provincial campaigns in York West. And, as James suggests, list sharing makes intuitive sense in Ontario given that national and provincial ridings are identical; national and provincial campaigns must cover identical geographic spaces with signs. Responding to these incentives embedded in identical ridings, national and provincial campaigns in the Ontario riding of London West have recruited the same local activist to act as sign chairperson.

Resource sharing can also take place when the local parties are not openly integrated. Given their status as volunteer organizations, sharing resources between national and provincial campaigns can depend on personal contacts and favours between activists. The process by which these resources are shared is generally informal because party activists who have acted as campaign volunteers in previous campaigns can control access to these resources.

Lawn signs are once again illustrative. A seemingly innocuous campaign position such as sign chairperson can take on great importance in subsequent campaigns at the other level when wooden stakes or steel signposts are required. If the former volunteer is involved in the campaign at the other level, the campaign might save a significant amount of money by recycling the stakes and signposts from the other level. But if the volunteer is obstinate or a single-level activist, the stakes and signposts might remain locked away in an unknown garden shed or warehouse, forcing the campaign at the other level to muster its own resources. In these cases, resource sharing is dependent on personal relationships and contacts between activists in the national and provincial campaigns.

Resources in BC ridings are often shared, though informally and even discreetly. Such discretion is necessary given that national and provincial Liberal campaigns are never fully integrated. This type of sharing takes place in the BC constituency of Richmond. The relationship between the national and provincial Liberal organizations in Richmond is complex. Although some activists sit on the national and provincial Liberal executives, relations between the Liberal MP and the three Liberal MLAs in Richmond range from warm to hostile.

Jordan, a national Liberal activist from Richmond who volunteers extensively in national Liberal campaigns and who sits on the national association executive, replicates the tense relationship between the national and provincial Liberal parties in Richmond in his own participation. Jordan is a single-level national activist who refuses to participate in provincial Liberal campaigns. His distinction between the national and provincial Liberal parties in British Columbia contrasts strongly with James's unitary conception of the national and provincial parties in Ontario.

Despite his rejection of the provincial Liberal Party, Jordan is not reluctant to ask provincial campaign volunteers to share their resources when they are required for national campaigns. To the contrary, he is likely to approach his personal contacts in the local provincial party if he believes that the national campaign can benefit from resources that the provincial party possesses:

If you happen to need something during a campaign, I know that I've gone over to the provincials and asked if I could borrow this or use this, and I've spent time in the office while I've been looking for things. They also, in turn, come to us when they're having a campaign and there's stuff we use in our campaign that they'd like to use ... Anything we have with computers, signage. Any kind of applications we have or where we get our stuff done.

Sharing resources between the national and provincial parties in Richmond is an informal process. As a result, a personal relationship with provincial Liberal campaigners is essential to resource sharing. "It can't be an official thing. If I went and asked, it would be because I know the person. Not because I know the party and not because I know the association. I would ask the person, 'can I borrow this?' Of course, they're not going to go through proper channels to give it to me." The personal relationships between national Liberals such as Jordan and provincial Liberals allow for a significant amount of resource sharing between the national and provincial parties in Richmond. Informal sharing allows these parties to maintain formal separation while nevertheless benefiting from cooperation. This informal sharing of resources in Richmond therefore contrasts with the open sharing in York West, where the national and provincial executives are more integrated with one another and where Judy Sgro and Mario Sergio have a close relationship.

Membership lists are another resource that can be shared between national and provincial campaigns in British Columbia. Lists are a valuable resource for local campaigns because they allow organizers to identify potential sign locations, campaign workers, and sympathizers who can be transported to the polls on election day. Cooperative former membership chairs can easily pass lists of party members at one level to the campaign at the other level.

Constituency associations recognize the value of their membership lists and can therefore impose severe security restrictions on them to protect the privacy of their members. In some constituencies, for example, the local membership chairperson carries an electronic key that periodically alters the security code required to access the association's membership lists. However, these are exceptional cases; party officials realize that they can do only so much to protect the lists from activists who wish to share them with other campaigns. Constituency associations generally lack the resources to protect their membership lists effectively. "The party's a volunteer organization," explains a party organizer from Ontario. "The membership list could be sitting on Joe Blow's computer at home, and he was the membership secretary, and then he quit. Then there's a leadership race, and he's like, 'hey, I got the list!' You can't control that."

The result of such membership list sharing, particularly within a context of dissimilar party systems, is that campaigns at one level pursue sympathetic activists from the other level in the hope of accessing its membership list. For this reason, former membership chairs can suddenly find themselves the subject of unexpected affection from campaign volunteers at the other level hoping to gain access to the lists. In other cases, national Liberals or Conservatives might actively seek the position of membership chair in provincial constituency associations so that they can subsequently provide those lists to national campaigns. "Membership chairs in each riding are one of the most sought-after positions generally because you have access to membership lists," explains one provincial constituency association membership chairperson from British Columbia. "During a federal election ... I was asked by the federal Liberal Party to turn over the [provincial] BC Liberal membership lists ... That's why those positions are highly sought after!"

The result of such sharing is that single-level activists in the provincial Liberal Party can be surprised by a call from the national campaign in the riding inviting them to participate, an invitation that many will accept. In this way, informal sharing of resources through personal connections between the two parties works to bind the national and provincial campaigns to one another despite the formal organizational separation of the two parties.

But in other cases, national and provincial campaigns are hesitant to share resources. Such unwillingness indicates the presence of differentiated campaigns. Resource sharing is typically absent when national and provincial campaigns share few formal or informal linkages. Where campaigns are not formally integrated, as they are in York West, and where few informal linkages between the campaign and the party at the other level exist, campaigns are unable to coordinate resources at the national and provincial levels and must instead muster their own resources.

The 2004 national campaign in the constituency of Fundy Royal illustrates how a lack of informal personal connections can deprive campaigns of valuable resources from the other level. Fundy Royal is a sprawling rural riding that encompasses seven provincial constituencies.

The rural nature of the constituency means that activists at the outer reaches typically feel excluded from the activities of the national constituency association, focused in the Sussex region in the centre of the riding. Such perceived exclusion extends to provincial Liberal activists in the provincial ridings of Petitcodiac and Riverview, in the far eastern corner of the national constituency. Local activists from Petitcodiac complain that they must drive at least an hour to attend national constituency association executive meetings. Despite the presence of a significant number of consistent party activists, these activists are generally unwilling to expend the time required to integrate fully their provincial associations with the national constituency association.

This dynamic in the provincial riding of Riverview is exacerbated by the boundary of the national constituency. Riverview encompasses growing suburbs on the fringes of Moncton, and many residents of the riding are employed in the larger city. Riverview previously existed within the national constituency that included Moncton, but the 2004 redistribution split the provincial riding between the ridings of Moncton-Riverview-Dieppe and Fundy Royal, and Riverview's Liberal activists awoke one morning to discover to their chagrin that they were suddenly residents of the national constituency of Fundy Royal.

The redistribution posed significant problems for Liberal activists on the Fundy Royal side of the boundary. By splitting a portion of Riverview from its previous national riding, the redistribution alienated activists from the political process. This alienation typically spread by word of mouth, as Kay, a local activist describes: "When it [the redistribution] excludes them, they tell their kids, they tell their friends, they tell their families ... So then everyone starts to get disillusioned, 'I'm not going to bother to vote.' My mother's ninety years old. She's not going to vote in Fundy Royal. She says, 'if they're not voting, why should I?'" Instead of participating in the activities of the national Moncton riding, these activists were now expected to participate in the activities of the faraway Fundy Royal constituency association. The distance of Riverview from the centre of the national association's activities in Sussex created obstacles for the continuing involvement of local Liberals in the activities of their national constituency association and in national campaigns.

The new constituency boundary was particularly grating for Liberal activists in Riverview since Moncton has generally elected Liberal MPs and is characterized by a vibrant local community of Liberals. The presence of a Liberal member of Parliament from Moncton does much to attract activists from Petitcodiac and Riverview to participate in that nearby association rather than in the activities of the Fundy Royal association. In contrast, Fundy Royal, dominated by the farmers of New Brunswick's rural Kings, Queens, and Albert counties, is a Tory stronghold.

As a result, Liberal activists on the Fundy Royal side of the constituency boundary have balked at the prospect of driving over an hour to attend party functions in Sussex and instead continue to participate in the activities of the national constituency association in Moncton. The national constituency association in Fundy Royal failed to build substantive ties with the small Liberal activist base in Riverview and with the provincial constituency association and activist base in that provincial riding.

The result of this lack of integration with the provincial party in Riverview was that the national candidate in Fundy Royal in the 2006 election could not reach out to the provincial constituency association to fill the gap left by a nascent activist base in the region. This dynamic was exacerbated by the nomination of Eldon Hunter, a businessman from the western section of the riding, as the national Liberal candidate. Whereas Marcelle Mersereau could depend on provincial activist bases to provide an organizational presence in most of the regions of Acadie-Bathurst, Hunter quickly discovered that the provincial association in Riverview was largely unavailable to him. This was because the activists in that constituency had maintained their substantive connections with the national association and the wider activist base in Moncton-Riverview-Dieppe rather than engage with the national constituency association in Fundy Royal. Rather than volunteering for Hunter, who was relatively unknown in Riverview, these activists simply crossed the constituency boundary to volunteer for the national Liberal incumbent in Moncton rather than participating in a campaign that was centred a distance away. Kay explains how the nature of the riding and the nomination of Hunter contributed to the disenchantment of local activists:

> Provincially, [activists in Riverview] are in the area where they live. They can partake federally too, but they're in the [national] Fundy Royal riding, which is huge. It's huge, and it's so far removed from them. In the last campaign, their candidate was Eldon Hunter ... For him to come here and work in this part of the riding, he didn't gain anything because people don't know him. He doesn't come from here. He's a distance from here. And they didn't connect with him, which I heard about him more than once. And it's nothing against him personally. It's just the way that the boundaries are laid out.

Campaign resources from the provincial level in Riverview were consequently scarce. Hunter could not depend on provincial Liberals in the riding to provide resources because those Liberals were largely active in the neighbouring national constituency of Moncton-Riverview-Dieppe. Facing the prospect of building a local campaign organization from scratch on short notice, Hunter's campaign largely abandoned the Riverview section of the riding. Whereas Marcelle Mersereau built a campaign organization from the provincial organizations throughout Acadie-Bathurst and exploited those organizations' campaign resources in the process, lack of access to the provincial organization in Riverview prevented Hunter from doing so.

Local Campaigns in a Multi-Level Context

Local campaigns exhibit significant diversity in the extent to which they are linked between the national and provincial levels, if at all. Local campaigns can be plotted along the continuum in Figure 4.1 with relative ease because the three indicators of integrated and differentiated campaigns tend to be related. Common inner circles are associated with similar groups of campaign volunteers, which in turn are associated with shared campaign resources. Conversely, distinctive inner circles in national and provincial campaigns tend to be associated with different groups of secondary workers, which in turn muster their own sets of campaign resources. The same can be said of mixed campaigns, which fall around the midpoint of the continuum. In other words, it is possible to treat integrated, mixed, and differentiated campaigns as wholes without accounting for variation in the three indicators presented.

Integrated campaigns are placed on the left side of that continuum, near the archetype. Marcelle Mersereau's 2006 campaign in Acadie-Bathurst provides a good example of a campaign that was strongly integrated with local provincial organizations. Mersereau constructed an inner circle composed largely of provincial constituency association presidents and officials from previous provincial campaigns. These inner circle members mobilized groups of provincial volunteers to work for the national campaign. And by accessing pre-existing groups of secondary workers from throughout the riding, Mersereau also gained access to the campaign resources associated with those groups. Provincial phone lists, for example, were used to canvass the towns of the riding, and other resources used by provincial workers in previous provincial campaigns, such as equipment for lawn and highway signs, were made available to Mersereau. The national campaign used many of the same campaign resources as provincial campaigns in the riding.

Mersereau's campaign demonstrates how national and provincial Liberal campaigns can be integrated by both common personnel and shared resources. But some campaigns are integrated with different parties at the other level. Wendy McMahon's provincial Liberal campaign in Columbia River-Revelstoke provides an example of an integrated local campaign within the context of British Columbia's dissimilar national and provincial party systems. This campaign was largely integrated with the national Conservative campaign organization in the riding. Although her inner circle consisted of friends and colleagues, McMahon also invited influential figures from the national Conservative Party into her inner circle. Those inconsistent members were influential in attracting national Conservatives to McMahon's campaign even though many of those activists were uncomfortable with the prospect of working for a provincial Liberal. In addition, these national Conservatives had access to the resources used in previous national campaigns and put them to use in McMahon's provincial campaign.

Mixed campaigns occupy the centre section of the continuum. These campaigns have characteristics of both integrated and distinctive campaigns. Rob Esselment's provincial Liberal campaign in Haldimand-Norfolk, for example, might be thought of as two conjoined campaigns – one a distinctive and personal organization centred on Esselment himself, the other situated in the local Liberal tradition of national-provincial cooperation. His inner circle consisted of friends and family participating solely to assist him. They were temporary, single-level activists with no connections to any national party. But his inner circle also included influential consistent activists from the riding with important linkages to the national party and incumbent MP. Secondary workers in the campaign consisted of young professionals – especially from a section of the riding, Haldimand County, in which Esselment was popular – and teachers who participated to defeat the provincial Conservative government. The consistent inner circle members, however, were instrumental in recruiting and attracting consistent activists to the campaign to act as secondary workers. These workers had access to local campaign resources, and Esselment, a neophyte candidate, benefited from their campaign experience.

Finally, differentiated campaigns fall on the right side of the continuum. These campaigns are confined to either the national or the provincial level and have few linkages, if any, to the party at the other level of the state.

Kwangyul Peck's campaign in the riding of Port Moody-Westwood-Port Coquitlam provides a good example of a national campaign that was differentiated. Peck can be thought of as an insurgent candidate; he brought with him a strong base of outsiders when he won the national Liberal nomination in his riding. His inner circle in the campaign consisted of friends and associates who had no connections to provincial politics; this inner circle was therefore distinctive from those of provincial candidates in the riding. In addition, the campaign's secondary workers, most of whom were recruited from a single local ethnic community, were motivated primarily to support Peck. As a result, his national campaign mustered a volunteer base that was largely distinctive from provincial campaign teams in the riding. And since the campaign had no linkages to provincial secondary workers, it was forced to muster its own resources.

This discussion illuminates dynamics of both change and continuity in campaigns. Local campaign organizations are episodic and can therefore transform from election to election. Different candidates, for example, tend to attract very different sets of campaign volunteers, who in turn produce different types of campaign organizations (Carty 1991, 175). Candidates such as Iain Black who build linkages to the party at the other level construct very different campaign organizations from candidates such as Kwangyul Peck with no such linkages. Local campaigns can therefore constitute themselves at different points along the continuum from election to election.

But campaign organizations also form within a context of local organizational traditions and must adapt to characteristics of local activist bases. These characteristics of the riding can limit the extent to which local campaigns shift along the continuum between elections. Integrated campaign structures are reformed prior to each election campaign in ridings such as Don Valley East, and local administrators have become used to working in similar capacities in these organizations. These integrated structures have outlasted the career of at least one incumbent member and are likely to survive beyond the current MP and MLA.

Finally, what is the impact of similar and dissimilar national and provincial party systems on the development of integrated, mixed, and differentiated local campaigns? Table 4.1 addresses this question by categorizing the national constituencies studied by the types of campaign organizations in each of them.

Ontario ridings tend to have integrated local campaigns. However, this appears to be a largely urban phenomenon. In contrast, campaigns in rural Ontario ridings such as Haldimand-Norfolk and Oxford are less integrated and therefore constitute mixed campaigns. These campaigns, which struggle to draw volunteers and resources from throughout the

Table 4.1

Integrated, mixed, and differentiated constituency campaigns

Integrated	Mixed	Differentiated
Ajax-Pickering[1]	Haldimand-Norfolk[1]	Perth-Wellington[1]
Don Valley East[1]	Oxford[1]	New Brunswick
Richmond Hill[1]	Fundy Royal[2]	Southwest[2]
York West[1]	Delta-Richmond East[3]	
Acadie-Bathurst[2]	Kootenay-Columbia[3]	
Saint John[2]	Port Moody-Westwood-	
	Port Coquitlam[3]	
	Richmond[3]	
	Vancouver Quadra[3]	

Notes: 1 = Ontario; 2 = New Brunswick; 3 = British Columbia

riding, share characteristics of both integrated and differentiated campaigns. Although Ontario campaign organizations tend to be integrated, clear differences between urban and rural campaigns suggest that characteristics of the ridings themselves can play a role in shaping local integration and differentiation in that province.

Local campaigns in New Brunswick also tend to be integrated. Campaigns in both Acadie-Bathurst and Saint John are strongly integrated between the national and provincial levels on all three indicators. However, local campaigns in Fundy Royal and especially New Brunswick Southwest are mixed and differentiated respectively. National Liberal campaigns in Fundy Royal struggle to attract volunteers and resources from throughout the sprawling rural riding. This is a particularly pressing problem in the Grand Bay-Westfield section of the New Brunswick Southwest constituency; in this area, local activists share no linkages to the national organization and therefore do not participate in national campaigns. Similarly, provincial campaigns are conducted entirely by a single-level provincial group. In this riding, then, differentiated campaign organizations predominate.

Dissimilar national and provincial party systems in British Columbia suggest that local campaigns are more likely to be differentiated than in Ontario and New Brunswick. In fact, this is not necessarily the case, for national and provincial campaigns in British Columbia tend to be characterized by mixed rather than differentiated organizations. Both national and provincial campaigns in that province rely on a core group of single-level activists to staff candidates' inner circles and secondary volunteer bases. But campaigns in British Columbia also tend to reach out to the party at the other level. Provincial Liberal campaigns therefore tend to be staffed by single-level provincial Liberals but also by national Conservatives and Liberals. This has important consequences for the wider informal relationships between national and provincial parties in British Columbia.

The literature suggests that national and provincial parties have separated their organizations so that they can campaign more effectively without being weighed down by the actions and electoral liabilities of their counterpart at the other level. Yet in the constituencies, most campaigns are either fully or partially integrated between the two levels, even in seemingly inhospitable environments such as British Columbia. National and provincial campaign organizations in many ridings come to resemble one another as they draw on identical personnel and resources; as a result, they blur the distinction between national and provincial for both Liberal activists and voters.

5
Small Worlds: The Riding Context

Same area, same people, same party.
— James, from York West

Geographically, we don't see each other much. So, yes, philosophically the parties are one, but in reality the constraints in
terms of distance and time and travel don't make it practical
for there to be a lot of cross-involvement.
— Don, from New Brunswick Southwest

From a multi-level perspective, the Liberal constituency organizations
in York West and New Brunswick Southwest could hardly be more different. York West is characterized by a strongly integrated Liberal organization, whereas the national Liberal Party in New Brunswick Southwest
is differentiated from the several provincial organizations in the national
riding. James and Don identify two reasons why this is the case, and
both relate to the character of the constituencies themselves. First, James
notes that York West is a coterminous national-provincial riding: both
the national and the provincial ridings encompass the same area and
thus the same people. The result is that the "same party" stretches across
the divide between national and provincial. But, for Don, the geography
of the riding shapes the nature of local party organization in New
Brunswick Southwest, a sprawling rural riding. Even though the national
and provincial parties are philosophically similar, they are separated by
distance, so it is impractical for there to be cooperation between the
national organization in one section of the riding and several faraway
provincial organizations. This chapter explores how the local context
shapes the types of party organizations that evolve in the ridings.

James and Don identify the two aspects of the local riding context that hold consequences for the operation of constituency party organizations and the conduct of local party life. The first relates to geographic and topographic characteristics of the ridings. Constituencies encompass vastly different spaces, shapes, sizes, and local idiosyncrasies. These local conditions are reflected in the structures and operations of the parties' constituency associations and campaign organizations (Carty and Eagles 2005, 19-20; Sayers 1999, 110).

The simple distinction made here is between densely populated urban ridings, where the geographic space of the riding is easily traversed, and sparsely populated rural ridings, where significant and sometimes treacherous distances separate communities of activists from one another. Organizing and campaigning in urban ridings take place within a geographic space that is generally accessible to the local activist base as a whole at both the national and the provincial levels. As a result, local campaigns in urban ridings tend to be centralized. Urban campaigns, for example, typically have a single campaign office that serves the constituency as a whole – there is no need for additional offices in small urban ridings. The campaign office can be supplemented by a few locations where activists can store campaign materials, carry out labour-intensive tasks, or work from home (Land 1965, 167; Sayers 1999, 167). But these locations only supplement the central campaign offices of urban campaigns.

In contrast, rural ridings can be thought of as inaccessible. In these constituencies, local party organizations and campaigns grapple with the challenge of performing their functions within a context of significant space. A large amount of space means that significant areas of the constituency are inaccessible to entire segments of the activist base. Activists in a town on one side of the rural riding will rarely interact with activists from a town on the opposite side, let alone be familiar with one another. These distinctive communities within the disparate pockets of rural constituencies result in geographically segmented activist bases (Sayers 1999, 111).

These bases engender significant challenges for party organizations and campaigns as they struggle to integrate such communities within their structures despite the geographic distances that separate them. Long-term activists on constituency association executives in rural ridings can deal with these challenges by recruiting executive members from the different regions of the riding. Local campaigns in rural ridings also tend to adopt a more decentralized model of organization. Rural campaigns can open several campaign offices that coordinate campaign activities in the different regions of the riding (Marland 2007, 5). In the 1988 national election, campaigns in the rural ridings of Fraser Valley West and Kootenay West-Revelstoke opened campaign offices in several different regions of those ridings (Sayers 1999, 111-12, 198).

The second aspect of the local context relates to electoral regime characteristics of the ridings, particularly differences between the boundaries of national and provincial constituencies. National and provincial boundary readjustment processes in Canada are formally separate from one another, which results in very different riding boundaries at the two levels. One practical consequence of distinctive riding boundaries is that national and provincial parties must maintain formally separate local structures and conduct formally separate local campaigns, both of which are organized in response to characteristics of the unique though overlapping ridings within which they exist (also see Bradbury and Russell 2005, 27-28). Furthermore, the geographic and ecological realities that shape these components of the local party can differ greatly between national and provincial ridings, particularly when several provincial constituencies exist within the bounds of a single national constituency or when national ridings encompass significant ecological variation. The result can be national and provincial local parties that differ greatly in both their organization and their operation.

The number of provincial ridings contained within national constituencies varies by province because this is generally a product of the size of the provincial legislature. Small provincial constituencies in Canada's less populated provinces fragment national ridings and therefore further compound the challenge of local integration in these ridings. At the time of this study, New Brunswick contained ten national ridings and no fewer than fifty-five provincial constituencies. In that province, then, national ridings were severely fragmented, especially compared with ridings in Ontario. National ridings in British Columbia were similarly fragmented, though not as severely as in New Brunswick. At the time of this study, there were thirty-six national and seventy-nine provincial constituencies in British Columbia, with the result that national ridings tended to be divided between two and three provincial constituencies.

In contrast, national constituencies in Quebec and particularly Ontario have never been so fragmented given those provinces' large provincial legislatures (Perlin 1980, 22). Instead, the number of national and provincial constituencies in the large provinces has always been more proximate than in the smaller provinces. The result of this congruence between national and provincial constituencies has been that local parties in the large provinces face fewer obstacles to coordinating resources and personnel between the national and provincial levels and therefore to the development of integrated local parties.

Indeed, relatively recent legislation in Ontario has produced an even closer congruence between national and provincial constituencies in that large province. The 1999 Fewer Politicians Act amended the Ontario Elections Act to link provincial riding boundaries to those of the national constituencies (Courtney 2001, 184). Subsequent amendments delinked the redistribution process for several sparsely populated northern ridings, but the vast majority of national and provincial ridings in Ontario, including all those examined in this study, continue to have identical boundaries. The result of this seemingly innocuous alteration to provincial constituency boundaries has been that the local organizations of national and provincial parties in Ontario face new opportunities for cooperation and coordination at the local level.

These differences in the structure of the local electoral regime have important consequences for the development of integrated and differentiated local parties in Ontario, British Columbia, and New Brunswick. Identical constituency boundaries create significant opportunities for the coordination of personnel and resources between the national and provincial parties by reducing the costs of cooperation. Such an electoral regime environment is therefore conducive to the development of integrated local parties. In contrast, distinctive constituency boundaries present obstacles to the coordination of resources at the national and provincial levels, obstacles that raise the costs associated with the development of integrated local parties. In these cases, differentiated local organizations are more likely to result, though local organizations in many of these ridings have developed mechanisms to facilitate the coordination of national and provincial efforts.

Four Types of Ridings

How do characteristics of individual constituencies shape the integration or differentiation of the local parties within them? Plotting ridings on the basis of geography and the similarity of national and provincial boundaries produces four distinctive types of constituencies. For the purposes of this discussion, I distinguish between ridings in Ontario, where each national riding contains a single provincial constituency, and those elsewhere. Doing so obscures differences between the large and small provinces and therefore in the relative fragmentation of national into provincial ridings. But the advantage of distinguishing between ridings in Ontario and elsewhere is that the impact of boundary congruence on local integration can be clearly explored in both urban and rural contexts.

Urban Ontario Ridings

Ontario's urban ridings are characterized by identical national and provincial boundaries; as a result, these ridings present no significant geographic obstacles to local integration. Furthermore, national and provincial parties organize themselves within identical geographic spaces – the national and provincial organizations confront similar challenges, and the process of local integration is simplified as a result. Urban Ontario constituencies therefore provide ideal local environments for the development of integrated local parties.

These urban ridings provide for relatively small geographic spaces within which activist bases develop. As a result, local organizers face few geographic obstacles to mobilizing activists to participate in party functions and campaigns at both the national and the provincial levels. In Richmond Hill, for example, local organizers brag that they are able to draw on local activists from throughout the relatively small urban constituency during election campaigns.

The identical national and provincial boundaries of these ridings also facilitate the participation of activists at the national and provincial levels. Groups of activists bound together by solidary relations or other characteristics are able to participate at both the national and the provincial levels within the same groups. Where national and provincial constituency boundaries differ, activists within groups formed during national campaigns can find themselves divided into several provincial constituencies during provincial election campaigns. Without the rewards provided by the benefits of membership in these groups, these activists can find themselves less interested in participating at the provincial level.

Boundary congruence, however, ensures that these solidary groups are not divided by several provincial constituencies. Local activists in Ajax-Pickering, bound together by strong solidary relationships, enjoy participating as a group on constituency events and in campaigns at both the national and the provincial levels and take for granted the role that identical national and provincial constituency boundaries play in allowing them to do so. Without identical boundaries, these activists would be divided into distinctive provincial constituencies.

Because the boundaries of Ontario's urban constituencies are identical and the ridings are relatively small, they also allow activists to develop specializations within both the national and the provincial constituency associations and campaigns. Local administrators are presented with opportunities to participate in similar capacities that reflect their interests in both the national and the provincial constituency associations. It is not uncommon in these ridings to find the same activists staffing identical committees in the national and provincial associations.

Local campaigners in these ridings are also provided with opportunities to develop their specializations in both national and provincial campaigns. Activists who have developed a specialization in coordinating literature drops, for example, organize drops in an identical manner during both national and provincial campaigns. One influential campaigner in York West bragged of her knowledge of the big donors in the riding and her ability to solicit donations from them, and she approached the same donors during both national and provincial election campaigns. The unified nature of Ontario's urban ridings allows activists to develop and duplicate these specializations at both levels of the state. In this way, the specializations of these local experts transcend differences between national and provincial elections.

By facilitating the participation of local activists in both national and provincial politics, Ontario's urban ridings constitute the ideal local context for integrated constituency associations to develop. Communications between national and provincial association executives are generally sustained by common members who sit on the national and provincial association executives as well as ex officio presidents. The ridings themselves present few geographic obstacles to the attendance of these members at national and provincial executive meetings. Furthermore, the proximity of activists in these ridings facilitates coordination of party events, since local partisans face few geographic obstacles to attending national, provincial, and joint events.

Cooperation between national and provincial constituency associations in these ridings is simplified by the presence of only a single provincial constituency association. Coordinating joint events involves cooperation between only two rather than up to eight constituency associations at both levels. National and provincial associations in urban Ontario are thus better able to coordinate their inter-election events to avoid exhausting the local membership and activist base.

The geographic characteristics of these ridings also allow for coordination between national and provincial campaigns within a context of relatively little space. National and provincial organizers and officials at both levels are typically familiar with one another, encouraging cooperation between integrated constituency associations. In York West, for example, members of the national executive can easily identify most members of the provincial executive and vice versa. In addition, local activists in these ridings are generally familiar with both national and provincial candidates. This familiarity in turn encourages volunteers to work in campaigns at both levels.

Identical national and provincial constituency boundaries are also important for the development of integrated local campaigns in urban Ontario. Because national and provincial campaigns operate in identical spaces, they are better able to coordinate campaign volunteers and resources during national and provincial elections. National and provincial membership lists are generally very similar in these ridings because those lists are drawn from the same population. Differences between the lists are quickly corrected when the lists are shared between national and provincial campaigns.

The geography of local campaigning in urban Ontario ridings is also very similar for both national and provincial campaign organizations. Since national and provincial campaigns take place in the same geographic spaces, they are likely to draw on the same base of volunteers to perform similar tasks at both levels. Both national and provincial campaign signs, for example, are likely to appear in the same prime locations within the riding. In York West, list sharing between national and provincial campaigns means that both campaigns are able to exploit the same locations. In these ways, the relatively small size and boundary congruence of these ridings combine to provide strong incentives for the development of integrated campaign structures.

Rural Ridings outside Ontario

Rural constituencies outside Ontario are both geographically large and contain two or more provincial constituencies within the national boundaries. As a result, the national and provincial local parties inhabit different spaces that contain communities with often divergent interests. Fragmented constituencies therefore present both geographic and electoral regime obstacles to local integration; the costs of integration in these ridings can therefore be prohibitive, and differentiated local parties are likely to result.

The rural nature of fragmented constituencies means that groups of activists in these ridings exist separately from one another in the small communities that dot the constituency. When these communities are isolated from one another, the activist bases within them can evolve distinctively, and as a result members can develop their own local customs and traditions. In the national riding of Kootenay-Columbia, for example, a vibrant Liberal activist base in the town of Revelstoke is separated from the wider Liberal community by both distance and a mountain pass that can be treacherous to drive in the winter months. The result of this isolation has been the development of an autonomous group of activists in Revelstoke. This group is closely bound together by long-term friendships and is viewed as a curiosity by other Liberal activists in the national riding.

The presence of several provincial constituencies within the boundaries of a single national riding encourages the development of autonomous, single-level communities of activists. Local activists in these fragmented national ridings encounter opportunities to engage with a local provincial organization that necessarily exists closer to the grassroots than does the national party. Partisanship in the provincial association allows local activists to make a difference within their immediate communities rather than in large national ridings. Smaller provincial ridings also allow these groups of activists to participate within the immediate social networks of activists in that local community rather than with a large and unfamiliar group of activists throughout the national riding.

These local influences are readily discernible in the small provincial constituencies that fragment New Brunswick's national ridings. Liberal activists in the island town of Shippagan, for example, identify closely with their small provincial riding, certainly more so than with the large national riding of Acadie-Bathurst. The provincial Liberal organization is thus perceived to be more accessible than its national counterpart. "Here in Shippagan, we have a small riding, which is Shippagan and the islands," explains Louis, an executive member from the riding. "So right there is a kind of attraction to get involved a little bit more [at the provincial level] because of the fact that we know the people." The same cannot be said of the large national riding, which includes members from faraway Nigadoo-Chaleur.

The provincial constituency association in Grand Bay-Westfield also provides local activists with opportunities to participate in the party within their own small community rather than the sprawling national riding of New Brunswick Southwest. Recognizing that Grand Bay-Westfield constitutes an outlying area within the large national riding, provincial Liberals plan several inter-election events designed to appeal to local activists' wish to participate within the context of their small town. "We really want to be involved in the community," explains

Glenda, a local executive member. "It's more than just getting the candidate elected, it's about becoming a part of the community."

The presence of an MLA encourages the development of autonomous provincial activist bases in these national ridings. Local activists focus on incumbent support and enjoy a more rewarding party life in provincial ridings where an incumbent is present (Carty 1991, 60). This rewarding party life in turn strengthens the commitment of activists to the provincial party and its local organization. As a result, MLAs in fragmented constituencies usually exercise significant influence over their local activist bases – one national official in a rural New Brunswick constituency derisively refers to provincial ridings as the "little fiefdoms" of MLAs. Given their influence within fragmented ridings, MLAs can either facilitate the integration of national and provincial parties or constitute an almost insurmountable obstacle to such integration. It is the combination of geography and a lack of boundary congruence found in fragmented ridings that helps to equip MLAs with this influence.

The development of distinctive activist bases oriented primarily toward provincial parties has consequences for the development of national constituency associations and campaign structures in rural ridings outside Ontario. The rural nature of these ridings means that constituency association executives face obstacles to recruiting executive members from throughout the national constituency. Even strongly committed activists might be unwilling to drive long distances to executive meetings or participate with a largely unfamiliar group of activists drawn from throughout the riding, especially when they can easily participate in the activities of a familiar provincial constituency association. In Fundy Royal, for example, Liberal activists in the Petitcodiac region are generally resistant to making the long drive to Sussex to attend executive meetings. Activists in Revelstoke, needless to say, balk at the prospect of driving for over four hours through a mountain pass to attend constituency association executive meetings in the town of Cranbrook. This isolation from the rest of the riding means that the local activist base in Revelstoke has never involved itself to a great extent in the riding's national constituency association, which suffers as a result of its inability to penetrate this section of the riding.

Differences between national and provincial riding boundaries accentuate the rural challenge faced by constituency association executives in rural ROC (Rest of Canada) ridings. Committed activists in the far-flung regions of such ridings generally feel closer to the provincial constituency association than to the federal counterpart. As a result, motivated activists might participate at the provincial level as single-level activists or focus their energies largely at the provincial level. Either way, the national association executive is deprived of the talents of activists who, through their joint participation at both the national and the provincial levels, might help to integrate the provincial association executive with that of the national association.

These ridings can allow for the integration of the national association and some but not all of the provincial constituency associations contained within the national riding. National constituency associations in fragmented ridings tend to be based in the primary population centres of the riding, with smaller groups of members – corporal's guards – inhabiting smaller towns and villages (Carty and Eagles 2005, 24). The geography of these rural constituencies dictates that the national association might be able to construct linkages with the provincial associations from ridings that are proximate to the population centre of the riding but will face difficulties building linkages with provincial associations from the more far-flung areas. The national association in Fundy Royal, for example, has several substantive linkages to the provincial constituency associations in the central Sussex and Hampton areas but has had difficulties building contacts with the provincial associations in the eastern regions of the riding, particularly Riverview and Petitcodiac.

This lack of integration has consequences for the joint planning of inter-election maintenance events by national and provincial constituency associations. Significant distances and the necessity of coordinating with a large number of provincial association executives mean that inter-election events will rarely be jointly coordinated between the national and all of the provincial associations. In addition, the geographic realities of these fragmented ridings mean that only a small fraction of the total activist base will turn out to national inter-election maintenance events.

Local campaigns in rural constituencies outside Ontario face similar obstacles when constructing groups of secondary workers throughout the riding. The distances that separate provincial organizations complicate national coordination of local campaign groups. This obstacle is not insurmountable – national campaigns in Acadie-Bathurst, for example, effectively build on the local organizations of their provincial counterparts – but the organization of integrated campaign teams is made more difficult in rural than in urban ridings.

These constituencies can present significant obstacles to the development of integrated parties at the local level. But these ridings also present opportunities for the development of such parties, even though the costs of integration are high. In these cases, provincial constituencies within the boundaries of a national riding can serve as building blocks for the development of a relatively integrated national organization, and this form of organization necessarily reflects the fragmented characteristics of the riding. Integrated constituency associations and campaign organizations can be found in Acadie-Bathurst, since local administrators and campaigners have attempted to adapt to the conditions of the large, fragmented rural riding. The national constituency association, for example, relies on several provincial constituency associations to staff the national executive.

Rural ridings outside Ontario also provide opportunities for national campaigns. These national ridings are characterized by distinctive groups of activists scattered throughout the different communities of the riding. Multiple provincial ridings mean that these activists generally feel closer to the provincial organization. By relying on provincial ridings as organizational units, national campaigns can construct formidable organizations able to generate both volunteers and resources within each of the distinctive pockets of large rural ridings. Marcelle Mersereau's national campaign in Acadie-Bathurst was constructed in such a federative manner. The national campaign depended on provincial constituency association presidents in each of the provincial ridings to recruit volunteers from local communities. However, the national campaign failed to integrate effectively with some of the provincial organizations in the Acadian Peninsula region of the riding.

Rural Ontario Ridings

In the ridings already examined, both geographic and electoral regime characteristics impact the costs of local integration in a predictable manner. Don Valley East provides an ideal context for the development of integrated local organizations; Fundy Royal is inhospitable to this type of organization. But other ridings exercise mixed, unpredictable influences on the development of integrated and differentiated local parties. Local parties in rural Ontario ridings face challenges to integration posed by significant distances. But since they are in Ontario, these ridings have identical national and provincial boundaries. Boundary congruence mitigates some of the differentiating impact of rural geography but can also prevent the formation of the sort of federative local organizations that have evolved in ridings such as Acadie-Bathurst.

Distinctive activist bases that develop in relative isolation from one another characterize rural constituencies. Outside Ontario, these bases are nurtured by several small provincial ridings that provide opportunities for activists to participate in their immediate communities. But these small political worlds do not exist in Ontario's rural ridings, where only a single provincial constituency exists within the boundaries of a national riding. Activists in these ridings are deprived of provincial organizations that exist in smaller communities than the national party; they therefore face no geographic incentive to participate with the provincial over the national party.

Boundary congruence alters the character of the local activist bases that develop in Ontario's rural ridings. The lack of a distinctively local party organization of the sort found in the New Brunswick towns of Shippagan and Grand Bay-Westfield means that local activist groups are less defined and coherent than in rural ridings outside Ontario. Local activists are less likely to develop their own customs and traditions separate from the national riding.

Local activists in the rural Ontario ridings of Huron-Bruce and Haldimand-Norfolk distinguish between the activist groups in the twin counties that make up these ridings. But these distinctive groups of activists do not have separate provincial constituency organizations to articulate their distinctive interests and provide opportunities for them to participate as small groups in provincial ridings. These groups also lack their own provincial MLAs; the lively party life that characterizes small provincial constituencies in New Brunswick's provincial ridings is therefore missing. These groups of activists are therefore less cohesive and their identities less defined than are similar groups in ridings such as Acadie-Bathurst, where Liberals readily identify with groups of local activists within their small provincial constituencies.

Rural ridings necessarily pose geographic obstacles to the integration of national and provincial constituency associations. But the presence of only a single provincial constituency association simplifies communication between the associations at the two levels. Rather than three or even seven ex officio members, national association executives in rural Ontario ridings require only a single executive member from the provincial level to maintain communications between the two levels. National and provincial executives in these ridings typically share at least one and often several executive members, facilitating communication between the two levels. In the rural constituency of Oxford, for example, national and provincial association presidents attend executive meetings at the other level to maintain relations between the two executives. The result is an open channel of communication between the national and provincial executives. This direct line of communication facilitates cooperation between the two executives and stands in stark contrast to the complex arrays of national-provincial relationships found in many ridings outside Ontario.

Cooperation in the planning of inter-election events is facilitated by identical national and provincial boundaries. In Haldimand-Norfolk and Oxford, the provincial executives rely on informal communicative linkages with members of the national association executive to facilitate coordination of inter-election events. In addition to holding joint events, the national and provincial associations in these ridings confer on the dates of national and provincial inter-election events to maximize turnout. But the rural nature of these ridings means that such events rarely see turnout from activists from throughout the constituency, and there are entire sections of the riding that lack any form of party life, whether national or provincial.

Local campaigns also reflect the geographic and electoral regime characteristics of Ontario's rural ridings. The rural nature of these ridings presents obstacles to the integration of national and provincial campaign organizations. Boundary congruence, however, mitigates this differentiating impact since the national campaign must coordinate with only one rather than several provincial organizations. The cooperation that characterizes national and provincial constituency associations in Oxford and Haldimand-Norfolk therefore easily extends to the national and provincial campaigns of those ridings.

However, the absence of several distinctive activist bases throughout rural Ontario ridings has consequences for the degree to which integrated campaigns can penetrate isolated communities throughout the ridings. In national ridings such as Acadie-Bathurst, the presence of small provincial constituencies encourages the development of a distinctive activist base in each community. The absence of several provincial constituencies within the boundaries of Ontario's rural ridings means that provincial activist bases are less developed and oriented to the local community. The extent to which national campaigns can draw on these activist bases to penetrate remote communities is therefore limited.

Yet national and provincial Liberal campaigns in these ridings exist within identical geographic spaces and therefore confront similar geographic imperatives with respect to rural campaign organization. National and provincial candidates confront similar issues, appeal to similar blocs of voters, attempt to raise funds and volunteers from similar sources, and adapt their campaign organizations to the geography of the same ridings. This occurs within a distinctively rural context, and the challenges that face candidates are therefore distinctively rural. Both national and provincial candidates grappled with the declining tobacco-farming industry in Norfolk County and turned to monied tobacco farmers for financial support. The candidates travelled to the same small towns of the riding and sought out the support of the same "local bigwigs" – influential community leaders – to generate secondary workers to staff their campaigns. And both candidates adapted their organizations to the rural nature of the ridings, for example by assigning lieutenants to run local campaigns in the myriad farm communities that dot the riding and placing their big campaign signs in the same prime locations along the riding's highways.

Urban Ridings outside Ontario
The final group of ridings are urban constituencies outside Ontario where national and provincial boundaries differ. Although small urban ridings facilitate local cooperation and integration, the presence of several provincial constituencies within the boundaries of a single national riding complicates cooperation between the two levels.

One defining characteristic of ridings such as Acadie-Bathurst comprises their distinctive regional activist bases oriented primarily toward provincial politics. In urban ridings, however, the proximate activist bases of provincial constituencies are less developed, less defined, and less distinctive. This is because activists in these ridings typically live only a short distance from one another and know one another quite well. In Richmond, for example, the small size of the national constituency and the proximity of the three provincial ridings mean that national and provincial Liberal activists are generally familiar with one another. Even national Conservatives describe how they run into national and provincial Liberal activists in the coffee shops of the riding, breeding a familiarity between communities of activists that is largely absent in sprawling rural constituencies.

Urban ridings outside Ontario are divided into several provincial constituencies. One effect of this division is that activists used to participating with one another in national campaigns can be split up into different provincial ridings, discouraging their participation at the provincial level. Liberals whose participation is linked to solidary relationships with activists from throughout the national riding are particularly likely to cease their involvement at the provincial level when they are separated into different ridings by distinctive national and provincial boundaries.

Other activists in these ridings, however, ignore provincial boundaries and participate wherever they like. The urban nature of these ridings means that activists are free to participate in the activities and particularly the provincial campaigns of their choosing. It is not uncommon in these ridings for activists who are less than enamoured of their provincial candidates to drive to adjoining ridings to contribute to those campaigns (Sayers 1999, 116). Needless to say, this option is not available to provincial activists in sprawling rural ridings, for whom exit is the only feasible alternative to participation in their provincial campaigns.

These ridings therefore enable whole groups of activists bound together by solidary relations or some other characteristic to work together on national campaigns and come together to work on certain provincial campaigns, regardless of the provincial constituencies in which they reside. The MLA in the provincial BC riding of Richmond East, Linda Reid, enjoys the support of women campaign workers who live in neighbouring provincial ridings but who nevertheless volunteer in her campaigns. These women justify supporting Reid over their own local BC Liberal candidates by pointing to her advocacy on behalf of women in provincial politics.

Similarly, activists in neighbouring Richmond-Steveston suggest that the riding's Liberal MLA, John Yap, benefits from the support of the local Chinese community, dispersed throughout Richmond. These local campaigners identify with Yap, an immigrant from Singapore with close ties to Richmond's Chinese community, and are willing to neglect their own provincial Liberal candidates to support him as the candidate in Richmond-Steveston. This is made possible in ridings where provincial constituencies are proximate to one another. In this sense, urban ridings containing several provincial ridings open up new possibilities for local activism at both the national and the provincial levels.

Urban ridings outside Ontario also present geographic incentives to the integration of national and provincial constituency associations. The proximity of activists in the national and provincial executives means that those executives can remain in easy contact with one another. Inter-election maintenance events can also be jointly organized between the national and provincial executives. However, the comparably large number of provincial associations within national ridings complicates coordination between the two levels. In Ontario, national and provincial associations are able to cooperate on a one-on-one basis; they are likely to be seen by local activists as partners. But outside Ontario, cooperation across the national and provincial levels in the planning of inter-election maintenance events, for example, is made more difficult by the presence of several provincial executives. Despite these difficulties, the relatively small size of urban-ROC constituencies means that inter-election events will enjoy the attendance of activists from throughout the riding.

In rural ridings such as Acadie-Bathurst, national constituency association executives face incentives to recruit members from throughout the riding. Since provincial associations are closer to groups of activists in each community, national executives in fragmented ridings benefit by drawing in representatives from provincial executives. In these ridings, success depends on recruiting activists from all the distinctive pockets of a large rural constituency. Provincial associations in urban ridings do not represent remote, well-developed activist bases in remote pockets of the constituency. Instead, activist bases in these ridings are generally familiar within the boundaries of a relatively small urban riding. The result is that there is less of an incentive for the national association actively to build the sort of federative constituency organization found in Acadie-Bathurst. In Saint John, for example, local officials make little to no effort to recruit the presidents of the provincial association executives as ex officio members. I was surprised to discover that those officials are not familiar with the federative organization of the national executive in Acadie-Bathurst as well as the campaign organization that flows from it.

These ridings entail some incentives for national campaigns to draw in campaign volunteers from the different provincial ridings that make up the national constituency. "When you're working on a federal campaign, usually those 200 people are all out," explains Tony, a party organizer from Saint John. "When you're working on a provincial campaign, they split up into the different provincial constituencies, the seven constituencies in greater Saint John." The presence of several provincial constituencies within the boundaries of these national ridings means that national campaign teams will necessarily be divided into different provincial ridings. This dynamic is particularly strong in ridings such as Saint John, where there is a significant number of provincial ridings.

However, the urban nature of these ridings lessens the imperative for national campaigns to recruit volunteers from the different provincial ridings present. In fragmented rural ridings such as Acadie-Bathurst, national campaigns attempt to recruit volunteers from provincial organizations because those organizations best represent the distinctive communities. However, in urban ridings, provincial organizations do not represent distinctive, inaccessible communities. As a result, the development of a cohesive national Liberal community in urban compact ridings is not difficult. The necessity of drawing provincial organizers and volunteers into national campaigns is therefore comparably weak, lessening the incentive for the development of integrated campaign organizations.

In urban BC ridings such as Port Moody-Westwood-Port Coquitlam, integrated campaign structures result from the need to overcome partisan differences between the national and provincial levels, not from the need to recruit groups of activists from different sections of the constituency. The result is that constituency association executives and campaign groups in these ridings are not clunky, federative organizations designed to accommodate a range of autonomous provincial organizations. Instead, they tend to be characterized by professional cadres of local activists with contacts throughout the small urban ridings.

The Local Context

This chapter situated local parties within their constituency contexts and argued that diversity in the integration of national and provincial local parties can be traced to incentives built into the constituencies themselves. The chapter is situated within a literature that emphasizes how the structure of constituency-level parties reflects incentives contained within the local community (Carty and Eagles 2005, Chapter 2; Sayers 1999, Chapter 7). However, the role of the local community in shaping the local organization is also a product of the lack of organizational control imposed on local organizations by the wider party. The autonomy of the local components of Canadian parties means that those riding organizations are particularly susceptible to local influences.

Certain types of constituencies necessarily characterize Ontario, British Columbia, and New Brunswick. There are few obstacles to the development of integrated local organizations in Ontario's urban ridings. As a result, the costs of integration in these ridings are low, and they constitute fertile grounds for the development of integrated local parties. But this is less true in the province's rural ridings, where great distances increase the costs of integrated parties and frustrate attempts by national and provincial activists to integrate local structures.

In British Columbia, urban ridings contribute to the confusion surrounding linkages between national and provincial parties. This is because national ridings in that province contain several provincial ridings proximate to one another. Rather than a single relationship between one national Liberal Party and one provincial Liberal Party – as is often observed in Ontario – these ridings allow national Liberal organizations to construct myriad and complex relationships with several provincial

Liberal groups, which in turn tend to be linked in some informal manner with the national Conservative organization present. These linkages with provincial organizations, all within the same national riding, can be strong in some cases and weak in others. National Conservatives might dominate some provincial associations and, from this position, frustrate attempts by the national Liberal Party to construct linkages between the two levels. And British Columbia's urban ridings allow national and provincial activists to abandon local organizations and travel relatively short distances to participate in the organizations that they prefer, with the result that candidates and MLAs cannot take the support of local campaigners for granted. In short, these ridings present both opportunities for and obstacles to local integration. As such, they contribute to the uneven and even confused lines of continuity between national and provincial party politics in British Columbia.

New Brunswick is a more rural province than British Columbia. The geographic and electoral regime contexts of most New Brunswick ridings impose high costs on the development of integrated local parties. This appears to be the case in Fundy Royal and particularly New Brunswick Southwest, where geography has played an important role in preventing integration between the national and provincial organizations in those ridings.

The experiences of national and provincial Liberal activists in the rural riding of Acadie-Bathurst, where a strongly integrated organization has been formed, provide a reminder that characteristics of the riding do not exercise a decisive influence on the development of integrated and differentiated local organizations. Instead, other factors, such as the similarity of national and provincial party systems and the orientation of incumbent members, play a role in concert with the nature of the constituency to shape the type of local organization. These three factors come together to shape the costs of integration and therefore the type of local organization that develops in each riding. And the presence of differing configurations of these factors in the constituencies helps to explain the diversity in local organization that characterizes the Liberal Party as a whole.

6
Little Fiefdoms: MPs, MLAs, and Their Local Organizations

Both of them would be out in the riding during elections. [MLA David] Caplan would be out going door to door for the federal party and vice versa. I can remember walking down the street with [MP David] Collenette and Caplan at the same time. It was a show of strength.
                              – Peter, from Don Valley East

Some of the MLAs are a little nervous about putting their organizations behind the federal candidate ... because, if it's a candidate that is not going to be popular or who is going to be a problem, then they would not want that to be reflected on them, particularly if the timing of the campaigns is going to be close together.
                              – Pierre, from Acadie-Bathurst

Peter and Pierre illustrate how incumbent MPs and MLAs can have radically different attitudes toward the party at the other level. In Don Valley East, national and provincial incumbents are very supportive of one another, even accompanying one another knocking on doors during national and provincial election campaigns. But Pierre's MLA was much more cool toward the national candidate in his riding and reluctant to provide organizational support to the national campaign. In both cases, incumbents send powerful messages to local activists such as Peter and Pierre about the proper form of local organization in their ridings; indeed, so powerful are these messages that one activist spoke of ridings as the "little fiefdoms" of their incumbent members. Just as local integration and differentiation are in part responses to the conditions of the ridings, so too do these different forms of local organization reflect the prefer-ences of incumbent MPs and MLAs.

The presence of incumbents transforms local party organizations in four key ways. First, constituency associations with MPs or MLAs are reoriented to provide incumbent support and tend to sponsor several inter-election maintenance events (Carty 1991, 60). Second, activists are more likely to get involved in local party organizations when an incum-bent is present since they view these organizations as more likely to facilitate the realization of their goals as activists. Third, re-election campaigns inevitably come to focus on the records of incumbents, who play important roles in election fundraising and campaign volunteer recruitment (Carty 1991, 174, 207). And fourth, incumbents also shape re-election campaign strategies, and incumbents' constituency offices and staff provide an immediate electoral advantage (Sayers 2007, 7). Given their influence over these four aspects of local parties, it is natural to expect that incumbents also play an important role in shaping the development of integrated and differentiated local parties.

However, the presence of incumbent MPs or MLAs does not lead to local integration or differentiation in a uniform manner. Some incum-bent members work toward the development of integrated party struc-tures by providing support to the party or candidate at the other level, whereas others strive to maintain a single-level, differentiated local organization.

Two key factors shape the orientations of incumbent MPs and MLAs to the party at the other level. First, incumbents encourage local integra-tion only if they believe that an integrated organization would aid their own re-election efforts. Some MPs view the party at the other level as an attractive ally in attaining support and warding off challenges from opponents. In contrast, other self-interested incumbents are eager to distance themselves from unpopular parties or candidates at the other level lest they be attached in the minds of voters.

Second, incumbents are constrained in the type of local organization that they can develop by local traditions and the national-provincial configurations of any pre-existing local organization. Incumbents pursue their own re-election within the context of a local organization that might already be integrated or differentiated between the national and provincial levels. Within the context of integrated local parties, incumbents are more likely to provide support to the party or candidate at the other level. In contrast, differentiated local organizations mean that incumbents generally face no expectation of providing such support.

Incumbents sometimes encourage local integration to gain access to different communities within the riding in the hope of attracting volunteers, donors, and resources of the party at the other level. Self-interested incumbents therefore face a particularly strong incentive to support integration when the party at the other level is very competitive because these organizations offer greater numbers of potential volunteers and resources. But when the organization at the other level is weak, incumbents are likely to conclude that integration entails greater costs than benefits. Since incumbents are primarily concerned with their own re-election, they are less likely to provide support for weak associations at the other level.

Local integration is particularly attractive to incumbents when the party at the other level has specific bases of strength within the constituency. These bases of strength can be geographic, or they can consist of non-geographic communities within the riding. For example, incumbents sometimes favour integration because the organization at the other level is strong in a particular region of the riding. In Haldimand-Norfolk, the provincial Liberal candidate in the 2005 provincial election built a strong base of support in Haldimand County but was less successful in Norfolk County. In contrast, the national Liberal MP had long-standing linkages to the farmers and communities of Norfolk County, and a strong national constituency association was therefore centred in that section of the riding. The provincial candidate in the riding favoured cooperation with the national party partially because he hoped to access that organization in Norfolk County and thereby remedy his own weaknesses there.

This attraction to integration for national incumbents is particularly strong in fragmented rural ridings where there are many small provincial ridings contained within national constituencies. By drawing on the strength of the provincial organizations that necessarily exist close to their communities, national incumbents hope to strengthen their own electoral positions in those communities. In Acadie-Bathurst, for example, national campaigns tend to be built on the local strengths of the many provincial organizations that exist within the boundaries of the national riding.

Other local party organizations are closely aligned with non-geographic communities of constituencies, and incumbents can encourage integration to access these communities. Associations and campaigns in urban ridings sometimes draw their strength from particular local ethnic communities, which can constitute rich sources of secondary campaign workers. Supportive incumbents work to gain access to these communities.

This dynamic is discernible in Don Valley East. The riding's MP, Yasmin Ratansi, won the national Liberal nomination in the riding partially by drawing on her strengths in the local Southeast Asian community. Ratansi maintains important linkages to this community and has attempted to act as its spokesperson in Ottawa; she therefore draws both volunteers and inner circle members from this community during her campaigns. For the provincial incumbent member, David Caplan, integration between the national and provincial associations gives him unprecedented access to that community. By encouraging local activists to campaign with Caplan, Ratansi provides the incumbent MLA with an important linkage to the community and a source of volunteers during his re-election campaigns in Don Valley East.

Providing support also allows incumbent members to prevent their partisan opponents from establishing bases of electoral and organizational strength at the other level, bases that can threaten the incumbent's re-election chances. Incumbent members are aware that MPs and MLAs can build strong personal local organizations, partially because incumbents attract participation from activists who would otherwise be uninterested in getting involved. But the election of a Conservative or NDP member at the other level might result in the development of a resilient Conservative or NDP organization, which can ultimately represent a base from which opponents can launch challenges on the incumbent member at the other level. For this reason, incumbents generally prefer to see Liberals elected at the national and provincial levels. This is especially true in Ontario ridings, where MPs and MLAs appeal for support from identical groups of voters.

However, incumbent members can also decline to offer support to the party or candidate at the other level if they believe that doing so will threaten their own re-election chances. Canadian general elections are characterized by a high rate of turnover, and incumbents, recognizing the precariousness of their positions, are generally unwilling to encourage integration if they think that doing so will threaten their own linkages to the constituency or the vitality of the organization on which they rely for re-election (Matland and Studlar 2004, 93). As a result, incumbents can consciously differentiate themselves from the party at the other level if that party is experiencing internal difficulties or is unpopular, especially within the constituency itself. In the period of this study, for example, the national Liberal Party was suffering through extensive negative media coverage of the Gomery Commission, investigating allegations of corruption in the former Liberal government. For many provincial Liberal incumbents, negative media coverage of the Gomery Commission provided a strong incentive to maintain a strict distance from the national party.

The ecological diversity of Canada's constituencies means that this incentive to maintain differentiation will present itself in different ways across the ridings. Although the national Liberal government introduced the national gun registry in 1995, many provincial Liberal activists in rural ridings report that the issue is still contentious. Provincial Liberal candidates and incumbents in rural ridings therefore have a special incentive to distinguish themselves from the national Liberal Party over the issue of gun control. Provincial activists in the rural Haldimand-Norfolk and Nigadoo-Chaleur constituencies, for example, identified the gun registry as one reason that provincial Liberal incumbents and candidates failed openly and enthusiastically to support national Liberal candidates. In sharp contrast, the party's stance was hardly a disincentive to supporting national Liberal candidates in city ridings, where the registry tends to be popular.

Incumbents might not support the candidate at the other level if the candidate is perceived to be particularly unpopular or it is thought that such support will undermine the incumbent's linkages to the constituency. Prior to the 2004 national election in Acadie-Bathurst, for example, Serge Rousselle won the nomination to run for the national Liberal Party. Unfortunately for Rousselle, many local Liberals came to the conclusion that he was a weak candidate, particularly because he had difficulties connecting with voters. "He's a good guy and all that, but he had a hard time gelling with the riding," explains one local activist. "A lot of people probably felt that he was not the right person. There's nothing wrong with his intelligence, but I think people felt that he had a hard time connecting with the ordinary person." As a result, local Liberal MLAs were less than enthusiastic in their support for his candidacy and did not strongly encourage their own supporters to work hard for Rousselle. In contrast, when Marcelle Mersereau was nominated to run for the national party in the 2006 election, the local Liberal MLAs thought that, given her prior electoral experience, she was a qualified candidate who stood a strong chance of defeating the NDP incumbent. They accordingly threw their enthusiastic support behind Mersereau and encouraged their local supporters to do so as well.

Another important reason that incumbents are less likely to actively support the party or candidate at the other level is because they wish to preserve the energies of local activists for their own re-election campaigns. Incumbents are aware of the time pressures felt by local party activists, especially in ridings with a tradition of integration, and how activists might deal with the pressures of activism in federations by prioritizing their activism at one level over the other. Consistent and inconsistent activists are expected to participate in national and provincial election campaigns, nomination campaigns, and leadership campaigns. The prospect of becoming "electioned out" is real, and incumbents worry that this point of exhaustion will be reached just prior to their own re-election campaigns. As a result, some incumbents gently discourage local activists from involving themselves in campaigns at the other level, much to the chagrin of those candidates hoping to add secondary workers to their own campaign organizations.

But incumbent members do not pursue their re-election goals within a vacuum. Instead, they pursue their goals within a local organizational context that often contains incentives for incumbents to provide support.

The presence of a common national-provincial activist base, for example, is an important aspect of this pre-existing organization. Where the national and provincial parties share a largely common activist base, activists tend to expect incumbents at both levels to get out and support one another during election campaigns. Incumbents in these ridings find it difficult to develop differentiated local parties, for activists used to integrated local structures typically find these attempts strange or even alienating. The result is that attempts by incumbents to build personal, differentiated organizations can alienate large segments of the consistent activist base, and incumbents themselves are aware of this danger.

In addition, elite relations between MPs and MLAs shape incumbent support. Incumbent members at the two levels might bring a personal commitment to one another. In these cases, MPs and MLAs can maintain both personal and professional relationships. These relationships can lead incumbents to support one another publicly and encourage their organizations to contribute to the campaigns at the other level. Good working relations between MPs and MLAs also send messages to the activist base about the incumbent at the other level that encourage participation and integration, whereas conflict between incumbents can create obstacles to participation.

Incumbent members generally value friendly personal relations with their counterparts at the other level. Incumbents at one level realize that they will have to interact with incumbents at the other level and, in some cases, work directly with them on local issues (Franks 2007, 39). This is especially true in Ontario, where national and provincial ridings are identical. Incumbent MPs and MLAs of the same partisan affiliation are generally capable of building good working relationships. This is partially because incumbents recognize that the election of a partisan opponent at the other level might make such working relationships problematic. Incumbents, for example, might be eager to gain credit for accomplishments in the riding and deny credit to the member at the other level. It is not uncommon to see MPs and MLAs from different parties sniping at one another, particularly in ridings where the national and provincial ridings are identical, though this sniping does not extend to constituency service. As a result, incumbent members offer support to maintain good working relationships between the two levels.

Four Types of Incumbent Support

The combination of incumbents' re-election goals and local riding conditions lead to different forms of support for the candidate or party at the other level. Two types of support, public and private, can be distinguished. Figure 6.1 illustrates the four ways that incumbents interact with parties and candidates at the other level.

By offering full support to the party at the other level, incumbents lower the costs of integration for local parties, providing opportunities for national and provincial organizations to coordinate resources and personnel between the two levels. In contrast, incumbents who offer neither public nor private support to the incumbent or who actively oppose integration at the other level raise the costs of integration, sometimes to prohibitive levels. It is very difficult for integrated local parties to develop in the face of incumbents who refuse to offer support to the party at the other level, so incumbents might therefore be thought of as possessing an effective veto over local integration, though many are hesitant to exercise such a veto given local traditions. In contrast, practical and superficial forms of support have a mixed and somewhat nuanced impact on the local parties.

Figure 6.1

Four types of incumbent support

	Public support	No public support
Private support	Full support	Practical support
No private support	Superficial support	Opposition/no support

Full Support

The first type of support lent by incumbent members to parties and candidates at the other level is full support. It consists of both private and public forms of support. Fully supportive incumbents provide private support by encouraging their supporters to participate in the activities of the party at the other level and by making their resources available to the candidate at that level. Such incumbents also lend public support to the party at the other level by openly encouraging cooperation. They attend events hosted by the association and participate in the campaigns of candidates at the other level. By offering both public and private support, openly supportive incumbent members play an important role in contributing to the integration of national and provincial local parties.

Fully supportive incumbents encourage cooperation and integration between the national and provincial organizations in several ways. They are privately supportive of integration within the contexts of their own constituency associations. Association executive meetings are ideal locations for incumbents to provide private support for integration, so fully supportive incumbent members generally attend executive meetings at the other level to present a united front across the national and provincial levels. In Don Valley East, for example, MP Yasmin Ratansi regularly attends provincial executive meetings, and MLA David Caplan attends national executive meetings. Their presence at these meetings sends important messages to the executive about the proper (integrated) conduct of local party life in Don Valley East, and both incumbents drive this lesson home by complimenting the other incumbent and praising the work of the other association. Their presence at executive meetings makes Ratansi and Caplan available to members of both executives; long-term party activists can thus develop loyalties to both the national and the provincial incumbents within the contexts of these meetings. Furthermore, both Ratansi and Caplan encourage the planning of joint inter-election maintenance events. In these ways, the MP and MLA encourage local integration by providing private, behind-the-scenes support to the party at the other level.

At inter-election maintenance events, openly supportive incumbents can publicly encourage integration of the national and provincial constituency associations. Both Ratansi and Caplan attend the annual Don Valley East picnic. Just as their presence at national and provincial executive meetings shapes the perceptions of executive members, so too does their presence at maintenance events send messages to the local activist base about the integrated nature of local Liberal politics in Don Valley East.

Fully supportive incumbents also play an important role in encouraging the development of integrated national and provincial election campaigns. They do so in both private and public ways.

Given their influence over their own campaign teams and local organizations, incumbents can play an important role in introducing candidates and incumbents at the other levels to organizers, secondary workers, and donors. Local executive meetings are a particularly good venue within which incumbents encourage secondary workers to participate in campaigns at the other level. In Don Valley East, both the MP and the MLA encourage their executives to get out and support the candidate during election campaigns. "When I was on his [Caplan's] executive, he encouraged all of his people to get out and support the federal party," reports Rod, an executive member from the riding. "And it's always been the same way with the federal association." "David and Ratansi support each other," confirms Peter, another member of the provincial executive. "David Caplan, he recommended that we all go and help with the federal election." Partially as a result of this encouragement, Ratansi and Caplan rely on largely common volunteer bases in national and provincial campaigns.

Incumbents also contribute to campaigns behind the scenes by encouraging donors to support the other candidate and campaign. This is especially the case for veteran incumbents with deep roots in the riding. Such incumbents have long-standing ties to the constituency and to local donors and can use these ties to put the candidate at the other level in contact with local donors and influential figures. Supportive incumbents are also likely to allow their various membership and sign lists to be shared with the organization at the other level.

Incumbents can also privately support campaigns at the other level by discreetly making their own campaign resources available to those campaigns. Constituency offices and incumbents' paid staff can play an important role in maintaining the local party organization and coordinating campaigns, since constituency offices provide valuable locations for organization, meetings, and storage (Sayers 1999, 84). Openly supportive incumbent members tend to make these valuable resources available to the incumbent or candidate at the other level. In Fundy Royal, for example, national Liberal candidates are sometimes sponsored by the provincial Liberal MLAs within the riding. As a result, national Liberal candidates can coordinate their campaigns in the large rural ridings through the constituency offices of MLAs. Instead of renting offices in several towns throughout the riding, national Liberal candidates can save money by coordinating the local campaigns in provincial offices. But national candidates must innovate to fill in the large gaps where Liberal MLAs are missing.

Fully supportive incumbents also offer public forms of support to campaigns at the other level. The most visible and important manifestation of public support occurs when incumbents openly campaign with candidates at the other level. Incumbents who wish to support the candidate at the other level can lead by example by actively working on the campaign. Incumbents visit campaign offices to energize the office staff, speak as representatives in the media on behalf of the candidate, attend rallies and public events to speak in favour of the candidate, and even go knocking on doors with the candidate.

Opposition/No Support

In sharp contrast, incumbents can offer neither public nor private support to the candidate or party at the other level. They might even actively oppose integration. Through their indifference or opposition, these incumbents exercise a differentiating impact on the national and provincial local parties.

John Wilkinson, the MLA from the Ontario riding of Perth-Wellington, is a good example of such an incumbent member. The provincial organization in the riding is focused on the re-election of Wilkinson, who, since 2007, has been a provincial cabinet minister. Rather than the broad integrated structure that characterizes many Liberal organizations in Ontario ridings, the provincial party in Perth-Wellington is dominated by a small and professional cadre of local advisers who are committed largely if not solely to Wilkinson's re-election. An important aspect of the professionalism of that organization is the maintenance of a strict distance from the national riding association, which has been bogged down in intra-party conflict. Hoping to avoid provincial entanglement in that conflict, Wilkinson's advisers privately encourage differentiation.

The private support for integration offered by Yasmin Ratansi and David Caplan in Don Valley East is therefore absent in Perth-Wellington. Wilkinson does not, for example, attend national Liberal executive meetings, nor does he provide encouragement to national Liberal activists in the riding. Furthermore, his local supporters share neither their lists nor their resources with the national association or national campaigns. Instead, the local party in Perth-Wellington maintains a strict organizational distance from the national organization in the riding. As a result, the weakened national organization in Perth-Wellington cannot piggyback on the organizational strength and wealth of the provincial group.

In addition, Wilkinson does not publicly support national Liberal candidates in Perth-Wellington. Whereas Ratansi and Caplan go knocking on doors together during national and provincial election campaigns, national and provincial candidates in Perth-Wellington conduct independent campaigns. Although national Liberal candidates stand to gain much from the assistance of Wilkinson, the dangers of integration with the divided national association dissuade him and his supporters from offering support.

The national and provincial Liberal organizations in Perth-Wellington have evolved a differentiated party structure in response to a variety of idiosyncratic local factors. By declining to lend public or private support to national candidates or the national organization, Wilkinson contributes to the ongoing differentiation of the national and provincial parties in the riding.

Superficial Support

Other incumbents offer support to the candidate or party at the other level but do so in a qualified manner. Incumbents who lend superficial support do so in public but not private ways. Superficially supportive incumbents publicly endorse and support candidates and might make appearances at events. Behind the scenes, however, these incumbents are either indifferent to the party at the other level or opposed to offering support. Whereas fully supportive incumbents happily marshal their resources and personnel to support the candidate at the other level, superficially supportive candidates are reluctant to do so. This is why such support is superficial: incumbents appear from the outside to be supportive, but away from public view in the trenches of local campaigning and organization these incumbents do little if anything to support the other candidate or party.

Roland Hache, the MLA for New Brunswick's riding of Nigadoo-Chaleur, offered superficial support to the national Liberal candidate in the riding of Acadie-Bathurst in the lead-up to the 2006 national election. Hache's local organization in Nigadoo-Chaleur is generally focused on his re-election. Hache took an active role in constructing a Liberal constituency association in the riding. He did so by recruiting Pierre, a popular community figure from the town of Beresford, to become the constituency association president. The selection of Pierre appears to have been shrewd since he has successfully constructed a constituency association that includes executive members from all of the disparate, close-knit communities of the riding. During election campaigns, Pierre and the other members of the constituency association form the basis of Hache's campaign organization and can draw on members from throughout the riding. Hache has consistently been re-elected since the 1999 provincial election, a testament to the strength of his local organization.

There is a long-standing tradition of national-provincial integration in Acadie-Bathurst, which exhibits itself in the organization of both local constituency associations and campaigns. The provincial organization in Nigadoo-Chaleur has traditionally played an important role in the campaign organizations of national Liberal candidates. But many local activists identified a reluctance by Hache to mobilize his local organization to support Marcelle Mersereau in the 2006 national election. For Hache, the unpopularity of the national Liberal Party in the rural riding attached costs to supporting it. Alan, a consistent Liberal activist from Nigadoo-Chaleur, explains why the large rural riding was generally inhospitable to the national Liberal Party:

> I'm afraid with the sponsorship scandal that we could have some problems. I shouldn't say this, but it's the feeling I have right now. People are a little frustrated. And two of the reasons are the sponsorship scandal and the gun registry. It [crime] may be a big problem in the urban areas and the big cities. But in this part of the province, people are sportsmen and hunters. It [the gun registry] affects a lot of people. And the cost of that program was so tremendous, you know?

Hache was well aware of the problems facing the national Liberal Party in northeast New Brunswick. Members of Mersereau's inner circle also knew that openly supporting the national party might cause future problems for local MLAs, especially since a provincial election was expected to take place within a year of the national election.

Provincial executive members from the riding report that Hache was concerned about the potential impact of offering support on the vitality of his own organization and the enthusiasm of the activists who make up that organization. Incumbents sometimes worry that local activists will become "electioned out" just prior to their own re-election campaigns, and Hache was no exception. More importantly, he was also concerned about the demoralizing impact of being involved with a national campaign that was challenging a popular incumbent MP.

From a wider perspective, it is clear that Hache faced strong incentives to adapt a non-supportive stance toward the national party and campaign in Acadie-Bathurst. Alan summarized Hache's behaviour in this episode:

> In the last federal election, the provincial MLA [Hache] ... didn't want to get so involved. I don't know ... whether he was afraid to lose some of his constituents. Because he knew that the people were frustrated, the Liberal people are frustrated. Therefore, if he gets involved, it might reflect badly on him in the next election ... So that's why he stayed back a little bit, that's why he didn't really want to get involved.

Instead of being fully supportive, Hache offered public support while gently discouraging members of his own organization from participating in the national campaign. Ultimately, his lack of open support might have had little impact on Mersereau's campaign. The tradition of integration and consistent partisanship in Nigadoo-Chaleur meant that provincial activists there did support Mersereau and worked on her campaign. In fact, those activists played important roles in her campaign, and she relied heavily on the provincial organization in Nigadoo-Chaleur.

Given that there is a tradition of integration in Acadie-Bathurst, Hache's superficial support was necessary to avoid alienating the local activist base, which consists largely of consistent activists. But behind the public lip service, Hache appeared to be concerned about the consequences of involving his own supporters too heavily in the national campaign.

Practical Support

Faced with contradictory incentives and disincentives to offer support, incumbent MPs and MLAs might wish to maximize the benefits of support while simultaneously minimizing its costs. In ridings such as Nigadoo-Chaleur, this means that incumbents offer superficial support: they benefit from publicly supporting the candidate or party at the other level while holding their own organizations in reserve in anticipation of their own re-election campaigns. But other incumbent members attempt to maximize the benefits of interaction with the party at the other level by providing private support while maintaining public neutrality. This can be referred to as practical support. Such an approach allows incumbent members to lend private support while avoiding the negative consequences of open, public support. As a result, candidates benefit from the organizational support of the other incumbent but not to the same extent as when the incumbent is openly and enthusiastically supportive.

The relationship between the Liberal MP and the provincial Liberal candidate in the constituency of Haldimand-Norfolk during the 2005 provincial election campaign illustrates some of the incentives that lead to practical support. Bob Speller was elected as a Liberal MP in the 1988 national election and was re-elected in the 1993, 1997, and 2000 elections. His local electoral success is partially attributable to his close connection with Haldimand-Norfolk's agricultural communities. In particular, Speller is identified by Liberal activists in the riding as an outspoken defender of tobacco farmers in Norfolk County. Although other politicians were condemning cigarette companies throughout the 1990s, Speller was lobbying for Norfolk producers and fighting against national anti-smoking initiatives. As he notes in a campaign letter,

> I have a long history of looking out for the interests of the tobacco sector in Norfolk, beginning with my earliest days as the Member of Parliament for this region ... During my time in Parliament, I also argued against increases in the excise tax on tobacco, often voting against my Liberal colleagues, and successfully lobbied for tax reductions in order to limit [cigarette] smuggling activity.

Speller was appointed federal agriculture minister in 2003 and in this capacity negotiated a $72 million aid package for tobacco farmers to transition to different crops, further enhancing his standing in the riding. In this way, he worked to secure his electoral base in Haldimand-Norfolk by taking on the roles of constituency representative and legislator (Studlar and McAllister 1994, 393).

Fenno's (1978, 8-18) conception of incumbents' re-election constituencies, the sections of the voting population likely to vote for incumbents, is useful here. A long-standing advocacy on behalf of tobacco producers endeared Speller to the farmers of Haldimand-Norfolk. Accordingly, he could depend on donations from wealthy tobacco farmers and on their support during election campaigns. In addition, his advocacy resulted in the loyalty of secondary campaign volunteers in rural regions but also in Norfolk County towns such as Delhi and Tilsonburg that are heavily dependent on the declining tobacco industry. By working on behalf of that industry and those reliant on it, Speller came to include those sections of the riding in his re-election constituency.

Like other incumbents, he could not be certain about the extent of his local support (Fenno 1978, 17-18). Accordingly, the agriculture minister constantly worried about his re-election constituency and worked to maintain his connections to it. This behaviour was also related to Speller's precarious position in Haldimand-Norfolk, hardly a natural Liberal riding. Like many Ontario Liberal incumbents during the 1993, 1997, and 2000 elections, Speller benefited from the presence of both Reform Party/Canadian Alliance and Progressive Conservative candidates who split the anti-Liberal vote between them, allowing him to win with remarkably small percentages of the local vote. The combined number of votes for these candidates in the 1997 and 2000 national elections surpassed votes for Speller, who was well aware that Haldimand-Norfolk would never be a safe Liberal seat.

Liberals had been less successful at electing candidates at the provincial level in Haldimand-Norfolk. The incumbent Conservative MLA, Toby Barrett, was elected in the 1995 provincial election and was re-elected in each subsequent election. Hoping to provide a credible challenge to Barrett, provincial Liberals nominated Rob Esselment as their candidate in the lead-up to the 2005 provincial election.

Esselment and Speller brought different strengths and weaknesses to their roles as candidates. Whereas Speller had cultivated a strong relationship with the rural producers of Norfolk County, Esselment, a young professional, had built a support base in the growing suburbs of eastern Haldimand County. In addition, Esselment had taken steps to access the network of local teachers in the constituency. Teachers' unions were strongly opposed to the Conservative government in the 1995 provincial election, and Esselment took advantage of this resentment by working to recruit teachers and educational support staff as secondary workers for his local campaign. "We had lots of teachers' groups there," reported one local campaigner. "We had teachers everywhere ... showing up to knock on doors in each of the towns."

Speller and Esselment had a complex relationship framed by their vastly different situations. By 2005, Speller was a veteran MP and cabinet minister. In contrast, Esselment was a neophyte candidate facing a veteran Conservative incumbent at the provincial level. Given Speller's experience and stature in the riding, Esselment had much to gain from his support. Conversely, Speller had more to lose by supporting an unpopular provincial campaign given his long efforts to build a resilient re-election constituency in Haldimand-Norfolk.

Although Esselment built a local campaign organization that focused on his strength among the young professionals of the constituency's suburban areas, two developments in the provincial campaign strained his local campaign. First, Liberal leader Dalton McGuinty promised to close the Nanticoke coal generating plant. Located in the riding on the shore of Lake Erie, the plant is generally recognized as the worst polluter among Ontario's power plants and was therefore targeted by the provincial Liberal Party for closure. The plant employs roughly 1,000 workers and is a major employer in the riding. The Nanticoke workers responded to McGuinty's promise viscerally, and Esselment's local campaign bore the brunt of their frustration. "The coal plant people weren't our best friends," one activist bemusedly observed.

Second, McGuinty promised to introduce a comprehensive anti-smoking campaign that would lead to reductions in cigarette smoking. In particular, he promised to raise taxes on cigarettes sold in the province. The promise alarmed Haldimand-Norfolk's beleaguered tobacco farmers and residents of the Norfolk County towns that service the industry. McGuinty's pledge placed Esselment in a difficult position, especially since the incumbent Conservative member, Toby Barrett, had worked to construct the sorts of linkages to tobacco producers that Speller had successfully built. Nevertheless, Esselment made efforts to gain support among electors attached to the tobacco industry in Norfolk County, including attending a tobacco farmers' auction.

Within the context of the 2005 provincial campaign, Speller faced contradictory incentives to supporting Esselment. On the one hand, Speller was a committed consistent Liberal, much like Ratansi and Caplan. For him, open support of provincial Liberal candidates came naturally. Perhaps more importantly, the Liberal activist base in Haldimand-Norfolk is largely consistent. Given the local tradition of national-provincial cooperation, particularly within a coterminous riding, activists looked to Speller to support actively the provincial Liberal candidate. Many activists would have been puzzled by any indication that he would not lend such support. In addition, Speller and Esselment shared a personal relationship and a common lineage, both having been raised in the town of Hagersville, Ontario. In short, Speller had both political and personal reasons to support actively and openly Esselment's provincial candidacy.

On the other hand, openly supporting Esselment would likely have alienated Speller's traditional supporters attached to the local tobacco industry. Having invested significant time and effort in adding tobacco farmers and those dependent on the industry for their livelihood to his primary constituency of supporters, Speller was hesitant to show public support for the provincial Liberal Party given its strong anti-tobacco stance. Furthermore, employees of the Nanticoke coal generating plant, who feared layoffs under a provincial Liberal government, would have viewed support for the provincial party as antagonistic.

Provincial campaign workers were well aware of the difficulties facing Speller. Noted Harvey, a prominent provincial activist,

> He [Speller] was probably looking at his own election coming up. Some of the provincial policies were very unpopular in the riding, from the coal power plant to the tobacco issues. He's traditionally been supported by the tobacco farmers as an advocate of theirs. So for his own political good, there wouldn't have been much benefit to tying himself to a provincial policy he had no part in making.

The national and provincial Liberal parties in Haldimand-Norfolk were traditionally integrated, but idiosyncratic developments during the 2005 provincial election threatened to divide the two parties. But instead of abandoning Esselment, Speller provided practical, behind-the-scenes support for the provincial Liberal candidate. He therefore played a role by supporting and encouraging national Liberal activists to get out and work for Esselment's provincial campaign. Harvey summarized Speller's role in that campaign:

> We saw [Speller] as an adviser ... His campaign team, they all came out ... We asked him more to feed his people and to feed anyone he knew into our campaign. And tell us who we should meet rather than be an active up-front person ... It was much easier to keep it at a higher level and [to have him] say, "I like this guy. I know what he's about. He's a good guy, he'll work hard."

Speller played a particularly important role in introducing Esselment to important and influential figures in the sprawling rural constituency. Speller's support for Esselment in this respect was invaluable since this access allowed Esselment to accumulate volunteers as well as donors for the campaign. A prominent provincial campaigner describes one memorable episode in which Speller introduced Esselment to a group of influential donors from the riding:

> There's actually a town in the riding where there is a very influential farmer who has a meeting every Thursday night in his garage. It's a big drive garage, and he's got couches, and he invites a whole bunch of people to come and just talk. Talk politics or talk agriculture or whatever.

And you have to get invited to come to this meeting. So Rob was able to get an invitation to this meeting. And basically, they all put him through the gears just to test him out.

Unknown to Esselment at the time, Speller had provided an access point to an important, well-established group of local donors and influential figures:

It has a garage door, and on the inside of it is a plastic covering. And he's had all the candidates and politicians that have been in for one of those blab sessions sign the wall. So he actually has quite a list of people and the year that they were there. So this was one of those behind-the-scenes things where, if someone hadn't told you about the politics of it, you would never even think that this guy's garage on this farm has had so many influential people. And there were cabinet ministers' names on the wall, and it was sort of surreal. And you had to get this invitation to go.

It is not clear whether Esselment's interactions with this group of donors aided his campaign. But the opportunity to present himself to the group was due entirely to the intervention of Speller, who "made sure that Rob got an invitation to come in to talk to them." In this episode, Speller illustrates the benefits of behind-the-scenes support for candidates, especially neophyte candidates such as Esselment.

Although Speller privately supported Esselment's campaign, he did not openly and enthusiastically support Esselment's candidacy – he did not provide public support for the provincial candidate. "[They] didn't do much door-to-door together at all," notes one provincial activist. The broad public displays of support found in ridings such as Don Valley East and York West were largely absent in Haldimand-Norfolk. For the most part, then, Speller's support for Esselment was behind the scenes and private. Speller is therefore a good example of an incumbent member who provided practical support to the candidate at the other level of the multi-level state.

Incumbent members might be privately supportive because they fear the negative consequences of publicly supporting the party or candidate at the other level. But this dynamic is in fact a two-way street. Candidates sometimes reject public support from the incumbent at the other level for fear of alienating potential supporters. But these candidates are happy to receive private, behind-the-scenes support from the member at the other level.

This dynamic was also apparent in the complex relationship between Esselment and Speller. Speller was reticent in his support for Esselment for fear of alienating segments of his local support base. But the national Liberal Party had burdened Speller with significant liabilities of his own in the rural riding. Esselment's campaign workers were well aware of the national party's local weaknesses, for they were hearing criticisms from voters over the actions of the national government. Notes one frustrated provincial campaign worker about his experiences while canvassing,

> During the provincial campaign, there seemed to be a lot of federal issues that came to the forefront. They were clearly federal jurisdiction. The same-sex marriage issue had come up. There were a lot of farmers that were still angry about the federal gun registry. And that was about the time that the [national] cabinet decided that they weren't going to go into Iraq. So a lot of these federal issues were at every doorstep.

As a result, Speller's lack of public support for the provincial campaign helped to differentiate the national and provincial parties in the minds of voters. In this respect, his lack of public support proved advantageous to Esselment. In the background, Speller drew on his long experience in the local organization to encourage local activists to get out and support Esselment. It was Speller's lack of public support that allowed Esselment to avoid taking responsibility for the unpopular actions of the national Liberal government.

In the same way, provincial candidates and MLAs in British Columbia can be eager to receive the support of national MPs and their organizations and vice versa. In Port Moody-Westwood-Port Coquitlam, for example, Iain Black benefited from the private support of James Moore, the riding's Conservative MP. But candidates and MLAs are generally aware that open support from national Liberal or Conservative MPs threatens the coalition nature of their provincial organizations, typically made up of both national Liberal and national Conservative partisans. As a result, provincial candidates and MLAs prefer to receive private, behind-the-scenes support from MPs.

This preference for private support can put provincial candidates and MLAs in a difficult position in their dealings with MPs. Consider the experiences of two Liberal MPs from British Columbia. Raymond Chan and Sukh Dhaliwal were the Liberal MPs from Richmond and Delta-South Richmond respectively. Both MPs have built strong local organizations in their ridings. Chan in particular is well known for his ability to marshal votes at intra-party meetings as well as at nomination meetings.

Prior to running for national office, Dhaliwal was an influential figure in one of Surrey's municipal political parties, the Surrey Electors Team. In the lead-up to the 2004 national election, Dhaliwal's nomination campaign recruited a significant number of party members to support his nomination bid. The local Liberal organization boasted 18,000 members in the lead-up to the nomination contest, most of whom had been recruited by Dhaliwal and his competitors for the nomination race. In short, both Chan and Dhaliwal were influential among significant groups of campaigners and voters in their ridings.

For provincial Liberal candidates and MLAs, Chan's and Dhaliwal's organizations represent rich sources of both secondary campaign workers and legitimacy in the different ethnic communities of their ridings. Provincial candidates and MLAs know that those organizations can be accessed by influential figures, particularly by Chan and Dhaliwal themselves. The trick for provincial Liberals is to access these national Liberal organizations without simultaneously alienating the significant number of national Conservatives also supportive of the BC Liberal Party.

Although Chan and Dhaliwal constituted rich sources of volunteers for provincial candidates in Richmond and Delta, the costs of association with the national Liberal Party in 2005 were high. Just as Esselment struggled with national issues during his provincial campaign in Ontario, so too were provincial Liberals in British Columbia wary of associating themselves too closely with the national Liberal Party. Of more importance in British Columbia, the sponsorship scandal had tainted the national Liberal Party and provided even greater incentives for the provincial party to distinguish itself from the national party. One activist describes the broad difficulties faced by the provincial Liberal Party as candidates attempted to differentiate their party from the national Liberal Party in the eyes of voters:

> At the BC Liberal level, one of the main concerns was that same-sex marriage was being debated at the federal level at the time. I knew that, at the provincial Liberal level, there was a huge concern that people with conservative right-wing views would not want to vote for the BC Liberals because some people – well, a lot of people, actually – don't know that there's a distinction between the federal Liberals and the BC Liberals. And that was a huge concern ... Or the corruption issue. Every riding for the BC Liberals was dealing with the Gomery thing.

Within this context, provincial candidates in Chan's and Dhaliwal's national ridings were conflicted. Would they reach out to Chan and

Dhaliwal to access their important local networks and organizations, or would they maintain a distance from the national party?

From a public perspective, provincial candidates appeared to reject Chan and Dhaliwal. In both cases, provincial candidates took steps to distinguish themselves from the MPs. Prior to the 2005 provincial election, for example, Chan attended a fundraiser for the provincial Liberal candidate in Richmond-Steveston, John Yap. Rather than valuing the support of an influential local MP, members of Yap's inner circle were spooked by the prospect of journalists drawing parallels between the national and provincial Liberal parties in Richmond. These inner circle members immediately called their contacts in the local media to distance their campaign from Chan and the national Liberal Party.

Sukh Dhaliwal put provincial campaigns in a similar situation when he attended a provincial event prior to the 2005 provincial election. Just as in Richmond, members of the provincial candidate's inner circle gathered to discuss how to deal with Dhaliwal:

> Sukh Dhaliwal let it be known that he was willing to throw his support behind us ... So we had a meeting about this, and we actually thought it was more of a liability. We actually asked the federal Liberals to back off. They wanted to support us, and we told them to back off because we didn't want to alienate the [national] Conservatives.

In both cases, provincial Liberal candidates were rejecting public support from national MPs, viewing such support as an electoral liability rather than advantage. The provincial campaigns appeared to be taking a route of caution rather than risking being linked to the national party, even if doing so meant that the provincial campaigns were denied access to Chan's and Dhaliwal's organizations.

However, the story behind the scenes was quite different. Provincial organizers drew on the practical support of Chan's and Dhaliwal's powerful local organizations. In doing so, they were able to access personnel and enhance the legitimacy of their candidates by attaching their names to important figures in the ridings' distinctive communities:

> He [Dhaliwal] was asked to stay away from the meetings. If there was going to be a public event, he was asked to stay away ... His supporters, well-known Liberal supporters, were asked to stay behind the scenes. To help out in the office, for example ... We definitely used his volunteer base, his networks, his phone list and mailing list. When we would talk to people in the Indo-Canadian community, we were authorized to say,

"we have Sukh's support." But if the media asked about it, well [we said], "we've had no discussions with Sukh Dhaliwal."

As a result, these campaigns benefited from rebuffing Chan's and Dhaliwal's public support while embracing their private support. In this way, provincial Liberal candidates walked the tightrope between public disavowal and private support.

Practical support is notable because it is hidden from public view and, to a large degree, from political scientists observing the lack of linkages between national and provincial parties. But away from public view, in the trenches of local campaigning and organization, incumbents might be providing invaluable practical support to parties and campaigns at the other level. Privately supportive candidates oversee the development of informal yet important linkages between the national and provincial parties, and local integration results.

The Roles of Incumbent Members

Incumbent members play important roles in shaping integrated and differentiated local party organizations. Fully supportive incumbents offer public and private support to parties and candidates at the other level. They can be seen at public association events and knocking on doors with candidates. Such incumbents are also active behind the scenes, providing resources and personnel to the campaign at the other level. These incumbents exercise an integrative impact on the local party. In contrast, non-supportive incumbents offer neither public nor private support: they maintain a strict distance from parties and candidates at the other level. In other cases, incumbents actively oppose the candidate or party at the other level. As a result, they contribute to local differentiation of the national and provincial Liberal parties.

Incumbents exist in a dynamic local environment that (1) impacts how they pursue their own re-election goals and (2) can provide incentives for them to offer public or private support to the party at the other level. The local party organization shapes incumbents as much as they shape those organizations. Incumbents are cognizant of the wishes of local association officials and the traditions of the local activist base. "They [constituency associations] are the local interpreters of party tradition," argues Sayers (1999, 217-18); "they, not candidates or parties, control local politics." As a result, "even a powerful incumbent ... cannot do just as he pleases." Incumbents can respond to local pressures by adopting a nuanced stance toward parties and candidates at the other level, offering either public or private support but not both. These limited forms of support – superficial and practical – do exercise an integrative influence on the local parties but not to the same extent as full support.

Incumbents' goals are shaped not only by constituency associations and local activist bases but also by the incumbent at the other level if one is present. Where both national and provincial incumbents are present, they might disagree on the type of organization that should be constructed in the riding. One incumbent might favour integrated structures, whereas the other might prefer to build an autonomous, differentiated local organization. In these cases, the latter incumbent typically prevails. Without the cooperation of both incumbents, attempts at integration are likely to founder – the reluctant incumbent holds an effective veto on local integration. In Perth-Wellington, for example, national Liberal activists yearn for a return to a broad integrated structure in the riding, mostly to benefit from John Wilkinson's successful campaign organization. Yet Wilkinson and his core supporters continue to oppose national-provincial cooperation, rendering local integration impossible.

However, organizational traditions and the local activist base can also play a role in overruling reluctant incumbents. Like Roland Hache in Nigadoo-Chaleur, incumbents can find that local activists are unreceptive to the development of a differentiated organization. Wilkinson is able to maintain a strongly differentiated local organization in a riding such as Perth-Wellington, where the Liberal Party does not have deep roots or a broad activist base at either the national or the provincial level. But any attempt by an incumbent to build such a differentiated organization in Don Valley East, for example, would likely fail given the long local tradition of integration and the vibrant consistent activist base in the riding.

Table 6.1 illuminates provincial differences in how incumbents offer support to parties at the other levels. Fully supportive incumbents are most likely to be found in Ontario. This is particularly true in the province's urban unified ridings. Only in exceptional cases do Ontario incumbents offer no support whatsoever to the party or candidate at the other level. This is the case in Perth-Wellington, where Wilkinson faces special local incentives to withhold support for the national party and candidate. Ontario, then, is a province where incumbents play an important role in integrating national and provincial local organizations. There is generally a long tradition of such support in these ridings. Incumbents are aware of these traditions and the expectations of local

Table 6.1

Incumbent support: Full support, superficial support, practical support, and opposition/no support

Full support	Superficial support	Practical support	Opposition/ no support
Ajax-Pickering[1]	Acadie-Bathurst/	Haldimand-	Perth-Wellington[1]
Don Valley East[1]	Nigadoo-	Norfolk[1]	Kootenay-
York West[1]	Chaleur[2]	Richmond Hill[1]	Columbia[3]
Acadie-Bathurst[2]	Saint John[2]	Delta-Richmond	Vancouver
		East[3]	Quadra[3]
		Port Moody-	
		Westwood-	
		Port Coquitlam[3]	
		Richmond[3]	

Notes: 1 = Ontario; 2 = New Brunswick; 3 = British Columbia

activists and typically respond by offering support. But that support does facilitate integration of the two parties, reinforcing the integrated structures and traditions that compel the incumbent to offer such support in the first place.

Incumbents in the New Brunswick ridings studied offered either full support or superficial support. Most of the incumbent MLAs in Acadie-Bathurst offered full support to Marcelle Mersereau in the 2004 election, both publicly endorsing her and rallying their own local organizations to assist her. This full support was essential to the construction of Mersereau's federative campaign organization in that election. However, Roland Hache in Nigadoo-Chaleur and most MLAs in the riding of Saint John offered superficial support to the candidates and parties at the other level. It might be concluded from the small number of New Brunswick cases that incumbents play a less important integrative role in New Brunswick than in Ontario.

BC incumbents contrast strongly with their Ontario counterparts. British Columbia's dissimilar national and provincial party systems make it difficult for incumbents to support openly candidates or parties at the other level. This is particularly true for provincial Liberal incumbents, who are careful not to alienate either the national Liberals or the national Conservatives within their support bases. Instead, an incumbent might lend or gratefully receive practical support from the incumbent at the other level. These forms of support make sense within a context of dissimilar national and provincial party systems and where there are high costs attached to support from the incumbent at the other level. In British Columbia, the threat is that open support from national incumbents will alienate provincial campaign workers and activists.

The importance of practical incumbent support in British Columbia provides a reminder that party system dissimilarity between the national and provincial levels does not necessarily rule out local integration or cooperation. Like activists, constituency organizations, and local campaigns, incumbents in that province have adapted to party system dissimilarity by crafting a mixed type of support that maximizes benefits and minimizes costs. Incumbents do offer support between the national and provincial levels in British Columbia, but, in sharp contrast to the open and enthusiastic incumbent support offered in ridings such as Don Valley East, incumbent support in British Columbia tends to be subtle and conducted behind the scenes. The same is true in ridings such as Haldimand-Norfolk, where incumbents and candidates are hesitant to embrace openly the incumbent at the other level.

In the final analysis, incumbent MPs and MLAs are more likely than not to support the party at the other level. Some form of support was provided in most of the ridings examined where a Liberal incumbent was present at one level. In some cases, the support offered was fulsome and enthusiastic. In many others, it was limited yet still helpful to the party or candidate at the other level. Only in a few cases was there no such support. This is not the outcome that one would expect to find between national and provincial parties at the two levels that are separate from one another. Incumbent MPs and MLAs, the key linkage between Canada's citizens and governments, generally continue to be preoccupied and involved with the politics of both levels of the multi-level state, with important consequences for how the parties are organized in the ridings.

7
Conclusion: The Local Political Worlds of the Liberal Party

Beginning in earnest following the 1957 national election, successive leaders of Canada's national and provincial Liberal parties faced new incentives to separate their parties from one another and have worked to fashion distinctive national and provincial organizations. But the grassroots activists tasked with building and maintaining the national party's local organizations in the ridings have never faced such incentives. To the contrary, they have always faced inherent incentives to construct and maintain integrated local organizations, and linkages between the national and provincial levels accordingly characterize many of these constituency parties. Turning our attention from the Liberal Party in Ottawa to the Liberal Party in the ridings reveals patterns of organization that often closely link national and provincial politics.

However, local Liberal party organizations also exhibit variation in the extent to which they are integrated between the national and provincial levels, if at all. In Don Valley East, local party structures obscure the divide between national and provincial; in contrast, differentiated local parties in Perth-Wellington strongly reinforce that division. Although there are inherent benefits to local integration, Perth-Wellington's national and provincial Liberal organizations demonstrate that other factors can diminish these benefits. Dissimilar national and provincial party systems obscure lines of continuity between the two levels; inhospitable local conditions complicate processes of local integration; and self-interested local incumbents can all but veto any form of national-provincial cooperation. In the absence of firm party rules dictating how constituency-level groups are to be organized between the national and provincial levels, grassroots Liberals are left to construct their own organizations, negotiating systemic, ecological, and political factors to arrive at the local solutions that best meet their needs.

This discussion suggests that there are few similarities to be found in how the Liberal Party's local groups organize themselves between the national and provincial levels. However, many local organizations face comparable situations, which means that similarities between sets of local organizations can be both detected and accounted for. Table 7.1 draws on the previous five chapters to organize ridings into four distinctive groups. Political scientists generally argue that Canada's separated national and provincial parties reinforce the existence of separate political worlds, but this analysis suggests that the parties have in fact contributed to the development of four distinctive types of political worlds in the ridings. The following paragraphs draw on the concepts and classifications developed in the previous five chapters to describe these different political worlds.

In the first group, national and provincial ridings constitute *one political world*. Integrated constituency associations and local campaigns characterize these ridings. Both the structures and the functions of these ridings' integrated constituency associations are linked between the national and provincial levels. National and provincial associations share executive members and maintain active forms of communication. Auxiliary units, where they are present, are linked in informal ways to both the national and the provincial constituency organizations and generally act as conveyer belts for local participation in both national and provincial politics. Party life in these ridings is distinctively integrated, since constituency associations organize joint party events and sponsor the events of one another.

As integrated campaigns, national and provincial campaigns in these ridings also share important linkages. Candidates' inner circles are often staffed by consistent partisans who play roles in the inner circles of both national and provincial candidates. Campaigns at both levels tend to draw on identical volunteer bases for personnel, and resources are openly shared.

Furthermore, local activist bases in these ridings tend to consist of consistent party activists who identify with and participate in Liberal politics at both national and provincial levels. In these roles, they encourage the development of integrated constituency associations and campaigns, which in turn reinforce consistent participation. Enmeshed national and provincial party organizations in these ridings mean that local activists exist in one political world. For these activists, national and provincial politics are hardly distinctive and not particularly separated from one another.

Table 7.1

The local political worlds of the Liberal Party

Province	National constituency	Party systems	Incumbent support	Local context	Constituency associations	Local campaigns
One political world						
ON	Ajax-Pickering	Similar	Full	Urban	Integrated	Integrated
ON	Don Valley East	Similar	Full	Urban	Integrated	Integrated
ON	York West	Similar	Full	Urban	Integrated	Integrated
ON	Richmond Hill	Similar	Superficial	Urban	Integrated	Integrated
NB	Acadie-Bathurst	Similar	Full/superficial	Rural	Integrated	Integrated
Interconnected political worlds						
NB	Saint John	Similar	Superficial	Urban	Mixed	Integrated
ON	Haldimand-Norfolk	Similar	Practical	Rural	Mixed	Mixed
ON	Oxford	Similar	N/A	Rural	Mixed	Mixed
NB	Fundy Royal	Similar	N/A	Rural	Mixed	Mixed
Distinctive political worlds						
BC	Delta-Richmond East	Dissimilar	Practical	Urban	Mixed	Mixed
BC	Port Moody-Westwood-Port Coquitlam	Dissimilar	Practical	Urban	Mixed	Mixed
BC	Vancouver Quadra	Dissimilar	No support/opposition	Urban	Differentiated	Mixed
BC	Richmond	Dissimilar	No support/opposition	Urban	Differentiated	Mixed
BC	Kootenay-Columbia	Dissimilar	No support/opposition	Rural	Differentiated	Mixed
Two political worlds						
NB	New Brunswick Southwest	Similar	N/A	Rural	Differentiated	Differentiated
ON	Perth-Wellington	Similar	No support/opposition	Rural	Differentiated	Differentiated

Local organizations in these ridings develop under circumstances where the costs of integration are low. Not surprisingly, such ridings are mostly in urban Ontario. Similar national and provincial party systems and the presence of urban coterminous constituencies have contributed to the development of integrated local parties in Ajax-Pickering, Don Valley East, York West, and Richmond Hill. For the most part, national and provincial incumbent members in urban Ontario provide full support – both public and private – to the party and candidate at the other level. These fully supportive incumbents are partially a product of the integrated local structures and traditions that characterize the ridings, but their public support and private support are conducive to the development and maintenance of such organizations. Only in Richmond Hill are incumbents less than fully supportive.

Where else might these local political worlds be found? Boundary congruence means that Ontario ridings comprise special local environments that are particularly hospitable to the development of integrated organizations. However, this effect is likely to be replicated in Canada's other large province, Quebec, where the number of provincial ridings is comparable to the number of national constituencies. The number of national and provincial ridings in Quebec is more proximate than in any other province besides Ontario, though they might overlap with one another rather than coincide. A closer confluence between national and provincial ridings lowers the costs of coordination and cooperation between the two levels. But Quebec's dissimilar national and provincial party systems also pose an obstacle to local integration, for the occasionally nationalist provincial Liberal Party has sometimes found it necessary to distance itself from its federalist national cousin in Ottawa. This divide can also discourage incumbent support in Quebec. Nevertheless, careful investigation of local Liberal organizations in urban Quebec would likely find the sort of local integration uncovered in Ontario's unified ridings.

The national riding of Acadie-Bathurst has played an important role in this study by illustrating the characteristics of integrated constituency associations and campaigns, and its exceptional nature should be noted. In this riding, as in urban Ontario ridings, national and provincial parties are strongly integrated, and local activists participate in what is essentially one national-provincial political world. Local organizations and campaigns in Acadie-Bathurst have adapted to the local environment and become quite integrated despite the presence of a fragmented rural constituency. Indeed, local Liberals in Acadie-Bathurst have built their integrated local party on the basis of the opportunities offered by several provincial ridings (and organizations) within the sprawling rural constituency. Acadie-Bathurst is therefore an important exception to the finding that fragmented rural ridings discourage local integration. The riding also illustrates how local parties are adaptive, in this case adapting to an inhospitable local environment to develop an idiosyncratic integrated local party well suited to the fragmented nature of the constituency.

In the second group of constituencies, national and provincial politics are linked less strongly than in the first group, and as a result these ridings might be thought of as *interconnected political worlds*. This group is distinguished by mixed constituency associations and, for the most part, mixed local campaigns. Structural linkages between national and provincial constituency associations in these ridings are largely absent; constituency associations are weaker in these ridings, and formal linkages between national and provincial executives are less common. Instead, integration is driven by consistent grassroots activists, and local campaigns tend to be characterized by mostly consistent members and volunteers, who informally link campaigns at the two levels.

Overall, linkages between the national and provincial levels in these ridings are somewhat weak. Rather than fully integrated constituency organizations and integrated campaigns, these ridings are homes to mixed local organizations. These weaker forms of integration can be traced back to the rural nature of the ridings, which complicates processes of local integration. Perhaps more crucially, limited linkages between the national and provincial levels reflect a lack of electoral and organizational strength in those ridings, since local integration requires the efforts of committed local administrators and campaigners willing to build linkages between the two levels. In all of these ridings, the Liberal Party is weak at both national and provincial levels. As a result, neither provincial nor national Liberal incumbents were present in either Oxford or Fundy Royal, and Haldimand-Norfolk's Liberal MP was defeated immediately following reunification of the Canadian Alliance and the Progressive Conservative Party in 2004. The lack of strong national-provincial linkages in these interconnected political worlds therefore demonstrates how a lack of electoral strength can hamper efforts at local integration. A cycle can result: the local parties are deprived of the benefits of full integration, which can impede success in future elections, which in turn prevents integration.

Ridings in this group are located in Ontario and New Brunswick and are characterized by (1) traditions of local integration and (2) largely consistent, integrated activist bases. Even where there are few formal linkages between the national and provincial association executives, local activists drive integration between the two levels, making little attempt to distinguish between the inter-election maintenance events and campaigns of national and provincial parties. As a result, these activists exist in separate yet interconnected political worlds.

The third group of ridings comprise *distinctive political worlds* for local activists. Unlike the ridings of the previous group, neither a tradition of local integration nor consistent, integrated activist bases characterize BC ridings. Facing dissimilar sets of parties and patterns of party competition at the national and provincial levels, voters and partisans are forced to distinguish between national and provincial parties. As a result, local cooperation comes neither naturally nor easily in these ridings. Rather, where it occurs, it results from the efforts of local elites, particularly members of some constituency association executives. In British Columbia, national and provincial constitute distinctive political worlds, yet party elites in the ridings sometimes reach between these worlds to integrate local effort and activity.

This occurs in Delta-Richmond East and Port Moody-Coquitlam-Port Coquitlam. In these ridings, local administrators on the national and provincial constituency association executives consciously work to construct informal linkages between national and provincial local parties. In some ridings, consistent activists take the lead in constructing linkages between national Liberal and provincial Liberal associations. In others, these linkages are built and maintained by inconsistent activists between the national Conservative Party and the provincial Liberal Party, demonstrating that partisan differences within a context of dissimilar national and provincial party systems do not necessarily constitute an insurmountable obstacle to elite cooperation in the ridings. But in Kootenay-Columbia, Richmond, and Vancouver Quadra, single-level elites on the national and provincial constituency associations have not constructed such linkages. Lacking local administrators willing to build relationships with any associations at the other level, these constituency associations have remained single-level loners.

All of the BC ridings studied are characterized by mixed campaign organizations. National and provincial campaigns share local campaigners in either candidates' inner circles or among secondary workers, and most campaigns are characterized by informal resource sharing between the two levels. These mixed campaign organizations exist in ridings with elite-driven constituency organizations, such as in Delta-Richmond East and Port Moody-Westwood-Port Coquitlam, as well as in ridings with differentiated constituency organizations, such as Vancouver Quadra, Richmond, and Kootenay-Columbia.

These unique forms of local organization must first be understood as a response to the incentives embedded in British Columbia's dissimilar national and provincial party systems. These systems greatly increase the costs of local integration. Instead of the broadly integrated organizations found in one political world ridings, activists in BC ridings have adapted to dissimilar national and provincial party systems by building organizations where cooperation between parties at the two levels is reliant on the intervention of local elites. Strikingly, there are no fully differentiated constituency organizations or campaigns in the BC ridings studied. Even in rural, fragmented Kootenay-Columbia, where there are high costs attached to integration, local campaigners have constructed national and provincial campaign organizations with important linkages between them.

Table 7.1 also suggests that the orientation of incumbents to the party at the other level plays an important role in determining whether constituency associations in British Columbia are mixed or differentiated. In both Richmond-Delta South and Port Moody-Westwood-Port Coquitlam, incumbents encourage cooperation between the national and provincial constituency associations. Practical incumbent support is well adapted to BC ridings, where Liberal MLAs must balance the support of national Liberal and national Conservative partisans. Such support also appears to impact the structures of the national and provincial constituency associations. Where incumbents fail to provide support or when no incumbent is present to do so, differentiated constituency associations are more likely to develop, as is the case in Vancouver Quadra, Richmond, and Kootenay-Columbia.

Dissimilar national and provincial party systems appear to be insurmountable obstacles to local integration. Yet activists in British Columbia have adapted to these obstacles and the conditions of their individual ridings to develop a unique brand of integrated local organizations. This illustrates the benefits of integration in the ridings and the adaptive capacity of local parties and indicates that some form of national-provincial linkage is likely to be found in even the most inhospitable environment. We would therefore expect to see these forms of local organization develop in other provinces with dissimilar national and provincial party systems. In Saskatchewan, for example, the provincial Saskatchewan Party maintains informal elite and personnel linkages with the national Conservative Party, though Saskatchewan Party officials are quick to deny the existence of any formal linkages to the national party (Mandryck 2006). And national Conservative and provincial Saskatchewan Party campaigns in the constituencies are generally staffed by similar sets of "local folks" (Esselment 2008, 22).

The fourth and final group contains both differentiated constituency associations and campaigns. These ridings therefore constitute *two political worlds* for local activists and citizens. In Perth-Wellington and New Brunswick Southwest, neither constituency associations nor local campaigns share important linkages. Constituency associations share few or no executive members and do not cooperate with one another in meaningful ways. Local party events are not hosted jointly, nor do national and provincial associations sponsor the events of one another. Local campaigns enlist different groups to staff their candidates' inner circles, and national and provincial volunteer bases are largely distinctive. Some campaign resources might be shared, but, because the national and provincial groups of secondary workers are distant from one another, this is rare. The result is that local activists tend to participate in either the national or the provincial party but not both. In these ridings, local structures and functions dictate that those activists do indeed reside in two separate political worlds.

In Perth-Wellington and New Brunswick Southwest, the costs of local integration are high. Distinctive local factors in each riding raise the costs of integration to prohibitive levels. In Perth-Wellington, this local factor is the opposition of the provincial incumbent member to any local integration, demonstrating the crucial effect that an incumbent can exercise on the organization of local parties. In New Brunswick Southwest, this local factor is the fragmented nature of the riding, where small provincial communities such as in Grand Bay-Westfield exist a substantial distance from the centre of the national organization. In both of these cases, one factor has raised the cost of integration to a prohibitive level, ruling out the development of any sort of integrated local organization.

To conclude this discussion, I should draw attention to the most striking aspect of Table 7.1: the lack of fully differentiated local parties. Canadian political scientists use terms such as "separated" or "disentangled" to describe the lack of organizational linkages between national and provincial parties, the implication being that the party organizations are largely autonomous. Yet in very few of the ridings studied do the local organizations of the national and provincial parties exist in two political worlds. Instead, some form of linkage or cooperation between the national and provincial parties is discernible in the vast majority of the ridings studied. The Liberal Party is an unevenly integrated party, but the local level is strongly weighted toward an integrated model.

The Liberal Party and Canadian Politics

What consequences do these findings hold for our understanding of the Liberal Party, federalism, and Canadian politics? First, this study illustrates that it is crucial to consider the roles of Canadian parties' constituency components in describing their overall national-provincial organizations. Observing the structures and activities of these local parties demonstrates that the organizational distinction between national and provincial politics in Canada is not as clear as previously thought. To the contrary, the national Liberal Party in many constituencies is strongly linked to provincial partisan politics, and these organizations structure local politics in such a way that the distinction between national and provincial is blurred. The Liberal Party might contest elections with pan-Canadian national campaigns, but its success in the ridings relies on local organizations often rooted in the politics of the provinces.

The efforts of national and provincial party leaders to disentangle their parties since the 1950s suggest that those parties are now distinctive, autonomous organizations, with the consequence that provincial parties are free to respond to the idiosyncratic competitive demands of their own systems without reference to the needs of the national party, which in turn has no stake in the outcomes of provincial election campaigns. Nevertheless, "while the federal field holds the glamour of the big league," observed Liberal organizer Gordon Dryden in 1965, "it is in the Provinces that one finds the basis of political power in Canada" (quoted in Wearing 1981, 27). What Dryden meant was that provincial parties and the elites attached to them were best able to maintain electoral machinery that existed closer to the communities of the nation and that national parties were therefore well served to draw on that machinery in their own campaigns. Canada's traditionally integrated parties embodied this principle in their reliance on regional ministers and provincial campaign organizations. This study demonstrates how the national Liberal Party has never evolved an organization that is completely free of linkages to provincial parties, even when the party system context in some provinces has become inhospitable to the continued existence of formal linkages. It is difficult in many ridings to distinguish between national and provincial party structures, and incumbent MPs and MLAs themselves are often deeply involved in both national and provincial politics.

These findings also have consequences for how municipal partisan competition is understood within the wider context of Canadian federalism. "[Because] Canadian parties are not engaged in the politics of local government," argues Carty (2002, 728), "their organizational roots in the communities they need to mobilize are inevitably weaker than those of parties in most other democracies." Carty's argument accords with other accounts of the Liberal Party as an elite cadre organization that stands above society, in sharp contrast to mass parties that are rooted within society. However, the seeming non-partisanship of municipal politics in Canada obscures important linkages between municipal electoral politics on the one hand and national and provincial politics on the other. The NDP, for example, has organized local branch parties to contest municipal elections in Vancouver, Winnipeg, and Toronto (Sproule-Jones 2007, 243).

National and provincial Liberals in the constituencies also organize covert branches to contest municipal office or have established informal linkages with explicitly municipal parties. For example, both national Conservative and provincial Liberal activists were intimately involved in the organization of Coquitlam First, a group of candidates who ran as a slate in Coquitlam's 2005 municipal election. These personnel linkages to the national and provincial parties in Coquitlam ridings meant that Coquitlam First candidates drew on the same base of campaign volunteers and resources as national Conservative and provincial Liberal candidates in the area. In Coquitlam, local activists and the organizations that they maintain are involved in the electoral politics of the national, provincial, and municipal levels.

Further research would likely turn up more linkages between national and provincial parties on the one hand and municipal partisan groups on the other. Indeed, the loose forms that allow for diversity in constituency-level organizations also allow those organizations and the personnel who staff them to involve themselves in municipal politics. One result of these findings is that national, provincial, and local are more strongly linked in their politics than was previously thought. The personnel of Canada's parties constitute such linkages, covertly if not explicitly. Far from the elite cadre portrayed in accounts of the Liberal Party as a brokerage party, it appears that the national party's organizational roots extend into both the provinces and the communities of the nation; in other words, from the very top to the very bottom of Canada's federal politics.

Analysts have struggled to explain why Canada's national and provincial parties have separated from one another and why national and provincial party systems are so distinctive from one another, especially when compared to parties and party systems in other federations (see, e.g., Wolinetz and Carty 2006). But these portraits of separated national and provincial parties do not take the constituency-level organizations of Canadian parties into account. The national Liberal Party might be formally separated from its provincial cousins, but the central components of the party do not impose this organizational separation on the fundamental components of their expansive organizations in the constituencies, which are often integrated between the national and provincial levels. The result of these divergent structures in the ridings is a significant amount of nuance in the national-provincial-local organization of the party. Such nuance is difficult to conceptualize in broad comparative studies of party organizations in multi-level states, where parsimony is a necessity. But conceiving of the Liberal Party as an unevenly integrated party allows political scientists to describe local organizational variation, which means that national and provincial parties are integrated in the ridings.

From a comparative perspective, these findings appear to reinforce the distinctiveness of Canadian party structures when compared to those of other democracies that employ geographic units of competition and representation. Whereas local campaigns in many developed democracies are extensions of the central campaign, the right of constituency associations to select candidates and the autonomy of local campaigns in Canada mean that local organizations maintain a distinctively local style (Sayers 1999, 222). This local style extends to the national-provincial configurations of local organizations, which can be traced back to the ecological and political characteristics of the constituencies that they exist within as well as characteristics of the national and provincial party systems in each province. The result is a significant amount of diversity in the national-provincial organization of these local groups.

However, it is important not to emphasize Canadian exceptionalism in this respect. This examination of the local components of the Liberal Party of Canada has revealed nuanced patterns of organization that hold important consequences for our understanding of Canadian federalism; the complex ways that the nation's dominant party organizes itself within this institutional context; and the ways that Canadians engage with their parties and the state. Similar analysis of party organizations in other multi-level states with constituencies might also reveal both significant variation and adaptability at the grassroots.

Appendices

Table A.1

National case study constituencies

National constituency	MP following 2004 election	Geography	Provincial constituencies (MLA in period studied)
New Brunswick			
Acadie-Bathurst	NDP	Rural	Bathurst (Liberal)
			Caraquet (Liberal)
			Centre-Péninsule (Liberal)
			Nepisiguit (Liberal)
			Nigadoo-Chaleur (Liberal)
			Lameque-Shippagan-Miscou (PC)
			Tracadie-Sheila (PC)
Fundy Royal	CPC	Rural	Albert (PC)
			Grand Lake (Liberal)
			Hampton-Belleisle (PC)
			Kennebecaisis (PC)
			Kings East (Liberal)
			Petitcodiac (PC)
			Riverview (PC)
			Saint John-Fundy (Liberal)
New Brunswick Southwest	CPC	Rural	Charlotte (Liberal)
			Fundy Isles (Liberal)
			Grand Bay-Westfield (PC)
			New Maryland (PC)
			Oromocto-Gagetown (PC)
			Western Charlotte (PC)
			York (Liberal)

▶

◀ *Table A.1*

National constituency	MP following 2004 election	Geography	Provincial constituencies (MLA in period studied)
Saint John	LPC	Urban	Saint John Champlain (Liberal) Saint John-Fundy (Liberal) Saint John Harbour (NDP) Saint John-Kings (PC) Saint John Lancaster (Liberal) Saint John Portland (PC)
Ontario			
Ajax-Pickering	LPC	Urban	Ajax-Pickering (Liberal)
Don Valley East	LPC	Urban	Don Valley East (Liberal)
Haldimand-Norfolk	CPC	Rural	Haldimand-Norfolk (PC)
Oxford	CPC	Rural	Oxford (PC)
Perth-Wellington	CPC	Rural	Perth-Wellington (Liberal)
Richmond Hill	LPC	Urban	Richmond Hill (PC)
York West	LPC	Urban	York West (Liberal)
British Columbia			
Delta-Richmond East	CPC	Urban	Delta North (NDP) Delta South (Liberal) Richmond East (Liberal)
Kootenay-Columbia	CPC	Rural	Columbia River-Revelstoke (NDP) East Kootenay (Liberal) Nelson-Creston (NDP)
Port Moody-Westwood-Port Coquitlam	CPC	Urban	Coquitlam-Maillardville (NDP) Port Coquitlam-Burke Mountain (NDP) Port Moody-Westwood (Liberal)
Richmond	LPC	Urban	Richmond Centre (Liberal) Richmond East (Liberal) Richmond-Steveston (Liberal)
Vancouver Quadra	LPC	Urban	Vancouver-Fairview (NDP) Vancouver-Point Grey (Liberal) Vancouver-Quilchena (Liberal)

Table A.2

Vote shares in national constituencies, 2004 general election

Constituency	Candidate (Party)	Vote share (%)
New Brunswick		
Acadie-Bathurst	Yvon Godin (NDP)	53.9
	Serge Rousselle (Liberal)	32.7
	Joel E. Bernard (Conservative)	10.9
	Mario Lanteigne (Green)	2.5
Fundy-Royal	Rob Moore (Conservative)	44.8
	John Herron (Liberal)	34.8
	Pat Hanratty (NDP)	16.2
	Karin Bach (Green)	3.1
	David Raymond Amos (Independent)	1.1
New Brunswick Southwest (St. Croix-Belleisle)	Greg Thompson (Conservative)	53.1
	Jim Dunlap (Liberal)	31.5
	Patrick Webber (NDP)	11.7
	Erik Matthew Millett (Green)	3.1
	David Szemerda (Action)	0.6
Saint John	Paul Zed (Liberal)	43.3
	Bob McVicar (Conservative)	33.6
	Terry Albright (NDP)	19.1
	Jonathan Cormier (Green)	2.2
	Jim Wood (Marijuana)	1.0
	Tom Oland (Independent)	0.8
Ontario		
Ajax-Pickering	Mark Holland (Liberal)	49.8
	René Soetens (Conservative)	33.6
	Kevin Modeste (NDP)	12.1
	Karen MacDonald (Green)	4.5
Don Valley East	Yasmin Ratansi (Liberal)	54.6
	David Johnson (Conservative)	28.0
	Valerie Mah (NDP)	13.2
	Dan King (Green)	2.9
	Ryan Kidd (Christian Heritage)	0.9
	Christopher Black (Communist)	0.4
Haldimand-Norfolk	Diane Finley (Conservative)	42.2
	Bob Speller (Liberal)	38.8
	Carrie Sinkowski (NDP)	14.4
	Colin Jones (Green)	3.4
	Steven Elgersma (Christian Heritage)	1.2

▶

◄ *Table A.2*

Constituency	Candidate (party)	Vote share (%)
Oxford	Dave Mackenzie (Conservative)	44.9
	Murray Coulter (Liberal)	30.5
	Zoé Dorcas Kunschner (NDP)	14.5
	Irene Tietz (Green)	4.3
	Leslie Bartley (Christian Heritage)	3.3
	James Bender (Marijuana)	1.7
	Kaye Sargent (Libertarian)	0.5
	Alex Kreider (Action)	0.2
Perth-Wellington	Gary Ralph Schellenberger (Conservative)	42.0
	Brian Innes (Liberal)	33.4
	Robert Roth (NDP)	15.6
	John Cowling (Green)	6.2
	Irma Nicolette Devries (Christian Heritage)	2.8
Richmond Hill	Bryon Wilfert (Liberal)	58.5
	Pete Merrifield (Conservative)	24.9
	C. Nella Cotrupi (NDP)	9.7
	Tim Rudkins (Green)	4.6
	Ellena Lam (PC)	2.3
York West/York-Ouest	Judy Sgro (Liberal)	64.7
	Sandra Romano Anthony (NDP)	15.3
	Leslie Soobrian (Conservative)	11.3
	Joseph Grubb (Christian Heritage)	5.7
	Tim McKellar (Green)	3.0
British Columbia		
Kootenay-Columbia	Jim Abbott (Conservative)	52.0
	Brent Bush (NDP)	23.8
	Ross Priest (Liberal)	17.9
	Carmen Gustafson (Green)	6.2
Port Moody-Westwood-Port Coquitlam	James Moore (Conservative)	40.9
	Kwangyul Peck (Liberal)	27.3
	Charley King (NDP)	26.4
	Richard Voigt (Green)	4.3
	Lewis Dahlby (Libertarian)	0.6
	Pat Goff (Action)	0.2
	George Gidora (Communist)	0.2
Richmond	Raymond Chan (Liberal)	44.5
	Alice Wong (Conservative)	35.3
	Dale Jackaman (NDP)	15.0
	Stephen H.F. Kronstein (Green)	4.3
	Allan Warnke (Action)	0.9

►

◄ *Table A.2*

Constituency	Candidate (party)	Vote share (%)
Vancouver Quadra	Stephen Owen (Liberal)	52.4
	Stephen Rogers (Conservative)	26.3
	David Askew (NDP)	15.0
	Doug Warkentin (Green)	5.6
	Connie Fogal (Action)	0.3
	Katrina Chowne (Libertarian)	0.3
	Donovan Young (Marxist-Leninist)	0.1

Table A.3

Vote shares in corresponding provincial constituencies

National constituency	Provincial constituency	Party	Vote share (%)
New Brunswick *(2003 provincial election)*			
Acadie-Bathurst	Bathurst	Liberal	48.5
		PC	47.1
		NDP	4.4
	Caraquet	Liberal	47.7
		PC	46.4
		NDP	6.0
	Centre-Péninsule	Liberal	47.4
		PC	46.6
		NDP	6.1
	Nepisiguit	Liberal	53.1
		PC	33.4
		NDP	13.6
	Nigadoo-Chaleur	Liberal	49.9
		PC	45.2
		NDP	4.9
	Lameque-Shippagan-Miscou	PC	60.1
		Liberal	35.7
		NDP	4.2
	Tracadie-Sheila	PC	56.3
		Liberal	35.6
		NDP	8.1
Fundy Royal	Albert	PC	53.6
		Liberal	38.7
		NDP	7.7
	Grand Lake	Liberal	62.1
		PC	29.2
		NDP	8.7
	Hampton-Belleisle	PC	44.2
		Liberal	35.7
		NDP	17.4
		Grey	2.7
	Kennebecaisis	PC	43.6
		Liberal	43.4
		NDP	13.0
	Kings East	Liberal	46.1
		PC	39.4
		NDP	14.5

▶

◀ *Table A.3*

National constituency	Provincial constituency	Party	Vote share (%)
	Petitcodiac	PC	60.6
		Liberal	32.2
		NDP	5.2
		Grey	2.1
	Riverview	PC	50.8
		Liberal	44.0
		NDP	5.2
	Saint John-Fundy	Liberal	47.7
		PC	40.1
		NDP	9.1
		Grey	3.0
New Brunswick Southwest	Charlotte	Liberal	49.4
		PC	28.0
		NDP	20.5
		Grey	2.1
	Fundy Isles	Liberal	52.7
		PC	43.6
		NDP	3.7
	Grand Bay-Westfield	PC	43.0
		Liberal	38.8
		NDP	10.8
		Grey	3.8
		Independent	3.7
	New Maryland	PC	45.7
		Liberal	43.0
		NDP	11.3
	Oromocto-Gagetown	PC	61.9
		Liberal	30.7
		NDP	5.6
		Grey	1.9
	Western Charlotte	PC	47.0
		Liberal	43.9
		NDP	9.1
	York	Liberal	49.3
		PC	42.7
		NDP	8.0
Saint John	Saint John Champlain	Liberal	40.0
		NDP	28.0
		PC	27.8
		Grey	4.1

▶

◄ *Table A.3*

National constituency	Provincial constituency	Party	Vote share (%)
	Saint John-Fundy	Liberal	47.7
		PC	40.1
		NDP	9.1
		Grey	3.0
	Saint John Harbour	NDP	43.4
		PC	28.9
		Liberal	27.7
	Saint John-Kings	PC	48.0
		Liberal	37.6
		NDP	12.1
		Grey	2.2
	Saint John Lancaster	Liberal	41.4
		PC	37.0
		NDP	19.2
		Grey	2.4
	Saint John Portland	PC	41.5
		Liberal	38.6
		NDP	19.9
Ontario *(2007 provincial election)*			
Ajax-Pickering	Ajax-Pickering	Liberal	49.6
		PC	34.0
		NDP	8.0
		Green	7.5
		Family Coalition	0.9
Don Valley East	Don Valley East	Liberal	55.6
		PC	25.0
		NDP	10.7
		Green	6.5
		Independent	1.3
		Family Coalition	0.6
		Freedom	0.3
Haldimand-Norfolk	Haldimand-Norfolk	PC	60.9
		Liberal	22.3
		NDP	10.5
		Green	5.2
		Family Coalition	1.1
Oxford	Oxford	PC	47.3
		Liberal	29.3
		NDP	11.4
		Green	8.8

►

◀ *Table A.3*

National constituency	Provincial constituency	Party	Vote share (%)
		Independent	1.7
		Family Coalition	1.6
Perth-Wellington	Perth-Wellington	Liberal	47.2
		PC	32.0
		NDP	10.1
		Green	7.8
		Family Coalition	2.0
		Independent	0.6
		Freedom	0.4
Richmond Hill	Richmond Hill	Liberal	47.8
		PC	34.8
		NDP	8.7
		Green	7.9
		Family Coalition	0.8
York West	York West	Liberal	55.0
		NDP	27.7
		PC	10.3
		Green	4.9
		Family Coalition	1.2
		Independent	1.0
British Columbia *(2005 provincial election)*			
Delta-Richmond East	Delta North	NDP	47.5
		Liberal	42.9
		Green	7.8
		Marijuana	1.0
		BC Party	0.9
	Delta South	Liberal	37.5
		Independent	33.1
		NDP	24.0
		Green	4.7
		Marijuana	0.6
		Independent	0.2
	Richmond East	Liberal	57.5
		NDP	33.0
		Green	7.6
		Independent	1.0
		Marijuana	0.9
Kootenay-Columbia	Columbia River-Revelstoke	NDP	51.7
		Liberal	39.9
		Green	8.4

▶

◄ *Table A.3*

National constituency	Provincial constituency	Party	Vote share (%)
	East Kootenay	Liberal	48.0
		NDP	43.7
		Green	8.3
	Nelson-Creston	NDP	58.8
		Liberal	26.7
		Green	12.4
		Marijuana	1.3
		Bloc BC	0.8
Port Moody-Westwood-Port Coquitlam	Coquitlam-Maillardville	NDP	47.0
		Liberal	44.6
		Green	6.3
		Marijuana	1.1
		Libertarian	0.8
		Platinum	0.3
	Port Coquitlam-Burke Mountain	NDP	48.1
		Liberal	43.7
		Green	6.9
		Social Credit	0.9
		Libertarian	0.4
	Port Moody-Westwood	Liberal	53.8
		NDP	37.4
		Green	6.3
		Your Political Party	1.7
		Independent	0.9
Richmond	Richmond Centre	Liberal	58.6
		NDP	32.5
		Green	7.7
		Marijuana	1.2
	Richmond East	Liberal	57.5
		NDP	33.0
		Green	7.6
		Independent	1.0
		Marijuana	0.9
	Richmond-Steveston	Liberal	59.2
		NDP	31.3
		Green	8.3
		Democratic Reform BC	1.2
Vancouver Quadra	Vancouver-Fairview	NDP	46.6
		Liberal	43.4
		Green	8.9

►

◀ *Table A.3*

National constituency	Provincial constituency	Party	Vote share (%)
		Sex Party	0.4
		Central Party	0.4
		Work Less	0.3
	Vancouver-Point Grey	Liberal	46.0
		NDP	37.7
		Green	15.1
		Marijuana	0.5
		Work Less	0.5
		Libertarian	0.2
		Platinum	0.1
	Vancouver-Quilchena	Liberal	67.2
		NDP	21.0
		Green	10.4
		Marijuana	0.7
		Libertarian	0.7

References

Beck, P.A. 1974. "Environment and Party: The Impact of Political and Demographic County Characteristics on Party Behavior." *American Political Science Review* 68, 3: 1229-44.

Bell, D.V.J., and C.M. Bolan. 1991. "The Mass Media and Federal Election Campaigning at the Local Level: A Case Study of Two Ontario Constituencies." In *Reaching the Voter: Constituency Campaigning in Canada,* ed. D.V.J. Bell and F.J. Fletcher, 77-114. Toronto: Dundurn Press.

Black, E.R. 1972. "Federal Strains within a Canadian Party." In *Party Politics in Canada,* 3rd ed., ed. H.G. Thorburn, 120-30. Scarborough: Prentice-Hall.

Blake, Donald. 1982. "The Consistency of Inconsistency: Party Identification in Federal and Provincial Politics." *Canadian Journal of Political Science* 15, 4: 691-710.

–. 1985. *Two Political Worlds: Parties and Voting in British Columbia.* Vancouver: UBC Press.

–. 1996. "Value Conflicts in Lotusland." In *Politics, Policy, and Government in British Columbia,* ed. R.K. Carty, 3-17. Vancouver: UBC Press.

Bradbury, J., and M. Russell. 2005. "The Local Work of Scottish MPs and MSPs: Effects of Non-Coterminous Boundaries and AMS." Report to the Commission on Boundary Differences and Voting Systems. http://www-server.bcc.ac.uk/.

Cairns, A.C. 1977. "The Government and Societies of Canadian Federalism." *Canadian Journal of Political Science* 10, 4: 695-725.

Carty, R.K. 1991. *Canadian Political Parties in the Constituencies.* Toronto: Dundurn Press.

–. 1992. "Three Canadian Party Systems." In *Canadian Political Party Systems: A Reader,* ed. R.K. Carty, 563-86. Toronto: Broadview Press.

–. 1994. "The Federal Face of Canadian Party Membership." In *Parties and Federalism in Australia and Canada,* ed. C. Sharman, 137-52. Canberra: Federalism Research Centre.

–. 2002. "The Politics of Tecumseh Corners: Canadian Political Parties as Franchise Organizations." *Canadian Journal of Political Science* 35, 4: 723-45.

–. 2006. "The Shifting Place of Political Parties in Canadian Public Life." *IRPP Choices* 12, 4: 3-13.

Carty, R.K., and W. Cross. 2006. "Can Stratarchically Organized Parties Be Democratic? The Canadian Case." *Journal of Elections, Public Opinion, and Parties* 16, 2: 93-114.

Carty, R.K., W. Cross, and L. Young. 2000. *Rebuilding Canadian Party Politics.* Vancouver: UBC Press.

Carty, R.K, and M. Eagles. 2005. *Politics Is Local: National Politics at the Grassroots.* Oxford: Oxford University Press.

Carty, R.K., M. Eagles, and A.M. Sayers. 2003. "Candidates and Local Campaigns: Are There Just Four Canadian Types?" *Party Politics* 9, 5: 619-36.

Chandler, W. 1987. "Federalism and Political Parties." In *Federalism and the Role of the State,* ed. H. Bakvis and W. Chandler, 149-70. Toronto: University of Toronto Press.

Chhibber, P., and K. Kollman. 2004. *The Formation of National Political Systems: Federalism and Party Competition in Britain, Canada, India, and the US.* Princeton: Princeton University Press.

Christian, W., and C. Campbell. 1990. *Political Parties and Ideologies in Canada: Liberals, Conservatives, Socialists, Nationalists.* 3rd ed. Toronto: McGraw-Hill Ryerson.

Clark, A. 2004. "The Continued Relevance of Local Parties in Representative Democracies." *Politics* 24, 1: 35-45.

Clarke, H.D., J. Jenson, L. LeDuc, and J.H. Pammett. 1980. *Political Choice in Canada.* Abridged ed. Toronto: McGraw-Hill Ryerson.

Clarkson, S. 2005. *The Big Red Machine: How the Liberal Party Dominates Canadian Politics.* Vancouver: UBC Press.

Courtney, J.C. 2001. *Commissioned Ridings: Designing Canada's Electoral Districts.* Montreal: McGill-Queen's University Press.

Cross, W., and L. Young. 2004. "The Contours of Political Party Membership in Canada." *Party Politics* 10, 4: 427-44.

–. 2006. "Are Canadian Political Parties Empty Vassals? Membership, Engagement, and Policy Capacity." *IRPP Choices* 12, 4: 14-32.

Denver, D., G. Hands, J. Fisher, and I. MacAllister. 2003. "Constituency Campaigning in Britain 1992 to 2001." *Party Politics* 9, 5: 541-59.

Deschouwer, K. 2006. "Political Parties as Multi-Level Organizations." In *Handbook of Party Politics,* ed. R.S. Katz and W.J. Crotty, 291-300. London: Sage.

Docherty, D.C. 1997. *Mr. Smith Goes to Ottawa: Life in the House of Commons.* Vancouver: UBC Press.

Dowse, R.E., and J.A. Hughes. 1977. "Sporadic Interventionists." *Political Studies* 25, 1: 84-92.

Dyck, R. 1992. "Links between Federal and Provincial Parties and Party Systems." In *Representation, Integration, and Political Parties in Canada,* ed. H. Bakvis, 129-78. Ottawa: Royal Commission on Electoral Reform and Party Financing.

–. 1993. *Canadian Politics.* Scarborough: Nelson Canada.

–. 1996. "Relations between Federal and Provincial Parties." In *Canadian Parties in Transition,* 2nd ed., ed. A.B. Tanguay and A.-G. Gagnon, 160-89. Toronto: Nelson.

Eldersveld, S. 1964. *Political Parties.* Chicago: Rand-McNally.

English, J. 1977. *The Decline of Politics: The Conservatives and the Party System.* Toronto: University of Toronto Press.

Esselment, A. 2008. "Fighting Elections: An Example of Cross-Level Political Party Integration in Canada." Paper presented to the Annual Meeting of the Canadian Political Science Association, Vancouver, BC, 4-6 June.

Fenno, R.F. 1978. *Home Style: House Members in Their Districts.* Boston: Little, Brown.

Franks, C.E.S. 2007. "Members and Constituency Roles in the Canadian Federal System." *Regional and Federal Studies* 17, 1: 23-45.

Jacek, H., J. McDonough, R. Shimizu, and P. Smith. 1972. "The Congruence of Federal-Provincial Campaign Activity in Party Organizations: The Influence of Recruitment Patterns in Three Hamilton Ridings." *Canadian Journal of Political Science* 5, 2: 190-205.

Jennings, M.K., and R.G. Niemi. 1966. "Party Identification at Multiple Levels of Government." *American Journal of Sociology* 72, 1: 86-101.

Katz, R.S. 1997. "Party as Linkage: A Vestigial Function?" *European Journal of Political Research* 18, 1: 143-61.

Katz, R.S., and P. Mair. 1992. *Party Organizations: A Handbook on Party Organizations in Western Democracies, 1960-1990.* London: Sage.

Koelble, T. 1991. *The Left Unravelled: Social Democracy and the New Left Challenge.* Durham: Duke University Press.

Koop, R. 2010. "Professionalism, Sociability, and the Liberal Party in the Constituencies." *Canadian Journal of Political Science* 43, 4: 893-913.

Koop, R., and A. Sayers. 2005. "Patterns of Federal-Provincial Party Membership in Canada since 1993." Paper presented to the Annual Meeting of the Canadian Political Science Association, London, ON, 2-4 June.

Land, B. 1965. *Eglinton: The Election Study of a Federal Constituency.* Toronto: P. Martin Associates.

Lawson, K. 1990. "Political Parties Inside and Out." *Comparative Politics* 23, 1: 105-19.

Liberal Party of Canada. 2009. "Every Voter Counts: The 308 Riding Strategy." http://www.liberal.ca/.

Mandryck, M. 2006. "Questions Still Remain about Saskatchewan Party." *Regina Leader-Post,* 24 February, B2.

Markku, L., and R. Taagepera. 1979. "Effective Number of Parties: A Measure with Application to West Europe." *Comparative Political Studies* 12, 1: 3-27.

Marland, A. 2007. "From Brochures to Web Sites: Candidates' Communication Suppliers in the 2000, 2004, and 2006 Federal Elections." Paper presented to the Annual Meeting of the Canadian Political Science Association, Saskatoon, SK, 30 May-1 June.

Matland, R.E., and D.T. Studlar. 2004. "Determinants of Legislative Turnover: A Cross-National Analysis." *British Journal of Political Science* 34, 1: 87-108.

McCall-Newman, C. 1982. *Grits: An Intimate Portrait of the Liberal Party.* Toronto: Macmillan.

Merolla, J.L., L.B. Stephenson, and E.J. Zechmeister. 2008. "Can Canadians Take a Hint? The (In)effectiveness of Party Labels as Informational Shortcuts in Canada." *Canadian Journal of Political Science* 41, 2: 673-96.

National Women's Liberal Commission. 2005. "Bylaws." http://www.nwlc -clfn.ca/.

Painter, Martin. 1991. "Intergovernmental Relations in Canada: An Institutional Analysis." *Canadian Journal of Political Science* 24, 2: 269-88.

Panebianco, A. 1988. *Political Parties: Organizations and Power.* Cambridge, UK: Cambridge University Press.

Perlin, G.C. 1980. *The Tory Syndrome: Leadership Politics in the Progressive Conservative Party.* Montreal: McGill-Queen's University Press.

Pond, D. 2005. "Imposing a Neo-Liberal Theory of Representation on the Westminster Model: A Canadian Case." *Journal of Legislative Studies* 11, 2: 170-93.

Rayside, D.M. 1978. "Federalism and the Party System: Provincial and Federal Liberals in the Province of Quebec." *Canadian Journal of Political Science* 11, 3: 499-528.

Regenstreif, S.P. 1963. "The Liberal Party of Canada: A Political Analysis." PhD diss., Cornell University.

Reid, E. 1972. "The Saskatchewan Liberal Machine before 1929." In *Party Politics in Canada,* 3rd ed., ed. H.G. Thorburn, 23-34. Scarborough: Prentice-Hall.

Reif, K.-H., and H. Schmitt. 1980. "Nine Second-Order National Elections: A Conceptual Framework for the Analysis of European Election Results." *European Journal of Political Research* 8, 1: 3-44.

Riker, W.H. 1964. *Federalism: Origin, Operation, Significance.* Boston: Little, Brown.

Russell, M. 2005. *Building New Labour: The Politics of Party Organisation.* New York: Palgrave Macmillan.

Sayers, A.M. 1999. *Parties, Candidates, and Constituency Campaigns in Canadian Elections.* Vancouver: UBC Press.

–. 2007. "Electoral Volatility and Political Party Organization in Canada and Australia." Paper presented to the Annual Meeting of the Canadian Political Science Association, Saskatoon, SK, 30 May-1 June.

Scarrow, S.E. 1996. *Parties and Their Members: Organising for Victory in Britain and Germany.* Oxford: Oxford University Press.

–. 2000. "Parties without Members? Party Organizations in a Changing Electoral Environment." In *Parties without Partisans: Political Change in Advanced Industrial Democracies,* ed. R.J. Dalton and M.P. Wattenberg, 79-101. Oxford: Oxford University Press.

Small, M.L. 2009. "How Many Cases Do I Need?" *Ethnography* 10, 1: 5-38.

Smiley, D.V. 1987. *The Federal Condition in Canada.* Toronto: McGraw-Hill Ryerson.

Smith, D.E. 1981. *The Regional Decline of a National Party: Liberals on the Prairies.* Toronto: University of Toronto Press.

Sproule-Jones, M. 2007. "Political Parties at the Local Level of Government." In *Canadian Parties in Transition,* 3rd ed., ed. A.-G. Gagnon and A.B. Tanguay, 241-54. Toronto: Broadview Press.

Stanbury, W.T. 1991. *Money in Politics: Financing Federal Parties and Candidates in Canada.* Toronto: Dundurn Press.

Stark, A. 1992. "English-Canadian Opposition to Quebec Nationalism." In *The Collapse of Canada?,* ed. R.K. Weaver, 123-57. Washington, DC: Brookings Institution.

Studlar, D.T., and I. McAllister. 1994. "The Electoral Connection in Australia: Candidate Roles, Campaign Activity, and the Popular Vote." *Political Behaviour* 16, 3: 385-410.

Tanguay, A.B. 1992. "Canadian Party Ideologies in the Electronic Age." In *Can-*

adian Political Party Systems: A Reader, ed. R.K. Carty, 464-89. Toronto: Broadview Press.

Thorburn, H.G. 1961. *Politics in New Brunswick.* Toronto: University of Toronto Press.

Thorlakson, L. 2006. "Party Systems in Multi-Level Context." In *Devolution and Electoral Politics,* ed. D. Hough and C. Jeffrey, 37-52. Manchester: Manchester University Press.

–. 2009. "Patterns of Party Integration, Influence, and Autonomy in Seven Federations." *Party Politics* 15, 2: 157-77.

Verba, S., and N. Nie. 1972. *Participation in America: Political Democracy and Social Equality.* New York: Harper and Row.

Wearing, J. 1981. *The L-Shaped Party: The Liberal Party of Canada, 1858-1980.* Toronto: McGraw-Hill Ryerson.

Whitaker, R. 1977. *The Government Party: Organizing and Financing the Liberal Party of Canada 1930-58.* Toronto: University of Toronto Press.

Whiteley, P., and P. Seyd. 1994. "Local Party Campaigning and Electoral Mobilization in Britain." *Journal of Politics* 56, 1: 242-52.

Whiteley, P., P. Seyd, and J. Richardson. *True Blues: The Politics of Conservative Party Membership.* Oxford: Oxford University Press.

Wolinetz, S.B. 2007. "Cycles and Brokerage: Canadian Parties as Mobilizers of Interest." In *Canadian Parties in Transition,* ed. A.-G. Gagnon and A.B. Tanguay, 179-96. Peterborough: Broadview Press.

Wolinetz, S.B., and R.K. Carty. 2006. "Disconnected Competition in Canada." In *Devolution and Electoral Politics,* ed. D. Hough and C. Jeffrey, 54-75. Manchester: Manchester University Press.

Young, L., and W. Cross. 2002. "Incentives to Membership in Canadian Political Parties." *Political Research Quarterly* 55, 3: 547-70.

Index

Printed and bound in Canada by Friesens

Set in Stone by Artegraphica Design Co. Ltd.

Copy editor: Dallas Harrison

Proofreader: Ann-Marie Metten